Violent Affections

FRINGE

Series Editors
Alena Ledeneva and Peter Zusi, School of Slavonic
and East European Studies, UCL

The FRINGE series explores the roles that complexity, ambivalence and immeasurability play in social and cultural phenomena. A cross-disciplinary initiative bringing together researchers from the humanities, social sciences and area studies, the series examines how seemingly opposed notions such as centrality and marginality, clarity and ambiguity, can shift and converge when embedded in everyday practices.

Alena Ledeneva is Professor of Politics and Society at the School of Slavonic and East European Studies of UCL.

Peter Zusi is Associate Professor at the School of Slavonic and East European Studies of UCL.

Violent Affections
Queer sexuality, techniques of power, and law in Russia

Alexander Sasha Kondakov

To all the victims of cruel authoritarian power

First published in 2022 by
UCL Press
University College London
Gower Street
London WC1E 6BT

Available to download free: www.uclpress.co.uk

Text © Author 2022
Images © Authors and copyright holders named in captions, 2022

The author has asserted their rights under the Copyright, Designs and Patents Act 1988 to be identified as the authors of this work.

A CIP catalogue record for this book is available from The British Library.

This book contains third-party copyright material that is not covered by the book's Creative Commons licence. Details of the copyright ownership and permitted use of third-party material is given in the image (or extract) credit lines. If you would like to reuse any third-party material not covered by book's Creative Commons licence, you will need to obtain permission directly from the copyright owner.

This book is published under a Creative Commons Attribution Non-commercial Non-derivative 4.0 International licence (CC BY-NC 4.0), https://creativecommons.org/licenses/by-nc/4.0/. This licence allows you to share, copy, distribute and transmit the work for personal and non-commercial use providing author and publisher attribution is clearly stated. If you wish to use the work commercially, use extracts or undertake translation you must seek permission from the author. Attribution should include the following information:

Kondakov, A. 2022. *Violent Affections: Queer sexuality, techniques of power, and law in Russia*. London: UCL Press. https://doi.org/10.14324/111.9781800082939

Further details about Creative Commons licences are available at http:// creativecommons.org/ licenses/

ISBN: 978-1-80008-295-3 (Hbk.)
ISBN: 978-1-80008-294-6 (Pbk.)
ISBN: 978-1-80008-293-9 (PDF)
ISBN: 978-1-80008-296-0 (epub)
ISBN: 978-1-80008-297-7 (mobi)
DOI: https://doi.org/10.14324/111.9781800082939

Contents

List of figures and tables   *viii*
Acknowledgements   *ix*
Series editor's preface   *xii*

Introduction: neo-disciplinary power   1

Part I: The authority of law   23

1. The legal field   27
2. From a place of indifference   48

Part II: Unruly sexuality   74

3. Russia in queer colours   77
4. The sexual subject of law   101

Part III: Affects, emotions and law   125

5. Power's affectual mechanisms   129
6. A catalogue of violent affections   146

Part IV: Techniques of power   170

7. 'Gay propaganda' as a meme   175
8. Conclusion: the global Memeticon   198

References   *211*
Index   *227*

List of figures and tables

Figures

2.1 Categories of anti-queer crime in Russia shown in years, 2010–16
7.1 Frequency of the 'non-traditional' meme complex in the titles of media publications and in court rulings relating to anti-queer violence in Russia, 2011–16

Tables

2.1 The range of legal categories in cases of anti-queer violence in Russia, 2010–16
2.2 Comparison of homicide sentences in cases of anti-queer violence in Russia, 2010–16
2.3 Social structure as reflected in cases of anti-queer violence in Russia, 2010–16

Acknowledgements

This book is a result of many structured and unstructured efforts, connections and aspirations. I am not able to mention all of them here, but I intend to give at least a sense of the book's origins, its crucial moments and its maturity. It was first conceived as an idea when I was working on the project 'Russian Expert Community and Human Rights Issues' (2016–17) supported by the MacArthur Foundation. When reviewing court cases on the application of the 'gay propaganda' law for that project, I came up with the idea of digging into legal databases further and searching for cases of violence against LGBT+ people there. I thank Oxana Karpenko and Dmitry Dubrovsky who took me on board with that project, as well as all its various participants who offered fruitful conversations, especially Alexander Verkhovsky who is a great expert on hate crime in Russia.

It was Rosa Luxemburg Stiftung in Moscow who supported my idea. Evgeny Shtorn – to whom I am hugely thankful for many things beyond this book – and I applied for funding for a quantitative project on hate crimes (2016–17). I thank Kerstin Kaiser and Elena Bezrukova for believing in us. I also thank the researchers on the project, the very talented Anastasia Tveritinova and Ekaterina Ivanova, as well as our artists Ekaterina Sotnikova and Polina Zaslavskaya, without whom the study would have looked very different. I also thank the Centre for Independent Social Research and Viktor Voronkov personally for hosting this project and I am grateful to Alexandra Berezkina for all her efforts in relation to it.

Certainly, the idea and the project have never been detached from LGBT+ activism and activist perspectives more generally. After all, I was dealing with the Russian government's direct crackdown on people's freedom of expression and, ultimately, their right to life. Hence, another dimension of this larger idea was a project entitled 'Sexuality Lab.', supported by the European Commission through the EIDHR Human Rights Incubator (No. 150068 from 19 December 2015). This portion of the project helped to keep our research team afloat for longer and expand it with Arseny Gabdullin and his technical expertise, and Andrey Tyukhtyaev and Ekaterina Khoninva who helped to collect media articles about violence against LGBT+ people. I thank Grigoriy Okhotin and Daria Rudanovskaya from the Human Rights Center Memorial who oversaw the larger project of which our Sexuality Lab. was only a part.

My idea then took a more individual turn as data were collected, calculations were performed and initial quantitative outcomes were presented to the public. Once I subjected the idea of hate crime to doubt, rethinking and reworking, the book really started to materialise. I initiated an internal conversation at the Woodrow Wilson International Center for Scholars' Kennan Institute, where I went with the project on hate crime against LGBT+ people in Russia and began my qualitative analysis of collected data (both court rulings and media articles). After a few months there I ended up with scepticism towards hate crime as a viable legal tool and many exciting thoughts about power. I am thankful to Matt Rojansky and William Pomeranz at the Center for their warm welcome.

This work continued as I moved to the Center for Russia, East Europe, and Central Asia (CREECA) at the University of Wisconsin–Madison. Alongside reading and analysing my collection of court cases, I reviewed a lot of theoretical literature there. The research seminar organised at CREECA was instrumental in enabling me to write up and publish my article 'The Influence of the "Gay-Propaganda" Law on Violence Against LGBTIQ People in Russia: evidence from criminal court rulings' in the *European Journal of Criminology* (first published in 2019). I rely on this article in Chapter 2, even though it is a very different text. I thank Jennifer Tishler and Kathryn Hendley for their continuous support, as well as all scholars at CREECA with whom I had a chance to discuss my ideas.

The first words of the book were written in Helsinki, where I was lucky to be appointed by the Aleksanteri Institute: Finnish Centre for Russian and Eastern European Studies of the University of Helsinki. I am grateful to Marianna Muravyeva who took me under her wing there, as well as to Markku Kangaspuro, Katalin Miklóssy and Judith Pallot. This was a very productive time, when I also wrote 'Regulating Desire in Russia', which was published in the *Research Handbook on Gender, Sexuality and the Law* (Edward Elgar, 2020) – thanks go to the editors Chris Ashford and Alexander Maine. I use some of it in Chapter 3. Most importantly, a different version of Chapter 7 was published as 'Non-Traditional Sexual Relationships: law, forgetting and the conservative political discourse in Russia' in *Conservatism and Memory Politics in Russia and Eastern Europe* (Routledge, 2021), which would not have happened without the involvement of the Aleksanteri Institute. I am grateful to the many people I met at the institute and Helsinki, as well as to all those who attended research seminars and conferences where I presented preliminary results of the project on which the book is based.

The book's last words were written in Dublin. University College Dublin was the first place to hear some of my Chapters 5 and 6 at a public seminar organised by the Centre for Gender, Feminisms and Sexualities. I am particularly thankful to Ursula Barry and Anne Mulhall for this. I then became UCD faculty, and I am grateful to School of Sociology colleagues, to Iarfhlaith Watson and Sara O'Sullivan, as well as many others who offered their insights during our regular seminars. I presented Chapter 7 there and received important feedback. I also presented Chapter 3 at the European University at St Petersburg and the University of California, Berkeley and thank Anna Temkina, Elena Zdravomyslova, Ekaterina Borozdina and Zachary William Kelly. I received very helpful comments at both events.

The book matured under the attentive eyes of its first readers, John Malcolm Anderson, Alexandra Novitskaya, Laurie Essig, Ekaterina Khodzhaeva, Davina Cooper, Maria Brock and Zachary Low Reyna. I am grateful to Richard Mole, Jeffrey Weeks, Eliot Borenstein, Annamarie Jagose, Valerie Sperling, Sharyn Roach Anleu and Kevin Moss for their suggestions regarding the book proposal. I appreciate the work done by UCL Press, especially by anonymous peer reviewers, my point of contact Chris Penfold and the Fringe series editor Alena Ledeneva. I am also immensely grateful to so many people I am not naming here but who had an impact on me and the book over the course of my career, especially at Q'ASEEES, the International Network for Hate Studies, EUSP, the International Institute for the Sociology of Law in Oñati and many, many other places. Not a single word here would have been written were it not for you all!

Series editor's preface

The **UCL Press FRINGE Series** presents work related to the themes of the UCL FRINGE Centre for the Study of Social and Cultural Complexity.

The FRINGE series is a platform for cross-disciplinary analysis and the development of 'area studies without borders'. 'FRINGE' is an acronym standing for Fluidity, Resistance, Invisibility, Neutrality, Grey zones, and Elusiveness – categories fundamental to the themes that the Centre supports. The oxymoron in the notion of a 'FRINGE CENTRE' expresses our interest in (1) the tensions between 'area studies' and more traditional academic disciplines; and (2) social, political and cultural trajectories from 'centres to fringes' and inversely from 'fringes to centres'.

The series pursues an innovative understanding of the significance of fringes: rather than taking 'fringe areas' to designate the world's peripheries or non-mainstream subject matters (as in 'fringe politics' or 'fringe theatre'), we are committed to exploring the patterns of social and cultural complexity characteristic of fringes and emerging from the areas we research. We aim to develop forms of analysis of those elements of complexity that are resistant to articulation, visualisation or measurement.

This volume examines anti-queer violence in present-day Russian society. Drawing on over 300 case studies of anti-queer violence, *Violent Affections* uses a 'bottom-up' methodology to embed this extensive empirical material within a framework drawing on queer theory and affect theory. In particular Kondakov's conceptions of the 'legal meme' and 'neo-disciplinary power' reveal the complex and fluid dynamics that relate social and political rhetoric to real-world violence. A ground-breaking addition to the study of not only the notorious 2013 Russian federal 'gay propaganda' ban but also to queer theory as such, this volume contributes to the examination of how legal and bureaucratic structures operate to constrain the lived experiences of LGBTQ+ individuals in Russia.

Alena Ledeneva and Peter Zusi
School of Slavonic and East European Studies, UCL

1
Introduction: neo-disciplinary power

I must begin with a warning. The materials presented in this book feature analyses of violent incidents, including cases of extreme violence that some readers may find disturbing and upsetting. Detailed depictions of these real stories behind criminal cases will be introduced at the outset of each part of the book in a specially formatted section like the one you are currently reading. It is possible to skip some of these sections if exposure to such materials is upsetting to you. Violence is one of the most hidden, yet ubiquitous, elements of our everyday life. My analysis exposes violence with the intention of intellectually reframing it in a way that – I hope – can help victims, criminals and society in general deal with it in a less traumatic manner. While some of this material may be upsetting, I think it is necessary to work with it as it brings us closer to a clearer understanding of violence and, therefore, to imagining paths to its elimination. What follows is the first of these stories.

In October 2011, police officers from Oryol, a regional capital south of Moscow, found 'a visibly injured body of an unknown man in a yellow woman's dress and nude-coloured tights'.[1] The body lay in a ditch located not far from a dam across the Oka River. Eighteen months later, Oryol district court sentenced three men for murder. In a 44-page ruling, the court reviewed a horrifying account of the events that led to the man's death. The victim, Oleg, was part of a group that had gathered in a small flat to relax and drink vodka. When two of the defendants arrived at the flat, seven other people were already there, including Oleg, Tatyana (the flat's owner) and her small baby. Most of them were quite drunk, and the new guests brought along two more bottles of vodka. In the courtroom, these two men claimed that during the time that elapsed after their arrival, there was a marked increase in tension between Tatyana and Oleg. Tatyana allegedly called him a person with 'non-traditional sexual orientation', requested money from him, and repeatedly bothered him. At one point, Tatyana took Oleg to her bed and 'sat on his face with her genitals, also trying to push her panties into his mouth'. He resisted, which she saw as proof of his homosexuality. One of the guests stood up for Oleg and was locked in a closet, only to be taken to a cemetery later where he was forced to dig his own grave, in which he was buried alive.

As the night progressed, Oleg was forced to put on the yellow dress and tights in which the police later discovered his body. The three defendants would soon be found guilty of beating him with their fists, feet and empty vodka bottles. According to the case file, blood was all over the place and Oleg could hardly walk when the drunken group took him to their car and drove in the direction of the Oka River dam. When they arrived, they opened the boot of the car and took Oleg out. He started to walk but fell into a nearby ditch, where he would lie for another week, unfound and eaten by maggots. The defendants left and headed to the victim's flat to pick up some of his belongings, including a TV, a microwave oven and a loudspeaker system. They returned to the original flat, where one of the defendants engaged in sex with Tatyana, and the rest of the guests had sex with another woman.

The events of that night were interpreted by the district criminal court as manslaughter (the man who had been buried alive luckily survived the assault and was simply ignored by the court). The judge held that the defendants did not have the intention to kill (this would have constituted murder), but simply caused injuries eventually incompatible with life (manslaughter). In establishing whether the victim was a gay man, the court reviewed a forensic examination of his anus, in which 'spermatozoa were not found'. The three attackers were sentenced to 8 and 9 years in a high-security facility – two of the men were already convicted criminals and therefore received one additional year on their sentences. The rest of the group were summoned only as witnesses, including Tatyana.

The cases of violence

This book deals with a particular set of criminal stories. Over the course of the following pages I review cases of violence which, in one way or another, relate to the victims' sexuality. In some jurisdictions around the world, many of these cases are referred to as 'hate crimes' based on the perpetrator's disgust towards their victim's sexual orientation or gender expression. Russia – where all my cases come from – is no exception to this. As my analysis in Part I of the book will show, despite its image as a lawless space, Russia has a perhaps surprisingly well-developed body of hate crime legislation, which is occasionally applied in cases of violence against LGBT+ people. Yet the letter of the law has only a marginal effect on the ways these cases are handled by the criminal justice system. Instead, a more complex configuration of power relations – I call it *neo-disciplinary power* – makes possible the ultimate form of the criminal stories scrutinised in this book. These power relations are the object of my interest and analysis. Structured by sexuality (as reviewed in Part II) and yet running wild across people's affects (analysed in Part III), they eventually manifest themselves in *violent affections* (detailed in Part IV).

The case above is illustrative of many contradictory facets of sexuality and affections with which this book deals. The perpetrators in the case actively sought to emasculate their victim by dressing him up in feminine garments. They associated male homosexuality with femininity in a quite literal sense. Furthermore, when the victim refused to engage in sexual intercourse with a woman, he was interpreted as homosexual, regardless of his motives and self-understanding. This led to him being dressed up 'as a woman'. The final scene of the evening hints at the perpetrators' own sexual insecurities when they engage in group sex with the women after committing a violent crime against a man whose sexuality had been questioned. In this act, I argue, they were trying – again, quite literally – to perform their fragile heterosexual masculinity, reinforce it, and demonstrate to each other their loyalty to the heteronormative order. Perhaps they were not really motivated by 'hatred' as such, but they definitely experienced a great variety of emotions that informed and guided their actions. The actions of the participants may look senseless, unreasonable and chaotic. Yet, I conclude that they were conditioned by *neo-disciplinary power* relations, which we can only study by tracing affects that position people and things in hierarchical relation to one another. This is exactly what I do in this book.

Violent Affections is the result of a thorough review of 314 stories like the one just recounted, in which victims' and perpetrators' sexuality played a crucial role in affectively shaping the crime scene. All these stories are criminal cases that were reviewed by the courts in various cities, towns and villages across the Russian Federation between 2010 and 2016. The following analysis is therefore a study of the Russian criminal justice system, too. In fact, law is an essential context of this research: it begins with an analysis of the effects of the 'gay propaganda' law introduced in 2013 and traces how it has been used as a tool to manipulate people's emotions by spreading a message of hatred of queerness. The study goes on to review what the legal system recorded as results of these manipulations: in other words, the incidents of violence (that I connect to the gay propaganda law) that were investigated and adjudicated within the official legal field. Hence, law is important in various respects here: it is central to my initial research question (how the gay propaganda law has influenced anti-queer violence) and it is also my primary source of information (the book is based on an analysis of criminal court decisions). It is also the context for all the criminal stories told in the book (by virtue of the stories being criminal). Ultimately, law is understood as a performative discursive field that impacts on affective power relations with its formal authority. *Violent Affections* investigates law's role and function in configuring these power relations.

The link between queer sexualities and the criminal justice system is currently being shaped by a relatively new analytic approach known as 'queer criminology'. In many respects, this book is a daring contribution to it. In simple terms, queer criminology is an approach that analyses the ways in which the criminal justice system deals with 'queers' – that is, historically, with people who were prosecuted for various activities outside heteronormative sexuality, mostly for same-sex intercourse and desires. Some societies in fact still have criminal statutes that punish voluntary same-sex intercourse between adults. Although 'non-queer' criminology may contribute to the study of these norms – and, in fact, has done so to a degree – it is queer criminology that seeks to 'both move LGBTQ people . . . from the margins to the center of criminological inquiry, and to investigate and challenge the ways that the criminal legal system has been used as a tool of oppression against Queer people' (Buist and Lenning 2016, 1). According to this interpretation, queer criminology is not a theoretical approach, but a field of academic study with a particular, identifiable research object: 'queers'. So long as the field of academic study requires a distinguishable focus – on 'the Queer community, which is to say the LGBTQ (lesbians, gay, bisexual, transgender, and queer) population' (Buist and Lenning 2016, 1) – it in many ways betrays the foundational premise of queer theory itself, which rejects the stable categorisation of sexualities, especially as confined in Western identity terms. After all, it initially appeared that queer theory was supposed to contest, not reproduce, sexual identities.

As one of the first overviews of the state of queer criminology reads, the extent of criminology's previous engagement with queer theory 'can be summarized in three short words: Not very much' (Woods 2014, 16). Jordan Blair Woods continues:

> . . . there is little to no theoretical engagement with sexual orientation and gender identity in each of the four major schools of criminology: biological, psychological, sociological, and critical. This lack of engagement raises concerns about whether existing criminological methods and theories apply to the experiences of LGBTQ people today, and whether queer criminologists can and should modify them to address sexual orientation and gender identity. It also raises key questions about the role of queer theories—which have been virtually excluded from criminological theories—to inform those modifications and to create new criminological frameworks. (Woods 2014, 17)

The tasks identified here seem to fall into two categories. First is the task of applying existing methodologies and theories to studies of 'queer' people in a criminal context. This task assumes the category 'queer' as an umbrella term for a number of knowable and expanding, but still exact, identity groupings. Successful research of this sort may well lead to practical solutions in criminal law reform.[2] My position, however, is sceptical of both criminal law reforms in Russia and the universal applicability of criminological (or queer) methodologies. I expand on this critique in Part II of the book, where I argue for asking good methodological questions.

The second identified task involves the conceptualisation of new theories and criminological frameworks that are queer in their logic and spirit. In *Violent Affections* I offer to elaborate on the latter of Woods' suggestions and create original queer criminological theories that open new horizons for the study of both criminal law and sexualities, as well as for the critical analysis of power relations more generally. My major theoretical concern lies with the multitude of power effects – that is, the stuff that power produces. Therefore, the main drive and contribution of the book is to explain how criminal law works as a producer of power-knowledge. My explanation is based on the context of contemporary dealings with queer sexuality in Russia, but my overall purpose is to identify and illuminate more general techniques and mechanisms of power.

Throughout the book, I draw on two major sets of literature in queer theory – the critique of identity and the understanding of affects as power relations – to offer my own contribution, which is given in Part IV. Unlike previous similar studies, I argue that power-knowledge operates through the production of many competing versions of truth rather than just one hegemonic version. To better grasp this, it is necessary to get rid of earlier metaphors that explained techniques of power in terms of the Panopticon. These explanations falter insofar as they necessarily represent power-knowledge as a regime of hegemonic truth production. In other words, they fail to account for the multitude and messiness of power effects. Instead, I imagine power flowing in contemporary informational societies and offer to replace the Panopticon with the Memeticon – circulating *legal memes* that fuel the workings of contemporary power-knowledge. Legal memes better explain how power works today as a set of contradictory, multiple and messy relations – neo-disciplinary power.

Neo-disciplinary power

As perhaps is already evident, my understanding of law and power aligns with their Foucauldian interpretation as discourse (Rose, O'Malley and Valverde 2006; Valverde 2010). Indeed, discourse is a site of social production through the workings of power. Discourse is not simply a collection of words, but a lively environment encompassing things, meanings and institutional arrangements that constitute both 'truthful' visions of the world around us and contestations of those visions (Brown 1993, 397). When people act they are conditioned by a version of truth that is shared among them as common sense. Michel Foucault argued that there are techniques of power operating in societies that 'produce reality' – in other words, this hegemonic version of truth (Foucault 1991, 194). One such technique is the classification of people into groups of dangerous and ill or respectable and sane. Once classified, we all 'know' how to deal with the individuals in each group, as well as what kind of behaviour is expected from us if we fall into one of these groups. Law – as discourse – is understood as a crystallised version of power relations configured through these techniques (Foucault 1978b, 92–3; Golder and Fitzpatrick 2009, 72). Yet this explanation of power relations allows for little to no messiness or variability in the workings and products of power that are becoming increasingly evident, including through the analysis of law (Amietta 2021; Taşcıoğlu 2021). Nevertheless, it is an influential interpretation, and it is the first brick in my own reading of neo-disciplinary power.

Foucault's definition of law has mostly been understood as a synonym of the rule of prohibition, and as such is focused primarily on the criminal legal process rather than other spheres of law (Hunt and Wickham 1994; Golder and Fitzpatrick 2009, 59–60). While my aim here is certainly to analyse criminal law, I still want to emphasise that Foucault's understanding of law cannot be reduced to any particular body of norms – criminal or otherwise.

Foucault's purpose in drawing a distinction between the law and discipline was to figure out law's new role in these power relations. Ben Golder and Peter Fitzpatrick have shown that Foucault indeed distinguished between a more 'positivist' version of conventional juridical power (sovereign law) and a more contemporary disciplinary form of power supported by law indirectly (Golder and Fitzpatrick 2009, 35–8). Whereas the former version is manifest in the practice of identifying crimes and applying punishments to perpetrators, the latter produces subtle effects in society overall. In other words, a criminal legal norm has two modalities at once: it *directly punishes* those who are proven to have committed a crime, and it *indirectly regulates* the behaviour of those who have not committed any crime. The first modality of law is *sovereign*, whereas the second modality is *disciplinary*.

This idea makes the law performative in two different ways. Firstly, it dictates a certain code of conduct: people who commit crimes go to prison by command of the law once they are caught. Secondly, the law is performative outside of its immediate application: people who do not commit crimes refrain from doing so out of fear of punishment and, hence, the discipline inscribed upon them relates to a legal norm that prohibits a would-be crime. However, the theory fails to account for much broader effects of law that may seem unrelated to any written norm at first glance but are still in fact produced, reproduced and enhanced through law's authority. In this book I am particularly interested in expanding the understanding of law's performativity further by exploring its role in the many counter-intuitive influences it may have on people's conduct. My main example here is Russia's 'gay propaganda' law. In a nutshell, the law is a piece of censorship legislation that prohibits the public spread of information about LGBT+ people under threat of immense monetary fines and detention (Kondakov 2019c). Its direct effects are both (1) the withdrawal of such information by order of the courts in cases against people who dare to speak up about LGBT+ topics in Russia, and (2) an enactment of self-censorship among people who would want to talk about LGBT+ issues but decide to refrain from doing so because of the threat of punishment. Yet I argue that the effects of this law reach much further than these two points alone suggest and result in a plethora of additional outcomes that can be captured by the concept of neo-disciplinary power. In *Violent Affections*, I especially focus on how this gay propaganda law has triggered anti-queer violence: how the law goes beyond its immediate enforcement and disciplinary effects. In one sense, then, the book can be seen as a search for a way to conceptualise this counter-intuitive, generative role of law.

One way to study law's multiple effects is to further expand the definition of law as discourse. Judith Butler significantly challenges the dichotomy between two previously mentioned modalities of law in her vision of performative power. She argues that sovereign and disciplinary types of power are not mutually exclusive. Butler contends that performative speech acts have been largely associated with 'legal instances: "I sentence you," "I pronounce you": these are words of the state that perform the very action that they enunciate' (Butler 1997, 81). But with hate speech, she shows that performative enunciations fall simultaneously both inside and outside the law – one is unintelligible without the other. Thus, if there is no hate speech legislation, the act of hate speech is not given the same importance as it would be if there were hate speech legislation. Both the crime and the law that punishes it require one another:

> Figuring hate speech as an exercise of sovereign power implicitly performs a catachresis by which the one who is charged with breaking the law (the one who utters hate speech) is nevertheless invested with the sovereign power of law. What the law says, it does, but so, too, the speaker of hate. The performative power of hate speech is figured as the performative power of state-sanctioned legal language, and the contest between hate speech and the law becomes staged, paradoxically, as a battle between two sovereign powers. (Butler 1997, 81)

Hence, the distinction between a sovereign version of law and the disciplinary power of law does not appear in this interpretation. My approach both acknowledges this idea and challenges it. I take this into account when investigating the power relations that have produced the materials under analysis: criminal court decisions, but also the violent incidents themselves and the sexual and emotional tensions that led to this violence. I look at power relations as they manifest in the texts of court decisions and I therefore analyse how the law punishes crimes against LGBT+ people. At the same time, though, I look at how the violence that the law punishes is also law's own product. However, for analytical purposes, I argue that it is important to figure out law's role within power relations rather than confuse law and disciplinary power with each other. Hence, Part I of the book is dedicated precisely to the institutional arrangement of law in Russia that allows law to create its discursive authority. The analysis in Part I shows that the legal field is intended to produce the ultimate truth about each case under the court's scrutiny by engaging in the reproduction of hegemonic knowledge about the victims' and perpetrators' relationships. And yet, what it produces is just one version of truth among many others: a version that is often valid in the legal field itself and within its institutional borders, but a version that also competes with powerful alternative meanings of reality outside the field that *Violent Affections* intends to illuminate.

The multiplicity of these versions of truth is evidenced in Part II, when I take a closer look at what is meant by victims' sexuality in criminal court rulings. As mentioned above, judges may rely on medical expertise in establishing victims' sexuality through forensic examination, although this is rather rare. Witness accounts of victims' behaviour is often another way, as well as material artefacts that may be telling (sex toys, porn films, accessories). All such 'proofs' are brought to the courtroom to establish that a victim can be classified in sexual orientation terms, usually given in a very specific bureaucratic formula: this is 'a person of non-traditional sexual orientation'. This all-encompassing legal category, not unlike the umbrella term 'queer', is meant to signal a range of sexual and gender experiences outside of reproductive sexuality without specification. In addition, the category stabilises this range of experiences as a body of relatively unchanging sexual patterns that define people once established by the court as truthful facts. At the same time, as my analysis in Part II will show, the category hides both a myriad of very different queer experiences and fluidity within those experiences, as they change depending on different conditions. Looking at sexuality from a queer perspective thus helps me demonstrate how hegemonic categorical language structures sexuality in sexual orientation terms as well as how discursive categories of sexual identity fail to grasp the multiplicity and fluidity of queerness in the cases under review.

Mechanisms and techniques of power

Foucault's failure to capture the multiplicity, complexity and messiness of sexual experience can be attributed to the understanding of power relations outlined above. While he offered a vivid and fluid notion of power relations, Foucault's theory still assumed – and rightly so – a certain degree of power's stabilisation and embodiment in only specific ways. In other words, although there might be many ways of being 'gay', only some of these are transformed and stabilised into hegemonic power-knowledge constructs of how to be gay precisely, because the production of knowledge is only done through particular authoritative types of expertise – medical or juridical expertise, for example (Halperin 2012; Weeks 2002). The Panopticon as a metaphor for power relations anticipated that this knowledge is shared by all bodies disciplined into 'knowing' it as if we all are subject to one single source of authority (the tower with guards in the middle of the structure): the all-seeing authority of expert knowledge. In fact, this expert authority is what transforms mere information into knowledge (Adler 2018, particularly chapter 2).

This vision of power as disciplinary was illuminating within the conditions of late modernity when Foucault wrote his major works. After all, information flows were indeed different back then because they were much scarcer than they are now, and only select information circulated as authoritatively legitimate (Brown 2008, 80). It was thus more reasonable to have certain criteria at hand to be selective and disseminate only certain types of information. It was also reasonable to air only information that was backed up by some kind of legitimate authority – that is, expert knowledge. Yet today, expertise is a much broader phenomenon: while there may still be relatively consistent beliefs in some types of authority, the production, dissemination and consumption of knowledge is no longer confined to elite expert professions. Rather, in the neo-disciplinary configuration of power, information in general is counted as knowledge. It produces truths for some and not for others: this or that piece of information suddenly operates here or there as productive of conduct, identities or relationships, but at the very same time it does not 'work' the same way every time or in every situation. In other words, fragmentation, multiplicity and fluidity are what characterise the production of knowledge in this neo-disciplinary environment, not guard-tower hegemony. Hence, I argue that the Panopticon is today insufficient to explain the workings of power. Instead, I propose that an important way to look at contemporary decentralised power-knowledge is as circulating pieces of information, or what we might call the Memeticon – the work of memes.

But first a clarification is necessary. In his works, as others have observed, Foucault rarely gives clear definitions of terminology and often tends to confuse readers with multiple versions of seemingly one and the same concept popping up in different forms in different writings (Valverde 2010). This is until a term *really* starts to matter. Thus, in *Discipline and Punish*, he introduces the Panopticon as either a *mechanism of power*, or its *technique*, or both. Foucault explains that the Panopticon is a representation of unconscious discipline that governs our conduct in everyday life as though it is an unwritten law, and in this sense it is the opposite of the law as a clearly stated written norm:

> Regular and institutional as it may be, the discipline, in its *mechanism*, is a 'counter-law'. And, although the universal juridicism of modern society seems to fix limits on the exercise of power, *its universally widespread panopticism enables it to operate, on the underside of the law, a machinery that is both immense and minute, which supports, reinforces, multiplies the asymmetry of power* and undermines the limits that are traced around the law. The minute disciplines, the panopticisms of everyday may well be below the level of emergence of the great apparatuses and the great political struggles. But, in the genealogy of modern society, they have been, with the class domination that traverses it, the political counterpart of the juridical norms *according to which power was redistributed*. Hence, no doubt, the importance that has been given for so long to the small *techniques of discipline*, to those apparently insignificant 'sciences' that give it a respectable face; hence the fear of abandoning them if one cannot find any substitute; hence the affirmation that they are at the very foundation of society, and an element in its equilibrium, whereas they are *a series of mechanisms for unbalancing power relations* definitively and everywhere; hence the persistence in regarding them as the humble, but concrete form of every morality, whereas they are *a set of physico-political techniques*. (Foucault 1991, 223, my emphasis)

Here and throughout *Discipline and Punish*, Foucault uses the terms 'panopticism', 'discipline', 'techniques of power' and 'mechanisms of power' somewhat interchangeably. But to make use of his theory of power, it is crucial to clearly differentiate between these terms. Foucault makes clear that the new disciplinary form of power is not law or the top-down application of force, even though these forms of power run concurrently with the discipline. Moreover, both types of power make people do things. While disciplinary power's *mechanism* of effecting subjection is not simple top-down enforcement, it still works by creating an impression of inequality and 'unbalanced power relations'. In other words, disciplinary power only works once a hierarchy between interacting subjects is established. Hierarchy is discipline's mechanism. Hence, its mechanism retains power's older top-down guise: it creates impressions of hierarchy in order to operate productively.

What is different, then, is *technique*. Disciplinary power's technique is the Panopticon – a way to generate hierarchisation: 'its universally widespread panopticism enables it to operate, on the underside of the law, a machinery... which supports, reinforces, multiplies the asymmetry of power' (Foucault 1991, 223). Therefore technique here is the way in which power enables its mechanism or moves in the world. Technique is the way in which power circulates and, eventually, reaches out to susceptible bodies it can colonise and hierarchise. This is why the Panopticon is disciplinary power's technique, not its mechanism: it is the way disciplinary power circulates, runs across societies, even before setting to work on bodies. As Foucault's theory of power develops across the four volumes of *The History of Sexuality*, this becomes crystal clear (Foucault 1978b; 1988; 1978a; 2021).

Techniques of power

Foucault's theory of disciplinary power-knowledge is best articulated in the first volume of *The History of Sexuality*, where he explains how this new method of power 'is not ensured by right but by technique' (Foucault 1978b, 89). How exactly power operates is central to its effectiveness and, in the example of 'the deployment of sexuality', it 'operates according to mobile, polymorphous, and contingent techniques of power' (Foucault 1978b, 106). Foucault develops this idea in more detail when he turns to the conceptualisation of power's techniques in volumes 2 and 3 (Foucault 1988; 1978a). There, he clarifies that techniques are practices of 'know-how' or skilful expertise – a practice that will 'guide action... in view of its ends' (Foucault 1988, 62). A technique is supposed to produce a particular type of human subject who is conditioned to do the 'right thing' in the moment. To be sure, Foucault argues that the techniques of power he uncovered tend towards both subjecting people to more disciplinary control and helping them escape the workings of power to find themselves truly emancipated, not simply resisting the power (Foucault 1978a, 43). While *Violent Affections* focuses on an analysis of how power controls, the latter point about emancipation from power also motivates and demands further analysis of the neo-disciplinary techniques of power relations.

Returning to the Panopticon, Foucault names it as one of the techniques of power that began to rise to dominance during European modernity and is often still seen in the design of collective spaces such as educational institutions, army and prison barracks, factories and workshops. This and other similar techniques marked 'the beginning of an era of "bio-power"' (Foucault 1978b, 140). The genealogy of the various techniques of power that Foucault outlines makes it clear that it evolved from ancient methods of self-control 'to the exercise of priestly power' in the Middle Ages, to 'educative, medical, and psychological types of practices' during modernity (Foucault 1988, 11). These latter practices were based on knowledge originating from 'legitimate' institutions of authority such as schools and hospitals, which could claim a monopoly on the production of truth. I argue that these once central techniques of power no longer hold sway. Contemporary neo-disciplinary techniques of power transform the Foucauldian, institutionalised forms of knowledge that guided our conduct to a multiplicity of information that triggers different things in different people and, as a result, impacts their practices. I argue that this is what characterises the neo-disciplinary power relations of today when *any information* is given the opportunity of becoming *knowledge* (a truth), regardless of the legitimacy of its source. Tracing the evolution of the neo-disciplinary techniques of power in current societies is the primary goal of this book.

If the techniques of power have really changed recently and if institutional forms of legitimate knowledge production are no longer as central to the way power operates, then what is the place of law in this new constellation? While juridical authority remained important for power relations in modernity, as shown above, this authority seems to have come under increasing contestation in our contemporary moment, losing its ability to generate persuasive, hegemonic truths. If there is no way for legal authority – or any other legitimate source of authority – to produce convincing enough knowledge, does it mean that the law has no say in the neo-disciplinary situation? To identify the place of law in this new constellation, I turn to an analysis of the ways in which law generates its authority through the practices of legal actors (lawyers, police officers, judges and the like). Pierre Bourdieu referred to the space where these actors perform as 'the juridical field' or the legal field. It is a self-referential discursive field of meaning production whose major product is paradoxically the law itself: the legal field generates the authority of law, which is on the whole relevant and understandable only to its insiders (Bourdieu 1987). Under the Panopticon, it is exactly this capacity of law to produce its own authority that gives it the opportunity to operate outside of the legal field with such power. However, in the neo-disciplinary configuration, the legal field may shrink to a self-sufficient system competing for recognition in the outside world. I continue this analysis in Chapters 1 and 7.

Despite the arguments discussed above (Golder and Fitzpatrick 2009; Butler 1997), Foucault always underlined differences between the law and disciplinary power. The law, even in its regulatory forms, was understood by Foucault as a top-down, older way of exercising coercion. In volume 4 of *The History of Sexuality* he proposes a telling analysis: if 'marriage' as an official procedure of recognition of the sexual bond between people is the face of the law, then 'virginity' is a disciplinary technique of power. Both discursive strategies control people's sexuality by limiting it. However, they do it in very different ways: marriage through the external imposition of symbolic authority, while the ideology of virginity gives the impression of 'a free individual choice that no precept could impose, either on everyone in the form of a law, or on some in the form of a commandment' (Foucault 2021, 166). In analysing neo-disciplinary power, my own task is to scrutinise the relationships between – figuratively speaking – marriage and virginity: between the law and discipline. Thus, it is insufficient to simply expand law's definition to include any performative effects it may have, nor is it analytically helpful to simply confine law to its positivist sovereign understanding. The task of defining law in the neo-disciplinary situation is the task of locating the impact of its authority on how power circulates – that is, its part in the performativity of power.

The power of memes

In arguing that power's techniques are now more appropriately viewed in terms of the Memeticon than the Panopticon, I challenge the idea that power-knowledge has a central source or that there is an organising principle at work in creating hegemony of knowledge through power relations. On the contrary, I argue that power runs unruly in various directions and that its truths are very much unstructured (even if they can under certain circumstances be structured in some particular ways). The way sexuality is (dis)organised in contemporary Russia, with many identity categories and sexual orientation terms coexisting and being treated interchangeably with a variety of other queer expressions, is a case in point (Essig 1999). While in some countries, especially the US, identity categories have been central to sexual self-understanding for many people, in other places around the world sexual identities are only one of many ways of expressing queer desires (Martin et al. 2010).

The authority of science, political struggles based on identity claims, and the use of a categorical sexual vocabulary in law (Godwin Phelps 2016) may create an impression of the centrality of sexual identities for the way we experience sexuality. Furthermore, the dominance of the US universities in knowledge production may reinforce this impression and spread it worldwide, especially when knowledge is expected to come from just a few sources. However, other examples show that there exist many alternatives and that none of them dominates the many sets of social, political and historical circumstances. My proposition to move beyond the Panopticon offers tools to better understand the lack of structure, messiness, fluidity and disorder that characterises neo-disciplinary power relations. In a situation where mere information becomes knowledge, it is memetics, or the science of information, that helps us realise how ideas move around even without authoritative institutional backup.

My interest in memetics aligns with Eliot Borenstein's interpretation of memes in cultural studies, most prominently in his *Plots against Russia* (2019), except that I interpret meme circulation as a technique of power (see also Jones 2020; Baker, Clancy and Clancy 2019). I see many similarities between how power currently operates – by converting any information into resonating knowledge – and the spread of conspiracy theories analysed by Borenstein. I expand on this point further in Part IV. What is important to note here is that memetics is used in the interdisciplinary studies of law, too (Menkel-Meadow 2021). Memetics pioneer Richard Dawkins has suggested that just like genes transfer encoded data used to reconstruct a version of an organism, there are memes that carry around concepts encoded in language and that replicate the information needed to reconstruct an idea (Dawkins 2016). Thus, memes are pieces of data, bits of information replicated in texts, speech acts or pictures. They refer to some original concept, but their living form changes because it depends on immediate contextual interpretation that may or may not accurately reflect the original concept. Legal texts are full of such concepts: ideas as ancient as Babylon and the Roman Empire reproduce themselves across the millennia, to be taken on board in the law that people currently use (Deakin 2011; Katz et al. 2011; Umali and Bañez 2013; Schaper 2014). Hence, memetics in law is a 'study of law's evolution' (Katz et al. 2011, 2); it is a computational positivist analysis of 'so called "legal memes": ideas, concepts, formulas and catchphrases which have become part of the deep structure of judicial doctrine' (Schaper 2014, 79). I deploy memetics to track legal memes in a very different kind of work. To begin with, I look at how legal concepts spread across other fields, not only in legal doctrine but outside the courtroom and legislative hall. Most importantly, so long as I regard legal memes as an element of power relations, I study how they impress upon people once they have reached them.

Previous legal scholarship used memetics to trace the historical development of the law as a 'cultural form' driven by 'Darwinian principles of heredity, variation and selection as apply to genes' and resulting in 'the emergence of [a] complex social institution' (Deakin 2002, 2). This evolution is seen as progressing from simple to more superior regulative systems (Stake 2001). In contrast, I use memetics to trace how information circulates regardless of its impact on any standard of progress and regardless of its relevance to a particular field (such as law). On the first point, I side with those who argue that 'memes, like organisms, will not evolve toward some preordained state of perfection. The memes that succeed in spreading throughout large segments of the population are simply those that are best adapted to being communicated . . . memes, like genes, will succeed if they are good replicators, whether or not they are correct or good for their human carriers' (Fried 1999, 298). In other words, memetics helps us to see how memes circulate, *not* how their circulation results in evolutionary improvement or growth over time. On the contrary, some memes may deteriorate and lose their ability to reproduce, taking down the larger discursive field in which they have been most commonly used (such as legal vocabulary). After all, the evolution of organisms ensured by the reproduction of genes has also had tragic failures, such as when the slow development of a species leads to its inability to adapt to a quickly changing environment and its eventual extinction. I believe that the law (as a vocabulary full of many strongly resonant memes) is probably far from extinction, but the possibility of it cannot be rejected.

As for the second point, I do not find it particularly fruitful to investigate the whereabouts of a meme only within a particular pool of memes such as legal vocabulary. An investigation like that makes the understanding of both law and memetics positivist and, therefore, limited. The law is positivist on that account because its definition is reduced to a corpus of written texts, and memetics is positivist because it is instrumentalised only to track and trace specific phrases, not ideas. My understanding of the law and memetics as applied to this analysis is very different. Throughout the book, I treat law as discourse – a collection of meanings that are much bigger than written laws. Therefore, my analysis traces meanings rather than words: the meanings that are encoded in words, but that may still appear in various forms – a variety of words and phrases. Take for example 'non-traditional sexual relationships', a phrase used in Russian courtrooms to refer to queer sexualities. This phrase alone cannot account for the entire set of signifiers used in the same manner – the meme complex (Umali and Bañez 2013, 77; Stake 2001, 880): 'non-traditional sexual orientation', 'homosexuality' and even 'gay love' should be added to the picture among many others (see Part II). At a certain level of abstraction, they all refer to the same idea of a type of sexuality different from heterosexuality. My analysis will pay close attention to a greater variety of forms that ideas can take in spoken and written language, reflecting the entire discourse.

In this book, I broaden the horizons of memetics by moving it from linguistics to the study of discourse. After all, memes are travelling concepts and ideas, not simply words (Dawkins 2016; Blackmore 2000; Fried 1999, 296). While tracing how ideas circulate cannot be as accurate as tracing how words circulate, the payoff can be bigger. My engagement with memetics in this book is intended to show how power operates via the spread and circulation of memes. Memes carry meanings that they impress upon those who encounter them. In Part III, I theorise this impression basing my arguments on Sara Ahmed's work (2004). I argue that while the circulation of memes is the *technique* of neo-disciplinary power, this impression they make once they reach a susceptible body is a *mechanism* of power relations. Thus, my overall proposition is simple: as memes circulate, they reach many different people; the catchier they are, the more people they reach; once they do, they make an impression; and this impression enables power to start working through the production of hierarchies, even if it does not necessarily work the same way in every case. I side with Ahmed in theorising impression as an affectionate involvement between subjects of power relations – an involvement that produces hierarchies.

The selfish meme

What do memes actually do that makes them a *new* technique of power relations? Unlike other interpretations of information, memetics presumes the agency of data bits: in other words, memes can act – they are not simply passive things that we utilise, they impose their own agenda (Dawkins 2016; Stake 2001; Fried 1999, 292). Conventional understandings of agency stipulate that only human beings can purposively act in ways oriented towards impact. Hence, to claim that memes have agency, too, means taking away some agency from humans: we are not in full control anymore; we are subject to other things that act on their own account. Jane Bennett's conceptualisation of distributed agency is informative in this respect: every action, she contends, emerges through the interactions and movements of diverse human and non-human actors.[3] On this view, agency does not belong to a single subject like a possession, but rather emerges through its enactment with others (Bennett 2010; 2005). This 'agency of assemblages' (Bennett 2005) is shared among many actors who 'do not exercise exactly the same kind of agency, but neither is it easy to arrange them into a hierarchy, for in some times and places, the "small agency" of the lowly worm makes more of a difference than the grand agency of humans' (Bennett 2010, 97). Memes' contribution to this assemblage of shared agency is part of the technique by which power circulates today.

One way in which memes contribute to distributed agency is through their 'selfishness'. To describe a meme as 'selfish' is to stress its reproductive process. In order to survive, memes must always be on the move, spreading, becoming catchy and, thus, prolonging their life. Ideally, memes that are good for people survive because their purposes align with those who can reproduce them. For example, a variety of basic safety rules survived in various folk proverbs and even acquired legal status across diverse generations and cultures simply because their presence helped the people who reproduced them in their speech and texts to survive. However, any perceived alignment of purpose in this scenario should be treated as coincidental and temporary because there are also memes that survive even though they do not carry any beneficial information for people (at least not for people in general). These memes may carry useless or even harmful information that can destroy people's lives. In other words, memes may achieve various goals and can even act against people: 'what if bad ideas are more like viruses . . . the virus has agency. It acts against our will. As noted above, ideas are replicators too. The better replicators have ways of making it into the next generation whether we want them to survive or not' (Stake 2001, 885). *Violent Affections* is about such memes, whose impact resulted in deaths, injuries and other forms of suffering endured by queer victims of crime in Russia. If words can kill, this book comes close to explaining how.

Another feature of memes' contribution to agency is that they always deliver slightly outdated messages. Memes hold us back; they do not really move us forward. Memes carry a *record* of data that has already been produced at least once. While they may trigger new interpretations of this data (information), the original is always already old. More importantly, memes reproduce only if the act of reproduction is instantly gratified (that is, it is beneficial at the very moment of reproduction), even if there is a possibility of extinction in the long run. These characteristics bring memes very close to their prototype: genes. Just as genes encode the environmental information of the moment, memes record and first resonate within the environment in which they were created. This poses both a challenge and an opportunity for memes. The challenge is that as the environment changes, memes (like genes) need to adapt to ensure their survival or they die. Opportunity arises because the memes that do adapt to the new environment get another chance to move on (Fried 1999). In any case, memes are 'conservative': they resonate best in the environment they are accustomed to.

'Non-traditional sexual relationships', the meme that signifies homosexuality in Russia, was created in a particular heteronormative environment in which queerness was seen as something that contradicts 'traditions', while 'traditions' were understood as something to be cherished by society. Imagine a different environment, in which 'traditions' are not a societal value to be upheld (for example, revolutionary Soviet society), and you might predict slim odds for this meme's survival. At the same time, this Soviet society was also heteronormative and, therefore, a different form of this meme – of the idea of homosexuality as inferior in some way – would still survive. For example, something based on medical professional terminology such as 'homosexualism' (Essig and Kondakov 2019) would feel relatively comfortable in the Soviet environment (which was generally hostile to diversity anyway). While these memes comprise a single meme complex (a combination of different forms of memes referring to a similar idea) and carry the same data (the difference between sexualities), they have to slightly adapt their form and the information they carry to respond to the environment in which they hope to reproduce. Certainly, if the environment changes (becomes less heteronormative or not heteronormative at all, for example), the homosexual meme complex will need to change significantly too or die out entirely. There are queer utopias premised on the presumption that sexual orientation will not matter in the future (the difference between sexualities will disappear). If memetics is correct, in order for the idea of sexual orientation to die, first the environment must become one in which sexual difference does not matter.

The organisation of the book

Throughout this book I advance a relatively simple argument. I contend that the way power circulates is changing from the Panopticon of modernity to the Memeticon of today's unruly times. This corresponds with the diminishing legitimacy of institutional authority such as that conveyed by law and other conventional institutions. Instead of a hegemonic shared truth sustained by the law, current power produces fragmented and fluid truths enacted across neo-disciplinary power relations. This argument is complex, though, because to show this change, I need to discuss a variety of very relevant, but not immediately connected, topics. I therefore divide these topics into four separate parts, consisting of two chapters each. The parts discuss the law, sexualities, emotions and memes. The two chapters in each part present theoretical and empirical arguments respectively.

Part I discusses the law. It is an opportunity for me to conceptualise law as a discursive field, simultaneously autopoietic (self-absorbent) yet porous (capable of exchange with other fields). The law features in the book as a prime example of the previously legitimate authority that seemed to play a crucial role in the thickening of modern power as it produced hegemonic truths with ease. Not coincidentally, one of the iconic incarnations of the Panopticon is the prison building – the place where legal decisions are executed. Since I want to show a new role for law in emerging neo-disciplinary power relations, I want to adapt its definition to the memetic discursive methodology. Pierre Bourdieu's idea of the legal field (1987), discussed in Chapter 1, does this job. Chapter 2 introduces the empirical material with which I work throughout the book: court decisions from 314 cases of anti-queer violence in Russia. I read them not as texts, but as manifestations of discourse in which power relations feature prominently. In my analysis I do not dwell on the facts of the cases. Rather, I conduct a descriptive and discursive analysis of the court decisions. Yet, I still read the cases as records that mirror a version of events that took place in cities, towns and villages across Russia. These records are unique and valuable sources of anthropological impressions about highly secretive phenomena: sex and violence.

Part I presents both a clear picture of the written law in Russia and many very messy legal practices: some descriptions of violence will sound bizarre, some people's decisions will not make sense, and courts' conclusions may leave you baffled. Part II will wrestle with this messiness by deepening the analysis of the court documents, only now focusing exclusively on the idea of queer sexuality expressed in them. Since this idea is manifested in messy, fluid and varied ways, I first discuss queer theory – a collection of mostly US literature meant for the analysis of sexualities beyond strict identity constraints and critiquing the concept of identity, while still investing in it. Queer theory is the glue that binds the entire book together: from Foucault to Butler to Ahmed and others, I draw a clear intellectual lineage to this literature. Chapter 3 works with this literature in two respects. Firstly, it remedies the US-centrism that obstructs a successful analysis of the Russian context with regard to queer theory. In doing so, I join the call for a global queer theory – a critical rethinking of queer theory as we know it (Liu 2015; Rao 2020). I argue for the legitimacy of asking classical queer theory questions, such as questions about power relations and using Russian knowledges to find globally relevant answers to them. Secondly, I outline the contribution of scholarship on queer Russia (Essig 1999; Healey 2018; Kondakov 2020b) to this global queer theory. This contribution helps me to structure the book's narrative and start building my queer theory of neo-disciplinary power relations beyond sexual identity concerns. Chapter 4 focuses on a discursive analysis of expressions of queerness in court decisions. It concludes by making sense of the fluidity, messiness and multiplicity of ways sexuality is expressed as opposed to simpler identity categories.

With the groundwork laid, Part III gets down to discussing how power works. This part is dedicated to the mechanisms of power. It explains why people do the things they do – in this case why they kill, injure or otherwise upset others once they feel a hierarchical sexual difference between them and their victims. In Chapter 5, I invoke Sara Ahmed's interpretation of 'affect' (2004) and discuss emotions more generally as a mechanism of power. While there are many ways to conceptualise emotions and affects, I argue that the understanding of affect as power relations is the one that helps me most in my queer criminological analysis. If power produces hierarchies, this is exactly what affect can do: affect is the way we feel others and is the first step in perceiving our relations to others once we encounter them. Chapter 6 analyses such encounters as recorded in the court decisions on anti-queer violence in Russia. I find that affect does not necessarily condition the creation of hierarchies, but when it does, we deal with a particular kind of affect – violent affections. Violent affections are feelings towards the other – they can entail both passionate and ferocious actions. As they necessarily conclude in murder, injury or malfeasance in the cases under analysis, they are by definition violent. Violent affections are one of the mechanisms of power that lead to violence.

I continue my analysis of violent affections in Part IV. This time, my aim is to present the techniques of neo-disciplinary power that trigger violent affections. In Chapter 7, I set aside the court rulings for a while and trace the lifespan of the Russian 'propaganda of non-traditional sexual relationships' meme complex. It was first introduced to me in 2013 when Moscow parliamentarians were discussing a federal ban on the 'propaganda of homosexuality'. I subsequently discovered the entire lifespan of the meme from its first invocation in the 1980s–90s to its temporary decline in 2016. My analysis in this part shows how the meme's lifespan and replicability match the level of anti-queer violence in Russia.

Chapter 8 is the book's Conclusion. Beyond the empirical and theoretical arguments that I have presented, here I give space to the question of further implications for my analysis beyond Russia and beyond studies of violence. I focus in particular on the place of law in this new configuration of power relations. Can law help us fight bad memes? What do we do with anti-queer violence if not? The Conclusion broaches these questions. In sum, this book is about breaking power by understanding how it works.

A Russian saying suggests that when one has power, there is no need to have intellect (*'sila iest' – uma ne nado'*). *Violent Affections* is based on the opposite sentiment: if we have the intellectual tools to identify and understand how power works, we may hope to create places where it is absent.

Notes

1. Source: Ruling 1-3/2013, Oryol. Fictional names have been substituted to preserve anonymity in this and all other cited cases. All quotes are translated from Russian by the author. Ruling titles reflect the index number of the court's internal registrar, year of decision and the place where the decision was taken. If the place is a provincial capital that gives its name to the entire province, then it stands on its own in the title. These files can be accessed through the official court decisions database at http://sudrf.ru.
2. Contemporary works in this area suggest, for example, that intersectional approaches may be a game changer in designing future hate crime legislation (Meyer 2015). With the growing body of queer studies of this kind, it is now evident that generating good ideas about updating the law is already a *fait accompli* in many 'gay friendly' jurisdictions. Now the time has come to expand these studies to under-researched areas and further apply the accumulated knowledge there. Certainly, with such expansion, questions of coloniality and the imperialism of knowledge production arise. I review these questions in Part II by positioning queer theory in relation to studies of Russia.
3. See an overview of these ideas in relation to law in Low Reyna 2020.

Part 1
The authority of law

A perfect crime

On 6 August 2011, a man, whom I shall call Misha, committed what seemed to him the perfect crime. Using a public computer in a library situated in a town near his temporary place of residence near Stavropol, Misha registered a new email account that he then used to activate a profile – including a fake picture taken from the internet – on a dating website. It took him only a week to find what he was looking for: a gay man to kill. Misha visited the library every day and exchanged messages with Sergey, a registered user on the dating website who indicated that he was a man looking for men. After making sure Sergey was indeed gay, Misha agreed to meet him one weekend in the large southern Russian city of Krasnodar, with which he had little connection. Misha rented a flat for several days in Krasnodar without showing his identity documents. Sergey and Misha met on a Saturday afternoon and drove towards the Black Sea in Sergey's car.

Instead of stopping by the sea – flooded with beachgoers from all over Russia, especially in August – the two men found an isolated meadow in the middle of a forest where they started a fire and prepared a picnic. When the time felt right, Misha hit Sergey with a stone and then strangled him with his bare hands. After committing the murder, Misha drove Sergey's car to a small village in the Republic of Adygea where he took a train to the sea city of Adler in Krasnodar Territory.[1] There, he packed his things and flew for more than 10 hours across Russia to his hometown of Shimanovsk in Amur Region.

Sergey's dead body would not be found for nearly a month, since nobody went to the forest on those hot days with the sea being so close.

Believing he had covered his tracks well, Misha felt deep satisfaction. However, he was arrested, indicted and sent back to Krasnodar Territory for trial in November of that same year. The pieces of the puzzle had been hard to put together: they required coordination between investigators in four different provinces (the location of the murder, the library computer, Sergey's abandoned car and Misha's home). The investigation started with an initial lead from Sergey's personal computer, on which the police found the following message exchange between the two men:

> Sergey: 'Hello, write to me if interested in chatting, I live not far from Krasnodar, work in the city, single, looking for a friend, decency guaranteed, dreaming of feelings and relationships. Sincerely, Sergey.' (31.07.2011)

Misha: 'Tell me please, Sergey, what kind of relationship are you looking for? And, well, how do you see all this? Sorry for so many questions at a time.' (31.07.2011)

Sergey: 'What does a man want: a bit of happiness, a close person by the side who one can hug in the morning, some intimacy, and the purpose to live for, then we'll see, I have a lot on my plate now, many prospects for development, I need someone by my side. As for intimacy, I can adapt to you, we'll do what you want. Hope it answers your questions.' (31.07.2011)

Misha: 'Surely!! Thank you for your great story! What do you do…? if this is not a secret for someone from the Internet.' (31.07.2011)

Sergey: 'I'm an engineer working on heating systems, it should result in a tourist project of the social kind, a lot of stuff, so let's meet, I don't bite.' (31.07.2011)

Misha: 'I'm really up for it!!! What would be the programme for our first meeting…?' (31.07.2011)

Sergey: 'Let's go to the sea over this weekend, we can meet any day really and chat, we can also go anywhere else, glad to meet you. Good night.' (31.07.2011)

Misha: 'Very well, Sergey!!!! I have to run now and please write to me what your schedule is for upcoming days (nights) evenings and we'll discuss it all tomorrow!!! Meanwhile I'll think how we can spend some good time together!! Cheers!! Till tomorrow!!' (31.07.2011)

Sergey: 'Hello!! I'm stuck at work now (tell you all about it when we meet), but literally tomorrow or the day after I'll be free as a bird – as soon as I fix this all, I'll call you and we'll make up a date, alright…?' (01.08.2011)

Misha: 'Alright.' (01.08.2011); 'Good evening, have you forgotten about me, maybe I have dreamt for no reason… I'm free over the weekend, we can do whatever you want, write me, hugs.' (02.08.2011)

Sergey: 'Hi!! Why forgotten…? I told you I was very busy at work! Tomorrow I'll be free, by the way I hope we'll meet on the weekend… if it's gonna be the sea or something else, we'll decide later! Are we not easy-going?!!!!!' (03.08.2011)

Misha: 'Hello, Sergey! it has been a hard day, I've had to go to Novorossiysk, the road is fierce, miss you, waiting for you to call, Misha.' (03.08.2011)

Sergey: 'I'll ring you tonight.' (04.08.2011) (1-121/2012, Severskaya, Krasnodar Territory)

The email account used by Misha led investigators to an IP address in the Stavropol public library named after the Russian poet Lermontov, as well as a pre-paid phone number. Suspicions arose when both the email address and the phone number turned out to have been used exclusively to communicate with Sergey. The Stavropol librarian testified that he clearly remembered a man coming in to use a computer in August, and he showed library activity logs to the investigators. The man was memorable because he had left the library when there had been a photoshoot of the premises for an exhibition. Furthermore, the librarian had looked over Misha's shoulder once and had seen that he was using the computer to visit a dating website. As for the phone, the last time it had been used was in proximity to Sergey's phone and the crime scene. Sergey's car had been captured by a road camera in the Republic of Adygea, driven by a man that looked like Misha. In the car, investigators found Misha's fingerprints and hair. They then followed his tracks to the city of Adler and the plane to Amur Region where he was eventually apprehended for the murder of a gay man.

1
The legal field

Unofficially hated

For a crime against an LGBT+ person to be classified as a hate crime, the perpetrator of violence must actively have targeted their victim because of their sexuality. In the modern world of digital technology, offenders often use dating apps and websites to search for, select and contact their victims. Misha in the case above did this and consequently left a digital footprint that led to his arrest. 'Hate crime' can be used as an official legal classification for a case. The legal professionals involved in a given investigation, from police officers to prosecutors and judges, must agree that the crime with which they are dealing is not a standard matter but a hate crime. Such a designation symbolically charges an act of lawbreaking and thus requires a symbolically charged response. Given that Russia is notorious for its official government-sponsored homophobia, it might be difficult to imagine that anti-queer violence could ever be elevated to the status of a hate crime within its jurisdiction. In this chapter, I outline both the theoretical arguments about the status of law and doctrinal details about the status of hate crime against LGBT+ people in Russian law. I argue that the situation is more complex than that fostered by any preconceptions of Russian homophobia.

Misha's case is an unusual but illustrative example to begin with. For starters, the case was properly and quickly investigated, and the victim's sexuality was recorded and evidenced. As for the sentence, which is supposed to be enhanced in hate crime cases, it was indeed harsher than would normally be given in a murder case. Misha's defence strategy was to reject the allegation of murder and say that his meeting with the victim was part of his personal research into gay people's lives. He claimed he was interested in why gay people were denied equality and understanding and so he wanted to meet one to find some answers. It was for this reason that he went to the forest with Sergey. Misha maintained that Sergey was still alive when he left him there; he said he was scared of being alone with a gay man and that was why he took Sergey's car and ran away. Given so much documented evidence to the contrary, provided by surprisingly good police work, the judge in the case did not decide in favour of Misha. It seems that the judge also took into account the hate motive that had become so obvious from the case file. In the following excerpt, the judge unambiguously states that Sergey was unequivocally targeted by Misha because he was gay:

> In this criminal case, the motive of unpleasant feelings to persons with non-traditional sexual orientation was evidenced by the fact that Misha chose a specific object – the life of Sergey – from the very moment when the idea of murdering a person with non-traditional sexual orientation crossed his mind, and in what had followed he did not pursue any other goals such as learning something new from talking to persons of non-traditional sexual orientation, although, according to the data from his email, he had every chance of so doing since many dating and chatting requests continued to end up in his inbox. (1-121/2012, Severskaya, Krasnodar Territory)

Yet while the judge clearly indicates that the perpetrator's motive is a negative attitude towards gay people as a group, notably he does not refer to 'hate' in his findings. Instead, he mentions 'unpleasant feelings', a legal term that reveals judicial reluctance to enforce hate crime legislation. Indeed, Misha was indicted and found guilty of violating Article 105, para. 1 of the Russian Criminal Code, namely premeditated murder, *not* a murder motivated by hatred, which is punishable under Article 105, para. 2, section L. The difference between these two clauses is that defendants are sentenced to between 6 and 15 years in the former case and between 8 and 20 years (also for life and to death) in the case of 'murder aggravated by hatred'. Since para. 2, section L was not cited, no hate crime was officially recognised in this case.

But this is not the end of the story. The judge sentenced Misha to 11 years in a high-security penal colony,[2] whereas most defendants (3,256 people) prosecuted under Article 105, para. 1 in 2012 were sentenced to between 5 and 8 years' imprisonment.[3] Misha was among 1,045 out of 7,577 people to receive harsher-than-average punishments in the range of 10 to 15 years. And all this despite the fact that Misha's personal characteristics played in his favour. According to his case file, Misha was a patriot and a 'volunteer', whose character was praised in court by a local police officer, an employer and village authorities; furthermore, he had never been in trouble with the law before this. These characteristics usually work towards a reduction in sentence. Given Misha's harsh punishment, could this judge have unofficially considered the hatred motive and increased the sentence as a result? In other words, might it be the case that while judges are reluctant to openly implement hate crime legislation because of socio-cultural homophobia, they nevertheless still believe that justice must be done, and therefore give longer sentences in cases of anti-queer violence? To answer this question, it is necessary to understand how the law works – and particularly how it works in Russia, as well as what the role of politics is in enforcing the law.

In this chapter I define the legal field and survey the Russian criminal justice system to offer an overview of the Russian legal context. This also gives me an opportunity to detail the main materials on which this book is based: the 314 cases of anti-queer violence that went through Russia's criminal justice system between 2010 and 2016. In Chapter 2 I offer simple descriptive statistics to acknowledge that the small numbers do not allow me to establish causation; they do, however, enable me to illuminate the data that I analyse qualitatively in the following chapters. My overarching question is why these cases made it through Russia's criminal justice system despite the hostile (homophobic) political context.

I turn now to look at criminal law as a source of authority in the discursive environment that structures, dictates and reproduces various practices for all parties involved in the legal process. In other words, I am looking for what law has to offer the configuration of power relations that runs through and across Russian society in various ways. I also review what Russian law actually says about hate crime in general and hate crime against LGBT+ people in particular. The analysis reveals both the ideas surrounding and the practice of law in Russia.

The legal field

As I outlined in the Introduction, the central claim of this book is that techniques of power have changed from organised ones, as reflected in Michel Foucault's Panopticon, to more disorderly and decentralised relations of power captured by the term 'Memeticon' because of the greater role information (or memes) plays in reproducing and delivering knowledge. I understand this analysis as a continuation of the work done by Foucault, who uncovered the idea of disciplinary power almost five decades ago. My claim is that conventional disciplinary power is evaporating and is giving way to neo-disciplinary power. While the law remains, its function changes. For Foucault, the law played a very important role in his theory of power, encompassing both the older, 'sovereign', top-down forms of power and also – although more paradoxically – disciplinary power's mode of transmission. But what role does law play in emerging neo-disciplinary power relations?

I mentioned in the Introduction that Foucault's commentators suggest that he distinguished between two interrelated modalities of law (Golder and Fitzpatrick 2009, 71–2). When the law is understood as a performative discourse, its sovereign modality is to make people obey what the written law says; in its disciplinary modality its task is to regulate people's conduct beyond the written law. Judith Butler has further argued that law is always both sovereign *and* disciplinary, and it therefore makes no sense to distinguish between these modalities of law (Butler 1997). Yet if the first idea defines the law, then how do we distinguish disciplinary power at all? If the Butlerian definition applies, then disciplinary power is barely distinguishable from the law and the disciplinary workings of power will sometimes appear to be confused with simple law enforcement. Because my analysis here intends to focus on the relations between law and power, it is analytically important for me to resist Butler's theoretical move and to separate the two. In contrast to Butler, then, I ask what the law does to power rather than whether or not law can be defined as disciplinary power.

In pursuing this question, I do not want to suggest that the law is simply a collection of legal texts, as any positivist analysis of the sovereign modality of law does. Nor do I want to deny legal texts their important place in contemporary law. Indeed, I analyse the texts of criminal statutes and criminal court rulings that have a clear impact on people's lives (in the form of punishments, for example). But I understand the law as something more than the sum of these texts. Without the support of the institutional arrangement of the criminal justice system, none of these texts would have any authority on their own. Pierre Bourdieu argued that for these texts to work properly, legal norms need to be embodied by a variety of actors within the legal field (Bourdieu 1987). The way these norms are embodied are through the habitual practices, the *habitus*, of legal professionals such as lawyers, judges and police officers. What they do forms – in part – what the law is, although, as others add, what 'lay people' and non-humans do about the law should also be included in its definition (Butler 1997, 142; Latour 2013).

The legal field is a discursive field defined by its thematic vocabulary (Dezalay and Madsen 2012). Bourdieu argues that societies consist of many porously delineated fields, each of which has its own set of norms and exchange values (accumulated in capital and used as sources of power) that ensure their predictable functioning and relative separation from other fields (Bourdieu 1984; 1987; 2013). Thus, there is a cultural field distinct from the political field, and the actors within these different fields will value different kinds of things and follow separate sets of norms corresponding to the practices within each field. In order to qualify as a legitimate actor in the legal field and, therefore, authoritatively use its resources, one has to possess the relevant credentials (a law degree, for example) and be able to utilise the relevant vocabulary (know the letter of law and its common interpretations). Legal actors become more authoritative if they accumulate good connections (social capital) or occupy higher offices (institutional capital) and so on. Certainly, various forms of capital amplify themselves – in other words, the rich find it easier to become richer. In addition, various forms of capital mediate each other: for example, in societies that ascribe less cultural value to femininity than to masculinity, women have fewer chances to advance in the legal field despite the absence of formal obstacles (Ivanova 2015; Schultz et al. 2021; R. Hunter 2015). At the same time, these various fields are interconnected, and figuring out their interconnections is important for my project.

In sum, the legal field is a type of discursive vocabulary and a space that contains sovereign and disciplinary modalities of law, legal norms and legal actors that embody them through their practices. Law as defined by legal texts can function effectively only when there is an entire system of practices backing it up: all the actors (judges, prosecutors, police officers), organisations (law schools, courts, prisons), rituals (investigation, hearing, punishment), etc., must act together. And indeed, they typically all function to maintain law's authority because their own positions and resources depend on it. If law loses its authority, all these lawyers and institutions lose their authority – and their privilege too. But law is also very fragile because its authority relies on external recognition within a larger social context – social recognition that what it serves can still be referred to as 'justice'. As I show in Chapter 2, justice is a thing constructed in the process of maintaining the authority of the legal field and the legitimacy of all these legal actors.

Thus, the legal field is an analytical way to describe the appearance of the law: if all actors within the legal field convince observers that what they do is justice, then it is the law. It seems, then, that the product of law is the law itself; or, at least, the product of the legal field is the law. What this means is that law is tasked with producing its own *authority*. Whether people are forced to follow the law, or they sincerely believe that following the law is a good thing to do, they are under the influence of the authority of law. In Foucault's theory of disciplinary power, law's authority is part and parcel of the Panopticon: it is instrumentalised to generate a shared hegemonic version of the truth without which the entire Panopticon cannot function. Perhaps there will be those who will challenge what the law says. Yet, many take whatever the authority of the law supports as common sense. This is law's function in disciplinary power relations: to authorise information and alchemise it into unquestioned truthful knowledge.

Over the course of the following chapters, I review the power of law to authorise in the neo-disciplinary situation. As my discussions will show, the legal field here turns into a sort of echo chamber rather than a commonly accepted authority. In other words, it does produce effects within itself, but it is losing its ability to influence other fields of social reproduction. So, while the law retains its capacity to reproduce its own vocabulary and its system of values for its institutional players, it no longer seems to be sufficient on its own for the production of legitimate knowledge externally. Like any other echo chamber, what the law authorises remains relevant to the law but is rarely heard outside of the legal field, where multiple versions of the truth are gaining similar legitimacy. Hence, law's function changes from guiding and enhancing information and authorising it to limiting the reach of information within legal boundaries and, therefore, defining it as merely legal.

Ordinary politics and law

Observers of the practice of law in Russia have stressed the politicised nature of Russian law (Muravyeva 2013a, 211). In other words, while legal professionals might try to maintain an appearance of judicial autonomy, they seem to be quite unsuccessful in this regard. Instead, the impression is that whatever President Putin personally (or the Russian government more generally) wants can easily be formalised through a court of law ruling. For example, courts can be tasked with advancing homophobia by discriminating against queer litigants and victims. Indeed, scholars tend to emphasise the culture of so-called 'telephone justice', whereby powerful actors make direct calls to judges to dictate the decisions they need (Ledeneva 2008). This results in distrust of the legal system and a sort of 'legal nihilism' (cf. Hendley 2012) among the Russian public that opposes the legitimate and authoritative appearance of the law.

These views of Russian law may be regarded as oversimplified, as though the law is driven solely by direct political pressure or is unused by the general population. But such views are actually substantiated by empirical observation. For example, in the 1990s Russian law was only just beginning to evolve; the rule of force remained dominant in everyday life (Volkov 2002; Stephenson 2015). Even after the legal system was established, Putin and the government clearly called judges – or communicated by other means – to demand certain decisions: to seize an oil company from non-loyal oligarchs (Kahn 2018) or to showcase a new conservative public order by punishing a feminist punk music band (Kondakov 2017d). Given that the courts have wide scope to turn non-legal decisions into enforceable judgments, it is reasonable to suggest that politicians want to use the power of the law to advance their agenda when circumstances permit (Silbey 1998). In Russia, circumstances are generally more favourable for achieving this than not. However, this applies only in exceptional cases – show trials and economic battles where important people feel it is worth going to the trouble of picking up the phone and calling the judge. This book is *not* about these exceptional cases. The analysis here is based on routine criminal hearings that those important people walking the corridors of power rarely become aware of. It is about everyday law in Russia (Hendley 2017).

Consider the case of Misha and Sergey introduced earlier. The victim was a relatively discreet queer man in his 40s who had previously been married to a woman. He was living with his mother at the time of his murder, but they had never discussed his sexuality, although she knew about it and testified in court accordingly. As for the murderer, he was a seasonal construction worker from a remote village on the Russian border with China, as well as a 'patriot' involved in government-led organisations created to promote 'proper' citizenship. Whether or not the ideas taught in these political organisations influenced his decision to find and kill a gay man remains a mystery. What is clear, though, is that this kind of politics is of little concern to President Putin, who would never conceivably have called the judge to press them about Misha's case. Thus, while both the veil of secrecy that surrounds Sergey's homosexuality and Misha's anti-queer vigilantism can be attributed – in part – to the Kremlin's hostility towards sexual diversity politics, it is not the same explicit kind of politics that we find in the cases of Pussy Riot and the Yukos Oil Company.

The Russian political context thus provides fertile ground for the capricious use of legal tools to suppress political opposition and benefit the economically powerful in cases that directly further their goals. In most cases, though, Putin's telephone line appears to be busy, and often justice must be served by the judges themselves in their everyday, monotonous scrutiny of mundane – if at times chilling – conflicts. In these mundane cases, what kind of politics operates? In my attempt to analyse the everyday politics of mundane law, I return to Pierre Bourdieu's analysis of the political dimension of law (Madsen and Dezalay 2013). In this account, Bourdieu regards the legal field as 'relatively independent of external determinations and pressures' (1987, 816) but at the same time dependent on external recognition. This independence is necessary to constitute the field as legal: it must maintain a certain level of autonomy through its own vocabulary, symbolic capital, hierarchies, etc. In other words, for this fragile social fabric to work properly, law should be determined by lawyers, judges and legal professionals whose legal competences are confirmed by trustworthy credentials and the various forms of capital they have managed to acquire through their careers.

However, the legal field remains authoritative only if it is recognised as legitimate by the outside world. In Bourdieu's own words: 'As the quintessential form of legitimized discourse, the law can exercise its specific power only to the extent that it attains recognition, that is, to the extent that the element of arbitrariness at the heart of its functioning (which may vary from case to case) remains unrecognized' (1987, 844). This is the definition of justice. I argue that only when a court ruling finds resonance with more general societal values can it be recognised as a legitimate decision. Even in the exceptional cases mentioned above, this societal resonance may have been provided by the fierce denunciation of Pussy Riot by some elements of the Russian populace or their dislike of the rich. In the mundane cases that I analyse, an aspect of this societal justice – at times cruel and bloodthirsty, at times kind and wise – is evidenced through the work of the sentencing that judges do. Judges do not simply implement the Kremlin's policies, rather they reproduce more general attitudes towards homosexuality or other markers of social inequality that play out in the cases before them.

Basing my enquiry on the above conception of the legal field, I argue that – unlike in more romantic versions of justice – what judges do is founded on prejudice and bias rather than equality and respect. Since judges, as actors in the legal field, are interested in the external recognition of their legitimacy, they have to follow public sentiment to the extent that they can and to the extent that they are aware of it. Therefore, even without the Kremlin exerting pressure on judges, it is in their interest to reproduce heteronormativity rather than gender and sexual equality, unless Russian society shifts to recognise these values (Gulevich et al. 2018). This is the kind of ordinary politics that can be found in everyday criminal justice in Russia. Indeed, Bourdieu suggests that the legal field is designed to support existing societal structures and biases, not to bring about a revolution (1987, 845). If that is correct, then the court decisions under analysis here are reflections of Russian society articulated from the privileged seat of the judiciary. Consequently, new questions emerge: What does society look like from the judge's vantage point? Are queer people understood as a vulnerable population worthy of protection via specifically designed laws? What other social markers of difference do judges take into account when making their decisions?

The codified law

Before I get down to analysing the documents produced by the criminal courts in the next chapter, it is necessary to take a closer look at the legal environment in which the courts operate. First I will offer an overview of the relevant criminal statutes in Russia, concentrating especially on those Criminal Code articles that refer directly to hate crime. I will also analyse some of the procedural norms that set out the rules on the investigation and adjudication of cases, because these norms explain how criminal justice should ideally take place. In many respects, the remainder of this chapter is a survey of the vocabulary legal actors use to create the appearance of law. I ask: What terms are available for legal actors to use? Which actors are involved in making justice appear? What procedural rites might these actors need to follow to make their work appear legitimate to insiders? To answer these questions, I analyse the texts of the criminal statutes that form the basis of the court rulings that I go on to study in Chapter 2.

The most visible parts of the criminal justice system are the texts of legal statutes. They are accessible to everyone both online and offline, as codified in the Criminal Code of the Russian Federation, which was adopted in 1996 and came into force in 1997. It replaced the outdated Soviet criminal code after the collapse of the USSR. The Criminal Code consists of more than 350 articles, subdivided into sections and paragraphs. It defines crimes and punishments, as well as setting out principles of the criminal justice system in current Russia. The provinces of Russia (subjects of the federation) do not have the right to adopt or implement their own criminal statutes. Crimes are listed in the Special Chapter (*Osobennaya chast'*), which starts with murder (Article 105). To date, the Criminal Code has been amended more than 250 times with additional articles and other revisions – it is quite a dynamic document. In some years – for instance in 2010, 2013 and 2014 – more than 20 new federal statutes amending the Code were introduced by the legislators.

Judges must refer to Criminal Code articles in their decisions and comply with the requirements that dictate the range of sentences that can be assigned to crimes. The Criminal Procedure Code of the Russian Federation (CPC), which was adopted in 2001, further clarifies the procedures involved in delivering justice. For example, it defines how cases should be handled, what evidence is admissible in courts, and how rulings are to be written and delivered. Another relevant code, enacted in 1997, is the Penal Code (*Ugolovno-ispolnitel'niy kodeks*) of the Russian Federation. This code defines how punishment is to be carried out. Various forms of prison facility are stipulated in this document, as well as rules on acceptable behaviour for convicted criminals in those institutions. These three codes comprise the core of Russia's criminal justice system – together with the country's international obligations and the higher courts' clarifications – although in practice the codified texts of national statutes take precedence over everything else. In other words, the codes signal and manifest the vocabulary of criminal law in Russia that legal professionals interiorise in their everyday work.

While the criminal codes are no more than texts of law and the forms of justice they convey depend on *interpretations* of those texts, it is still worth looking at some of their articles. I began this research with the idea of searching for anti-queer hate crime. But is violence against LGBT+ people even criminalised? The answer is ambiguous. Article 63 of the Criminal Code defines aggravation when considering sentencing for a crime. Before 2007, that article, contained within Section E, recognised 'hatred or animosity' motivated by ethnic, racial or religious bias as aggravating circumstances together with 'revenge for rightful actions of other persons' and motives to commit a crime to hide another crime. Other sections listed further aggravating circumstances; hate as such did not have a place of its own. In 2007 this was remedied, and Article 63 was edited and expanded to define aggravation as 'the commission of a crime motivated by political, ideological, racial, ethnic or religious hatred or animosity, or motivated by hatred or animosity towards any one social group'. How did this change come about?

A legal novelty

Most probably, the language of hate crime legislation arrived in Russia from the outside. If this is so, and hate crime is indeed a concept foreign to the Russian criminal justice system, then it explains why the application of hate crime legislation is so rare and why so many legal professionals in the field are unwilling to embrace it (at least until the notion is domesticated; clearly, many legal notions enter a national jurisdiction from elsewhere). The Soviet criminal code contained one mention of 'ethnic or racial animosity and discord' as an aggravating circumstance in murder (Criminal Code of the RSFSR 1960, Article 102, Section M). It also had a separate Article 74 that prohibited 'violations of ethnic and racial equality' (Dubrovskiy 2020, 725). This is as close as Soviet law got to punishing hate at the time. Notably, in the new Russian Criminal Code, the Soviet term 'discord' was replaced by 'hatred'. Work on the wording of the 2007 amendments was prompted by the Organisation for Security and Cooperation in Europe (OSCE), broadly a Cold War institution set up as a meeting point for Western and Socialist states (Morozov 2005), especially its Office for Democratic Institutions and Human Rights (ODIHR). Russia (and originally the USSR) is a member state of this organisation and is open to scrutiny for human rights and rule of law violations. As a collective body, the OSCE cannot be said to advance a purely 'Western' perspective (whatever that means), since Russia's membership of the organisation ensures that it contributes to its functioning. Yet it does exhibit a degree of bias towards Western legal notions and discourse.

Pressure from these agencies started with two Plenary Meeting decisions in 2004 that partially resulted from the United Nations' (UN) and the Council of Europe's previous work, especially the European Commission against Racism and Intolerance's (ECRI) General Policy Recommendation No. 7 (2002).[4] One decision concerned anti-semitism and instructed states to combat 'hate crimes, which can be fuelled by racist, xenophobic and anti-Semitic propaganda' (OSCE 2004a, 1). The other stressed the importance of anti-discrimination and hate crime legislation, as well as prompting member states to record and generate better statistics in this area (OSCE 2004b). ODIHR would indeed assume the role of collector of hate crime statistics from 2009,[5] and in all its governing documents pays particular attention to gathering numbers (Katsuba 2021). Programmes were further put in place to assist member states with writing hate crime legislation and composing good datasets for the OSCE. For example, in a 2005 report, *Combating Hate Crime*, an incident record template was offered for law enforcement in member states. The template included 'sexual orientation' under the rubric of 'discrimination type' (OSCE 2005, 103). A reading of this report, however, does create the impression that hate crime laws are foreign not only to Russian law but to European law as a whole. The report constantly stresses the superiority of hate crime legislation in the USA and Canada, while paying significantly less attention to various methods of combating prejudice in European jurisdictions, not to mention Soviet experiences.

Further reports and recommendations published by these authoritative institutions strengthened the understanding that hate crime legislation and its monitoring by law enforcement agencies across OSCE states was of high importance for European bureaucracy. Sexual orientation was not insisted upon as one of the necessary avenues of law's intervention; rather, the documents focused on hate crime by arguing for the necessity of protecting 'ethnic minorities'.[6] It is important to note that the reports were not confrontational in nature towards Russia. On the contrary, they were written in cooperation with the Russian authorities and stressed the advantages of what had already been put in place in the country.

With the development of LGBT+ activism in Russia around the same time (Kondakov 2013b; Stella 2013; Buyantueva 2018; Mikhaylova and Gradoselskaya 2021), homophobia became more articulated as a response to the increased public visibility of queerness and therefore evoked reasonable, albeit brief, responses by relevant international bodies, including the OSCE. A report of 2006 discusses verbal attacks on LGBT+ people in Poland, Latvia and Russia – in all three cases the insults were directed towards activists who tried to organise street events (OSCE 2006, 28–9).

In summary, the Russian government (just like many other governments in Europe) was subjected by international bodies to a thorough review of its efforts at fighting discrimination and hate crime between 2002 and 2006. I have sketched only an outline of this review, with emphasis on the role of the OSCE, but the point is that hate crime was of particular concern to international agencies and, consequently, it had trickle-down effects (Sundstrom, Sperling and Sayoglu 2019; Kerf 2017). While some interventions were more or less direct, most of this work instead produced the conditions for legal and institutional reform, namely the dissemination of relevant terminology through training programmes and sharing of documents; pressure due to the constant reqirement to report back to pan-European and UN agencies;

empowerment of local civil society organisations (most notably the SOVA think-tank and the Moscow-Helsinki Group) in the sphere of hate crimes; and pointing out inconsistencies and pitfalls in current legislation. Given that all this was introduced through the language of fighting ethnic biases, no 'sexual' triggers were flagged at the time and the Russian government remained relatively calm: there was no opportunity to retaliate with the 'traditional values' discourse (which would be the case in the near future). In the absence of 'red flags' and in response to this flow of requests, critique and information, the Russian government initiated amendments to its criminal law. The updating of hate crime law, including aggravating circumstances under Article 63, was one of the visible outcomes of this work.

Hate and sexuality

In relation to the queerness that concerns me in this book, the introduction of the notion 'social group' in Russian law in 2007 is especially relevant (Kondakov 2017a). This new wording in Article 63 gave hate crime its own paragraph (revenge et al. were moved to a different place) and the list of punishable prejudices increased with the addition of 'politics', 'ideology' and 'social group' as possible targets of hatred. This latter notion is queers' entry point into law. As the Constitutional Court of Russia opined in 2014, citing *inter alia* Article 63:

> The sphere of freedom of sexual self-identification presumes the existence of objective differences in sexual identity and the possibility for, as a rule, adults to choose any non-violent or not implying threat of injuries variances of sexual behaviour, including those that are disapproved of by the majority from their ethical, religious or other perspectives . . . This constitutional principle implies unacceptability of limitations on rights and freedoms or of institutionalisation of privileges dependent upon affiliation with any one social group, which includes persons with a particular sexual orientation. (Constitutional Court 2014, para. 2.1)

In other words, the Constitutional Court confirmed that LGBT+ people are covered by the term 'social group'. This decision does not mean much, though, because in the Russian legal system the lower courts follow statute law, rather than the precedents of other (even higher) courts.[7] Those who wish to apply the idea of 'social group' in queer cases may be a little more confident to do so now – if they ignore the overall social context – but, generally, unless this opinion of the Constitutional Court is codified with another amendment to the Criminal Code, no judge feels obliged to interpret 'social group' in this particular manner. In fact, of the 314 incidents of anti-queer violence that I analysed in my research, hate crime legislation was cited by the judge only six times. Of these cases, in four the defendants were convicted, in one the defendant was found incapable of assuming guilt due to mental health, and in the final case the parties reconciled and the charge was dropped. Interestingly, though, all these cases except for the last one happened before the Constitutional Court decision anyway.

Article 63 must be considered by a judge every time they decide a sentence. Usually they cite the article simply, saying, 'no aggravating circumstances were found'. However, there is another procedural trick. If the aggravating circumstance is listed in any other clause on which the sentence is based, then the judge does not need Article 63 at all and only has to check that the crime has been classified appropriately and cite the relevant section of the applied article (see Kondakov 2021b). Put more simply, many criminal articles already contain a hatred motive (using the same wording as Article 63) that enhances sentencing for various forms of physical and psychological violence (Articles 111, 112, 115, 116, 117), murder (105), threat to kill (119), recruiting minors in hate crimes (150, para. 4) and offences against the public (213, 214). The way this works procedurally is that, say, Article 105, para. 1 punishes (intentional) murder, and in para. 2, Section L it adds aggravating motives of hatred (including towards a 'social group'). Thus, if Section L applies, the murderer goes to prison for a longer period. The same goes for crimes that do not involve physical violence: Article 282 bans hate speech through '[a]ctions directed to incitement of hatred or enmity and deprivation of a person's or group's dignity based on sex, race, ethnicity, language, descent, religion or membership in any one social group'. However, despite this well-developed hate crime legislation (which would nearly satisfy ODIHR), none of it is met with enthusiasm by the Russian judiciary in cases of anti-queer violence.

Ritualistic rules of the game

Perhaps all these criminal articles simply fail to fit the incidents that occur on the ground? How does a judge actually decide which article to apply? Are they really in control of classifying a case (matching events to a criminal article)? A murder is a murder, but deciding what particular kind of murder it is may prove tricky. Russia follows the so-called 'neo-inquisitorial' model of criminal justice. This means that a lot of emphasis is put on the investigation that takes place before the court hearing; consequently, investigators – rather than judges – are the most powerful actors in the Russian legal field (Dzmitryeva et al. 2015; Solomon 2018, 190). A typical criminal case starts with the reporting of an incident, usually to the police. According to the procedural rules, such a report may be produced by a witness, a perpetrator, a victim or by the police themselves due to discovery of an object that may involve a breach of the law (for example, a dead body). The responsible law enforcement agency has three days to make a decision about the event – a term that is extended to 10–30 days in some circumstances (CPC Article 144) – whereupon one of three things must happen: a criminal case is opened; the allegation is rejected; or the report is redirected to a different authority.

In complex criminal cases, the report together with preliminary information obtained by the police are taken to the Prosecutor's Office (*Prokuratura*) to decide on jurisdiction (who should lead the investigation). Generally, there are three major options here. If it is a matter of private prosecution in which the victim is responsible for compiling the case file and presenting it in court, the incident may go directly to justices of the peace, who preside over small cases including minor felonies such as private prosecutions (battery is a classic example).[8] All other relatively minor – but not privately prosecuted – cases and moderate felonies stay within the police's jurisdiction, where the Investigation Unit has the right to open a case file and start a criminal enquiry. Meanwhile, all major cases go to the Investigative Committee of Russia (ICR), a sort of Russian FBI, which collects evidence for the government. CPC Article 151 delineates these jurisdictions with a list of criminal articles corresponding to each of them.

The investigation must be concluded within 2 months of opening a case, although this deadline is usually extended for another 3 months or in exceptionally complicated cases for a year (CPC Article 162).[9] The case file and indictment composed by either the ICR or the police are then handed over to the prosecutors. They review the case and, if it looks like a criminal law violation, with the alleged perpetrator well established and evidenced, they confirm the indictment and direct the case to the court. Again, the clock is ticking and normally a prosecutor must make up their mind within 10 days (CPC Article 221).[10] Criminal cases where the maximum sentence is less than 3 years' imprisonment go to justices of the peace for the first-instance decision. Graver cases are tried in federal courts. The first-instance federal courts are city and district courts in Russia.

The courts are also on the clock: once a case is with a judge, they have to decide how to proceed within 14 to 30 days. The case can be returned for further investigation, be given a preliminary hearing or be tried in full. Preliminary hearings are closed, and the judge can reject cases. In contrast, trials are public and end with an acquittal or conviction. Procedural law does not stipulate how long a case can be heard in court before the final decision must be taken. It only regulates the terms of arrest of an accused and dictates that 6 months is the maximum time the state can keep someone in jail before ultimately deciding their case (CPC Article 255). In 'grave' and 'particularly grave' crimes, this term can be given 3-month extensions many times over. This 6-month deadline seems to be the only indication in procedural law of time limits that a judge cannot exceed – though as we see, even here they are flexible. Overall, though, cases are normally decided much faster, because judges, just like other actors in this field, are incentivised to process cases quickly rather than take the time to think about them. One such incentive is the number of cases they have to deal with. Around 10,000 justices of the peace and approximately 15,000 federal first-instance judges all over Russia decide nearly a million criminal cases each year and – on top of that – almost 10 times that number of civil, administrative and procedural cases (Andrianova 2018; Paneyakh, Titaev, and Shklyaruk 2018; Court Department 2021).

Thus, according to the procedural rules, the criminal process in Russia is a rather strict, rigid and detailed framework of 'set moves' that leaves very little space for discretion. The rules of the game are designed to prioritise quick solutions in short timeframes. In addition, criminal procedure relies heavily on documented evidence submitted to the court. As a result, a case file is a collection of papers created using templates, written in accordance with procedural requirements. All actors in the legal field are obliged to check that the rules for composing such papers were followed in the earlier stages of a case. Every action of every actor (investigators, prosecutors and judges) has a document template of its own, which adds police and court clerks to the ranks of legal actors because they actually produce these papers. The result is that by prioritising the endless creation of paperwork, the criminal process ensures that the actual incident that took place in physical space pales into insignificance next to the paper-pushing elements involved in the case. These documents are what the judges review in their courtrooms and base their decisions on. Indeed, Agnieszka Kubal suggests that these state-produced documents actually take precedence over other types of evidence in the courtroom. She analysed a case in which a document presented by the prosecution in the courtroom was in obvious contradiction to the testimony of a person who was physically present in the same courtroom; for the judge the document took priority over the person because it had been produced by the state (Kubal 2018, 107).

Similar evidence of papers taking precedence over empirical reality has come up in my analysis of court rulings on anti-queer violence. I want to emphasise this reliance on paper in the Russian courts because it uncovers a peculiar set of power relations within the legal field as well as the field's artificial constitution of justice. In the cases I reviewed, if, in the courtroom, a defendant stated something that contradicted their earlier statement recorded by the investigation and presented in the form of a signed and sealed document to the court, the paper version was regarded as more truthful. Judges argue, in fact, that they have no reason to cast doubt on such documents, because they have been created following procedural norms:

> The disputes of [the defendant] that multiple violations of criminal procedural law took place during this criminal investigation, that initiation of the criminal case against him was illegal and unreasonable, that the criminal case was fabricated – the Court recognises as invalid. The decision to open the criminal case was taken by a proper person in official capacity after considering the matter and sufficiently taking into account the grounds that indicated the signs of possible commission of crimes by [the defendant]. In its form and content, the decision to open the criminal case follows requirements of the criminal procedural law. (1-205/2014, Moscow)

This reasoning is incredibly formalistic. A lot is at stake here: clearly, if investigators have in fact manipulated evidence, they should be investigated themselves and convicted for obstruction of justice, while the defendant should walk free. But who wants to spend all this time on an additional investigation if on paper the defendant looks guilty as hell and the police as righteous as can be? In refusing to look beyond the documents provided by the investigation, judges ally with other legal actors in the field at the expense of defendants' rights. In other words, they make their internal professional solidarity more important than the concerns of the romantic version of justice.

Copy, paste, repeat

One result of this process is that power relations and social bonds between legal actors are created. Formally, on the one hand, it might be claimed that this rigid process helps the criminal justice system safeguard the delivery of justice in a situation where there is little trust in legal actors. Since investigators, prosecutors and judges might be corrupt, the law limits their discretion and requires that their every step be documented. On the other hand, the system can also be understood as a very powerful instrument in the hands of legal actors who can easily manipulate it, with results that stand far at odds with justice. Given that legal professionals know how to produce a valid paper that often carries more legal heft than empirical reality and given that they hold an almost full monopoly over the production of such documents, these procedural steps open a space for fabricating versions of events that benefit the legal actors themselves, rather than justice. Justice is delivered – if at all – only as a by-product of this procedure. Or rather, what is delivered as justice is a very formalistic version of it.

The central element in this system, as I see it through my analysis, is the indictment. As previous research has shown, decisions are overwhelmingly made at the stage of investigation, before the indictment is issued, rather than in courtrooms (Paneyakh, Titaev and Shklyaruk 2018; Solomon 2018). The indictment is another piece of paperwork, this time outlining the investigator's argument against the accused. It contains nearly all the necessary information to compose a verdict: names, description of the alleged criminal offence, classification in accordance with criminal articles, evidence from prosecution and defence, aggravating and extenuating circumstances, personal characteristics of the accused, etc. (CPC Article 220). The prosecution adds its desired sentence. Now, if the judge finds that a violation under the criminal article has indeed taken place, they typically compose a ruling using very much the same structure as the indictment (CPC Articles 307, 308), adding their reasoning to it (the descriptive section of the verdict) and details of the sentence (their resolution). If a judge wants to save time, the most resource-efficient way to do this is to copy and paste from the indictment straight into the ruling. This is exactly what happens, as analyses of criminal procedural practice clearly show: scholars call this unofficial judicial writing practice 'copy-pasting' not as a metaphor, but to reflect actual techniques of judicial writing in Russia (Dzmitryeva et al. 2015; Kondakov 2017d; McCarthy 2018; Kahn 2018).

What this means for justice is that the actual decision as to the guilt of the accused is made privately and among legal actors who are incentivised to obtain guilty verdicts (investigators and prosecutors). While criminal court hearings are open to the public, criminal investigations are not. What goes on behind the closed doors of police precincts and jails rarely gets acknowledged publicly. Imagine an investigator who is working on a murder case. They have a suspect who they simply feel is guilty (possibly only by association because the person is, say, homeless and the investigator's prejudice connects this status with delinquency). But to transform this feeling into a convincing argument takes time – and time is running out. The investigator could ask for an extended deadline, but their colleagues and superiors will say the case is too simple to take that much time. Besides, the other cases will not solve themselves – and there are heaps! Another option is to close the case without solving it since the suspect cannot be located, but this reflects badly on performance indicators and there will be other cases during the year that will have to go this way because they will not even have suspects. So why not put the effort into 'convincing' an available suspect to admit their guilt and sign a blank paper that has already been generously endorsed by a friendly lawyer whom the prosecution can claim represented the accused? Given the conditions, this often seems like the best bet. It saves time for everyone, except of course for the alleged criminal who will have to serve their time behind bars.[11] Such pragmatic solutions may not necessarily take place in every instance, but the entire system leans that way.

It is helpful to think of the habitual practices of a given legal field as gravitating towards one of two poles: one is the pole of high professionalism, where justice is a value not to betray; the other is the pole of self-survival in the legal field, with little regard for justice as a value but producing a version of justice as a formality. The formal practices of legal actors in Russia, carried out as embodied, habitual ones in their professional field, gravitate towards the latter pole. In this way, the texts of procedural norms appear to actually amplify this instinct towards pragmatic practices of survival at the expense of romantic justice.

In the case of Misha and Sergey presented earlier, it appears that the investigators did not have to fabricate evidence. The accused thought he had covered his tracks well, when in fact he had left many traces that were easily transformed into evidence and valid documents. He used a computer with an identifiable IP address from a state-run library; he used a phone that marked his locations and calls that were obtained via the telecommunications company, which was capable of producing signed and sealed logs; he appeared on a traffic camera maintained by the road police; he purchased train and flight tickets using his identity documents; and his face was seen by people he interacted with and whose interviews were recorded following the requirements of the CPC. In other words, due to these specific circumstances his case was proved based on paper, which, because of the clarity and documented character of the evidence, gravitated towards the romantic version of justice.

However, there are many cases in my database that relied primarily on self-incriminating testimonies of the accused. I now turn to my detailed analysis of these cases. The aim throughout is to understand the role of legal actors in deciding them, the set of societal values they maintain, and the driving force behind the adjudication of everyday incidents of anti-queer violence in Russia.

Notes

1. In order to make more explicit the hidden colonial administrative categorisation of Russian provinces, I offer translations rather than transliterations of their names. 'Territory' is *Krai* in Russian, and it usually presumes a large piece of land that includes smaller portions of officially recognised indigenous lands (commonly called 'Autonomous Districts' and 'Autonomous Republics' within the Territories). In addition to 'territories', there are 'Republics' (*Respublika*) that belong entirely to one colonised people (referred to as a 'title nation'): for example, the Chechen Republic or the Republic of Tatarstan. Finally, there are 'Regions' (*Oblast'*) that are supposedly neutral or historically 'Russian', even though they can also be lands colonised by the Russian Empire both to the west and to the east of the Ural Mountains. Examples include Bryansk Region and Tomsk Region. I think these translations better reflect the taxonomy of imperial governance that transliterations obscure.
2. According to Article 16, para. 9 of the Penal Code, defendants can be imprisoned in various types of penal facility. The following are the most common, ranging from mild to harsh: settlement colony (a monitored, non-secure village that one cannot leave until the sentence has expired); medium-security correctional colony; high-security correctional colony; maximum-security correctional colony; and prison confinement. Secure colonies are designated zones with many barracks where inmates live and where various facilities are located (such as canteens, groceries and cinemas). People are usually allowed to move around these zones. As for prisons, inmates are confined within a single building for the entire day, except two hours a day designated for outside exercise. The different categories of security define the degree of liberty inmates have in terms of spending money, visits, receiving post, leisure, outside walks, etc.
3. For these kinds of statistics I consult data from the Court Department of the Supreme Court throughout the book (Court Department 2012).
4. Before the Russian war on Ukraine in 2022, Russia was also part of the Council of Europe, where the ECRI had functioned since 1993/4. The ECRI's General Policy Recommendation No. 7 (2002) urges the combating of hate speech in relation to racism and xenophobia.
5. See publicly accessible hate crime data collected by the ODIHR at http://hatecrime.osce.org.
6. For example, the Council of Europe's 2006 review of the situation in Russia focused exclusively on discrimination and hate speech biased towards ethnic and racial minorities: 'There has been an alarming increase in the number of racially motivated crimes in recent years and hate speech has become more prevalent in the media. Incidents of discrimination, including in access to residency registration, remain high' (Council of Europe 2006).
7. The Constitutional Court can instruct legislators to introduce changes to relevant statutes if it wants a particular decision to be codified and become mandatory for the lower courts. If this is

not done, the Constitutional Court's decision does not serve as a precedent; it can only be used by judges to strengthen their arguments rhetorically. In this particular decision, anyway, the Court ambiguously opined on the 'unacceptability of limitations of rights and freedoms or of institutionalisation of privileges dependent upon affiliation with any one social group'. Hence, in the strangest of logic, the question arises as to whether 'special' protection of a historically disadvantaged social group from crime can be understood by the Court as 'privilege'.
8 Only three Criminal Code articles could be prosecuted by a private person in 2010–16; the number is even lower now.
9 The case can also be paused, and there are other tools available to investigators to extend the process, but in general the aim is to resolve the case as quickly as possible.
10 The case can also be returned for further investigation if the prosecution believes the findings are incomplete, but this time the investigators have only 1 month to conclude their work properly.
11 There are good investigative journalist reports on the various illegal techniques that the police use, prosecutors approve and judges formalise through court decisions (Golunov 2020).

2
From a place of indifference

Another law

One of the requirements of the law in Russia is to publish every court decision in an open-access database so that people can easily review crucial information about justice. Rulings from all over Russia have been published in anonymised form on this official database since 2010. All court decisions are indexed so as to be easily explorable using search terms. An alternative database was launched around the same time by independent lawyers and existed until 2018.[1] After realising that simply collecting court statistics on the application of hate crime legislation was not enough, I used both of these databases to search for cases of anti-queer violence, regardless of the way they were officially classified. I collected the cases from 2010 to 2016 – the three years prior to the 2013 'gay propaganda' law and the three years after its adoption, which also happened to be all the available years in these two databases at the time. Detailed accounts of my methodology and the processing of search results are published elsewhere (Kondakov 2017c; 2021b; Kondakov and Shtorn 2021).

The following keywords were used to compile more than 3,000 documents that mentioned something queer: *netraditsyonnyi* (non-traditional), *gomoseksualizm* (homosexuality), *muzhelozhstvo* (buggery), *lesbiyanstvo* (lesbianism), *transseksual* (transsexual) and *menshinstvo* (minority).[2] After a brief reading of these documents, the sample was narrowed down to unique, first-instance court cases of anti-queer violence. In total, incidents with 314 victims were documented between 2010 and 2016. These cases form the backbone of my current analysis, which shows how law is practised by the legal actors within the boundaries of the legal field.

The central question of this chapter is what version of justice – or societal attitudes towards queerness – judges reproduce in their decisions. If the task of the legal field is to maintain the authority of law by amassing legitimacy through confirming society's general views about social structures and hierarchies, then a reflection on general societal attitudes towards LGBT+ people should be an essential part of the reasoning behind criminal court rulings. Do legal actors employ the law to protect queer victims? Or do they find ways to exonerate perpetrators of anti-queer violence?

To begin with, any legal decision is bound to some extent by the text of statute law. The law is relatively clear in saying that LGBT+ people in Russia must be protected from hate crime under the banner of 'social group'. This protection is guaranteed by three different types of legal tools in the domain of criminal law (Mason 2009, 326): a Criminal Code article defining the hate motive as an aggravating circumstance in any crime; enhancement of punishments in cases of violent offences with a hate motive; and a criminal article that punishes the expression of hate. The list of possible grounds for hate does not explicitly refer to sexual orientation or gender identity, but this interpretation is possible through the notion of 'social group', which, as the Constitutional Court has already confirmed, should be expanded to LGBT+ people. Despite all this, the practice of adjudicating cases of hate crime by citing relevant legislation is basically non-existent. What do the Russian courts use instead to decide cases of anti-queer violence?

When I use the term 'violence' in this research, what I mean is a set of interpretations of the events under scrutiny as violations of criminal law. Hence, my sample is restricted to officially reported and recorded incidents of violence. Among the 314 cases, in 185 instances only one criminal article was applied to convict the perpetrator. In all other cases (129), the crimes were complex enough to involve convictions citing several different criminal articles. This can happen, for example, when a defendant kills their victim and then steals their belongings and is therefore tried for both murder and theft. Judging from the available case files, many perpetrators decide to take something from the crime scene after they commit a murder. In addition, a defendant can be held accountable for various crimes in a single trial with different victims involved in the process: those killed for flashing queerness or those assaulted for their valuables. Not all the facts of a case, therefore, are of particular relevance to my analysis. Thus, using NVivo, I reconstructed the events of all the crimes according to the court rulings and singled out the one criminal article that governed that part of the ruling where a

Table 2.1 The range of legal categories in cases of anti-queer violence in Russia, 2010–16

Criminal code article	No. victims	Category	Class
105.1	67	Murder	Homicide
162	51	Assault	Violence
161	45	Robbery	Larceny
111.4	41	Manslaughter	Homicide
105.2	20	Aggravated Murder	Homicide
111.1-2	18	Serious Injury	Violence
163	18	Extortion	Larceny
116	13	Battery	Violence
119	7	Threat to Kill	Violence
112	6	Moderate Injury	Violence
107	5	Affect Murder	Homicide
158	4	Theft	Larceny
159	4	Fraud	Larceny
30.3 (105, 112)	3	Attempt (Murder, Injury)	Violence
115	2	Light Injury	Violence
127	2	Abduction	Violence
30.3 (161)	1	Attempt (Robbery)	Larceny
126	1	Kidnapping	Violence
108	1	Self-Defence Murder	Homicide
113	1	Affect Injury	Violence
117	1	Torture	Violence
139	1	Burglary	Larceny
213	1	Hooliganism	Larceny
282	1	Hate Speech	Violence

queer person was victimised. In cases where several criminal articles were applied to the queer element, I prioritised the gravest conviction (say, murder over robbery). All other criminal articles were recorded in my database in a separate column. This helps me present a picture of queer victimisation as documented by the criminal justice system in Russia. And it also suggests very explicitly that this picture reveals just the tiny tip of an iceberg, not only because many criminal encounters are not officially accounted for at all, but also because even for a sensible representation of this sample in my research, it was necessary to trim down the complexity of the cases further.

Table 2.1 lists the criminal articles that the defendants in my sample were found to have violated. All cases that reached the courtroom concluded with the discovery of violations of criminal statutes. And while there were no clear acquittals, later in this chapter I shall discuss the strategies that judges in Russia use to semi-officially resist the prosecution. For now, the table needs some unpacking. First and foremost, the range of criminal articles is relatively small. In total, 21 articles are cited in the analysed cases. As evidenced from the short description categorising these cases (taken from the Criminal Code), the majority of instances involve quite serious crimes, with two types of murder, violent assault, robbery and manslaughter being among the top five and totalling 224 victims out of 314. Each line of the table is shaded, showing severer crimes on a darker background.[3] As one can see, the darker shading is concentrated in the upper lines of the table (sorted by victim numbers from high to low), signalling that graver crimes are prosecuted with more frequency.

This descriptive analysis suggests that the cases that reach the courts may be those that the criminal justice system deems worthy of prosecution or those that prosecutors have to deal with anyway (for example, cases involving a dead body that require an official response from law enforcement). In contrast, more 'minor' cases (say, light injury or battery) perhaps rarely get drawn into the criminal justice system, not only because queer victims may refrain from reporting them due to fear of the police, but also – even if they do report – because the police may not process such cases, considering them frivolous or undeserving of attention.[4] Legal professionals may have some discretion when deciding to record a case and then classifying it one way or another, consciously choosing the governing article that benefits their career or helps them go about their daily work as effortlessly as possible. In an ideal world (the world of statute law theorists at least), the job of investigators and prosecutors is to match the circumstances of a case to the definitions of crimes as set out in the legislation (properly classifying incidents in accordance with the Criminal Code taxonomy). In reality, these professionals work to construct a narrative for the public hearing of a case – both in Russia and elsewhere – regardless of how closely the actual events match the charges they decide to pursue. In other words, they opt for constructing a limited set of narratives which they know how to prosecute instead of looking for a statute that best fits the situation. Yet, the job of constructing a particular – and preferably convincing – narrative that can lead to a specific conclusion of guilt is a very different job from both matching events to abstract legal notions and serving justice as a value. While justice may be served as this narrative is built, this is not ultimately necessary for the narrative itself. Newer and less familiar statutes (such as Russia's hate crime articles that emerged in 2007) are particularly vulnerable to being ignored in these circumstances simply because legal professionals are not sure how to use them. I expand on this process in the following sections.

Types of crime

Another analytical operation shown in the table above is the grouping of various crimes into general classes (column 4). I sorted the cases into three groups: homicide; violence; and larceny. These categories are very broad and do not correspond to the legal categories but represent the *type* of incident from the perspective of the victim. Thus, 'homicide' includes all crimes that resulted in a victim's death, be it premediated murder, unintentional manslaughter or something classified as self-defence or killing someone under affect. The approach taken in Table 2.1 is that where there is a dead body, there is homicide. While homicide is of course a form of violence, a separate class labelled 'violence' includes only cases where the victim survived an assault. It is another broad category, comprising torture and serious injury together with relatively minor crimes such as battery. Finally, 'larceny' in my sample always goes hand in hand with violence (victims are intimidated and assaulted before their belongings are taken from them), but in the courtroom these crimes are presented as purely 'economic' crimes and the defendants are charged with taking away property, not damaging human bodies. These incidents range from habitual robberies to more queer-specific extortions. Figure 2.1 represents these categories across the years of observation (2010–16). While these statistics are merely descriptive due to the small number of cases involved, they merit a few important remarks.

Figure 2.1 Classes of anti-queer crime in Russia shown in years, 2010–16

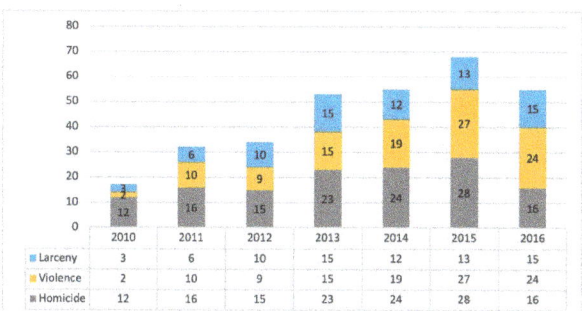

Initial observations provoked by the chart are that the total number of crimes grows over time until 2015 and then goes down somewhat, from 68 to 55 victims in 2016. In 2010 the system returned only 17 results, with 12 of them being homicides. This number grows every year and jumps to 53 in 2013, and then shows continuous growth for two more years. This is the year Russia adopted the gay propaganda bill; there was very prominent discussion of queer issues in the Russian media both before and after the bill's signing (Pronkina 2016). It is not unreasonable to assume that the bill and its discussion hinted at the idea that queer people are vulnerable and, therefore, are easy targets for various kinds of crime. Another observation to note is the distribution of various types of incident. Whereas larceny fluctuates from 10 to 15 victims in 2012–16, non-fatal violence shows continuous growth over time and, even after the overall decrease in cases in 2016, it does not return to its previous level. As for fatal violence, its share of overall yearly cases increases from 12 in 2010 to 28 in 2015 and only then drops to the 'pre-propaganda' level of 16 victims.

These numbers are very low for statistical calculations of dependencies and correlations without significant errors. This is why a direct link between the growth in cases and the adoption of the 'propaganda' bill cannot be made. Instead, I will look for more qualitative explanations.

It was around 2012 when a group of violent so-called vigilantes, 'Occupy Paedophilia', spread across Russian towns and cities. The group had a very vague idea of 'paedophilia' and many of its local chapters confused it with male homosexuality. Their activities were structured around 'safari hunting' people they located on gay dating websites and apps (Essig 2014, 45; Favarel-Garrigues and Shukan 2019, 6). After identifying a victim, they would meet them, intimidate them, beat them up and then record their homosexual 'confessions', which were then published on social media. The cases where victims were not identified as 'paedophiles' by a court of law ended up in my sample.[5] Criminal charges against various chapters of this vigilante group were prosecuted across Russia, its initiator was sentenced for crimes unrelated to gay-bashing, and the group's activities deteriorated under law enforcement pressure by 2015.[6] In my sample, some of the cases were still under consideration by regional courts even in 2016, but their major contributions to these statistics had already been made by then. Most of these cases also involve multiple victims. Moreover, the influence of this group reaches far beyond 'vigilantism': the group engaged in extortion and inspired 'copycats' interested exclusively in using queer victims' vulnerable position to their own advantage. These criminals were mostly concerned with identifying 'easy victims' for robberies, and gay men turned up as an opportunity to explore.

Finally, when in 2015 homicides and violent cases peaked at 28 and 27 victims, respectively, many of the cases in the latter group concerned minor offences. Some of them concluded with decisions that found the defendants guilty but released them by pardoning due to the 70th anniversary of Victory in the Great Patriotic War. Given this narrow window of opportunity – the pardon was valid for charges presented in the anniversary year of 2015 – some cases that would not normally be prosecuted due to their frivolousness reached the courts (such as minor robberies, battery and light injuries). Police precincts were interested in recording such cases because they knew that for the judges a guilty verdict without punishment meant quick and satisfying decision making. All parties were happy. The police improved their indicators, the courts improved theirs, and the perpetrators walked free with mild consequences and, therefore, no intention to appeal.

Classifying crimes

According to studies of the Russian judiciary (Volkov and Dzmitryieva 2015; Ivanova 2015; Dzmitryieva 2021), judges come from two sources: they either originate in the courts, starting as clerks and later receiving legal education and advancing to the judiciary; or they come from the prosecutor's office and to a lesser extent from investigative agencies. All other pathways for legal professionals to join the judiciary are marginal. Combine this 'doorkeeping' with the power bequeathed to law enforcement agencies through the procedural law highlighted in Chapter 1, and it becomes clear that so-called 'accusatorial bias' in delivering criminal justice is inevitable (Solomon 2018). Once they have moved to the judiciary, former prosecutors and investigators evidently favour their ex-colleagues in the handling of cases. Or they may simply understand very well the everyday job-related hardships of prosecutors and side with them because of it. As for former clerks, they have wide experience of composing verdicts for judges early in their careers. In other words, it is their hands that perform the copying and pasting. Although some members of both groups may resist the tendency to subscribe to this habitus, most of them follow the norms embedded in the Russian legal field and do not consciously temper their actions (Volkov and Dzmitryieva 2015; Solomon 2018; Dzmitryieva 2021).[7]

Hence, I interpret legal professionals as a tight-knit group that prefers to work for its own benefit by minimising external pressures and achieving performance indicators rather than prioritising the delivery of justice. While the latter must feature in their work, too, justice takes another form. This helps to explain why the cases I reviewed orbit around a very limited range of criminal articles. These articles are familiar to all the actors in the legal field as they proceed, blinkered, in a flock along their professional path. In these circumstances, murder is murder. Black is black. But 'hate crime' murder – while it appears in Russian criminal law – is an unknown hue: few judges have ever tried to adjudicate it. Indeed, there is no evidence that such a case would stand in a first-instance or appellate court. On the contrary, there is much evidence that the majority of judges would likely fear to step outside the box and implement a little-known criminal article. In this environment it is easy to see why no one would risk trying something new, something foreign, something that has no clear pattern and no evident rewards. In sum, when classifying a case, investigators and prosecutors seem to seek a balance between what will be relatively unsurprising but still somewhat convincing in a courtroom. Meanwhile, a first-instance judge seeks to meet the expectations of the higher courts, fearing that a successful appeal would hurt their career progression and salary (Dzmitryeva et al. 2015). This is why the majority are happy with typical, common cases. The result is that despite the efforts of international institutions, hate crime does not seem to have taken root in Russia, at least not for the 'social group of homosexuals'. Instead, Russian courts try anti-queer cases as ordinary crimes in order to draw as little attention as possible to their verdicts.

Consider a case of murder heard in the Moscow Region court in Orekhovo-Zuevo in 2011 (1-108/2011, Orekhovo-Zuevo, Moscow

Region). Anatoly was quite drunk when he met his former workmate Lyubov on a pedestrian bridge across the River Klyazma. They were happy to see each other after so many years and decided to spend some time together. They met at 10am, went to a market to buy jogging trousers for Lyubov, then walked to a nearby forest situated by the local psychiatric clinic and strolled around until 1.30pm. They walked, talked and drank alcohol, seemingly enjoying each other's company. However, as soon as Lyubov mentioned that she was a lesbian, Anatoly's violent affections surfaced. He decided to have sex with Lyubov to prove her wrong. Lyubov resisted and took a jack-knife from her pocket, but Anatoly grabbed it and stabbed her 27 times in the chest.

In the courtroom, Anatoly's version of events was inconsistent, but the prosecution produced his authorised confession; Lyubov's mother repeated her previously signed testimony that her daughter was a lesbian; and Anatoly's friend recalled how the defendant had revealed his crime to him. Anatoly had also taken and sold his victim's phone, which had been traced and was presented to the judge with full documentation. Only the jack-knife was never found. The defence argued that the case should be reclassified as manslaughter (Article 111, para. 4), but the court took the side of the prosecution, reasoning that stabbing someone in the heart establishes intent to kill (Article 105, para. 1).

Why was Anatoly not charged with a hate crime? It seems that there was enough evidence to establish this charge (para. 2, Section L): there was both the victim's mother's testimony that her daughter was a lesbian and the revelation in court that Anatoly's intention to kill Lyubov emerged precisely at the moment when he 'obtained information about [her] sexual orientation'. Yet, as the court established, 'no aggravating circumstances in this case were found'. As a result, Anatoly went to a high-security facility for 7 years 8 months. This is 4 months fewer than the minimum sentence for a hate crime murder.

In this case, the prosecution had all the necessary evidence in their hands. The only thing they needed to do was classify the case properly as a hate crime. Such a move would not have challenged the overall narrative, nor would it have upset any of the legal actors involved. The investigators would still have had their case successfully closed with a proper accusation; the prosecutors would still have had a conviction. If the decision were challenged in an appellate court, it would probably only have reduced the sentence by dropping the hate crime element and upholding the conviction, so the first-instance judge would not have suffered either. The judge himself could not reclassify the case and impose severer charges, certainly, since nobody had asked for it. Doing so would infringe the defendant's right to a fair trial because a judge can only reduce charges, not add new ones.

In my sample, there are 23 cases where judges reclassified the charges in the courtroom as they evaluated the arguments presented to them and decided to reduce sentences – this they can do. One of the cases is of particular relevance. It was heard in Novosibirsk in 2015 (1-721/2015, Novosibirsk). The three assailants found their victim on a gay dating website and decided to 'teach him a lesson', as they stated in the courtroom. One of them met the targeted man at an agreed spot and dragged him into a car, where they all intimidated the victim. They asked him questions about his sexual orientation, beat him up with a rubber baton, and took his money, phone and credit card, which they were able to use after extracting the pin code from him, stealing around EUR 800.[8] The prosecution presented charges of assault aggravated by the intersectionality of racial hatred and hatred towards any one social group – the victim was a gay man from a former Soviet republic in Central Asia. The judge nevertheless argued, despite the defendants having clearly stated their motives of hate:

> The court concludes from the analysis of presented evidence that no proof supports the aggravating circumstance of commission of this crime neither based on racial hatred or enmity, nor based on hatred or enmity towards any one social group, as it has been suggested in the indictment.

Since the hate crime charges were rejected, the three defendants were charged with assault without aggravation and were sentenced to between 2 and 2.5 years in a medium-security penal colony. One idea we can take from this is that the hate crime legislation has indeed failed to take root in Russia and there is even active reluctance among judges to apply this law. However, another aspect to consider is that it appears that judges do after all have a certain amount of discretion, notwithstanding their culturally prescribed boundaries within the legal field. In this case, this freedom was used against the victim, who turned out to be not only gay but also a member of an ethnic minority that is associated in Russia with low social standing and labour migration (Voronkov, Gladarev and Sagitova 2011; Kubal 2019).[9] The defendants, on the other hand, were young college students with 'Slavic' surnames who identified as heterosexual. Considering this, the judge may have taken into account the wider context of social discrimination and hierarchisation that she herself could observe from her privileged position and sought to uphold a version of justice that supported these social inequalities. Moreover, the defendants' social prejudices may have centred primarily on the victim's ethnic and national markers rather than his sexual ones. In other words, by deciding the case the way she did, the judge appears to be defending privileges – in this case ethnic privileges – instead of remedying social injustices.

In considering judges' biases more generally, I will go on to explore more deeply the implicit societal hierarchies that judges maintain when conveying a version of justice in their rulings. Ironically, one might call it 'social justice', in the sense that it deploys specific power relations spreading across society and manifesting inequalities on which society operates.

Semi-acquittals

The main element of a ruling that judges decide relatively autonomously is the actual sentence. Here, judges have a degree of discretion that they can use to convict someone for a term not exceeding that requested by the prosecution, and it can be a suspended term for a number of years or real time in prison. The prosecution present their vision of the sentence in the courtroom, but the judge may offer a different, more lenient sentence. When a judge does this, it does not appear to upset the legal field as identified earlier. So, how do judges sentence? Let me first sketch out some rulings where judges' use of discretion was minimal and sentences were mild.

Three cases from my database can be referred to as semi-acquittals. In all three, the judges confirmed that the defendants had violated criminal law, but in two cases the parties reconciled in the courtroom and in the other the defendant was found incapable of assuming guilt and was sent for compulsory psychiatric treatment. In the first two cases, criminal charges were brought only in their 'economic' aspect: the accused had attacked gay men and taken their belongings. The physical attacks themselves were not regarded as crimes, whereas the thefts were. Yet because the defendants had reimbursed their victims during the trial, they were set free. In two further cases, the defendants were found guilty but granted amnesty immediately.[10] I count these as two more 'acquittals'. Thus, if all these cases count as acquittals to at least some extent, then five cases out of the total 314 comprise an acquittal rate of 1.6% in this sample. The Russian criminal justice system is regarded as having a high accusatory bias with acquittals 'well under 1 per cent' (Khodzhaeva and

Shesternina Rabovski 2016; Solomon 2018, 170). Peter Solomon, for example, believes – as I do – that while full acquittals are indeed rare, various methods of diverging from prosecutors' versions should count to some extent as acquittals (Solomon 2018).

Another way of unofficially resisting the prosecution without explicitly siding with the defence is to sentence with a suspended term of imprisonment. In such cases the defendant is found guilty and sentenced to a term behind bars, but the sentence is suspended on condition that the defendant visit a parole officer periodically and commit no more crimes. Their criminal record still shows the conviction, but, if they behave, at least they do not serve their term in an actual prison. In my sample, terms of imprisonment were suspended in cases totalling 56 victims. The longest suspended term was 4.5 years in the case of a violent assault, home intrusion and 'moderate' physical harm (three criminal charges). The shortest term was 6 months in the case of extortion decided without judicial review of evidence under a 'plea agreement'.[11] The median number of suspended years in these sentences is 2 (average 2.1).

Suspended sentences are expected to be awarded for minor crimes (such as low-value robberies, theft or 'light physical harm'). Indeed, 20 instances in the sample involved very minor charges, where the perpetrators simply attacked queer people in the street and took their mobile phones or battered them. Some of these minor crimes were aggravated because they were committed in groups, but they still resulted in suspended sentences. In crimes against eight victims, the charges were very severe and fell under paragraphs 1 and 2 of Criminal Article 111 (serious injuries). This kind of damage is associated with loss of physical abilities and with risk to the victim's life. It is regarded in law as the second-most serious category of crimes. In this article, the higher limits of the sentence are 8 and 10 years' imprisonment in paragraphs 1 and 2 respectively (without lower limit). Still, sentences ranging from 2 to 4 years were suspended. One case may serve as an example of what exactly this involves (1-296/2016, Petropavlovsk-Kamchatsky, Kamchatka Territory). In 2016 in Petropavlovsk-Kamchatsky, a man stabbed another man five times in his chest and head. The victim's face and body were 'disfigured forever', as the judge on the case copied from the indictment. Aggravated serious damage to health (Article 111, para. 2) stood in court, but the case was heard under a plea agreement suggested in the courtroom and the sentence of 3 years was suspended.

In sum, a huge range of criminal charges (from battery to serious injuries) can be resolved with suspended sentences. Does this also hold true in cases where the victims lost their lives?

Table 2.2 Comparison of homicide sentences in cases of anti-queer violence in Russia, 2010–16

Article	Formal classification	No. of victims	Average terms in queer cases	Max. statutory term	Range of the most common sentences[a]
111,4	Manslaughter	41	7.25	15	5–8[b]
105,1	Murder	67	8.8	6–15	5–8[c]
105,2	Aggravated murder	20	18.1	8–20[d]	15–20
Total		128	10.5		

[a] Statistics taken from aggregated published sources of the Supreme Court for 2010–16.

[b] With the exception of 2016, when the most common term was 3–5 years.

[c] The preference for 5–8 years was marginal and the second-most common term was 8–10 years.

[d] Life and capital punishment are also indicated in the article.

Homicide sentences

In my analysis of homicide cases, I focused on 121 court rulings that convicted defendants for killing a total of 128 queer people. I excluded a few affect and self-defence murders and analysed three different types of homicide: (1) Manslaughter, Article 111, para. 4; (2) Murder, Article 105, para. 1; and (3) Aggravated Murder, Article 105, para. 2. Defendants were convicted for 10.5 years on average (9 years median) and no suspended sentences were awarded or possible in this category of crimes. Note also that the Article 111 charges were complex cases that involved additional charges in 9 of 41 cases and out of 20 aggravated murders 18 involved additional charges. As for simple murder, 27% involved additional charges, which in real numbers was 18 out of 67. Moreover, two murder cases were reclassified as manslaughter. Table 2.2 gives a better sense of the variety of sentencing in these three types of homicide and puts each in the context of the overall adjudication of such crimes. As the table shows, judges in the analysed cases tended to lean towards the higher margins of the most common sentences in each respective category, especially in the case of simple murder.

Manslaughter sentences on average fall within the most common range of terms of imprisonment in my study. Although at 7.25 years the statistic leans towards the range's highest point of 8 years, the Supreme Court statistics cannot determine what sentences comprise this range category (5–8 years) and the majority of sentences may well be at the higher end. Therefore, it is unclear whether judges in queer cases are harsher in their punishments than judges overall. However, the average number of 7.25 years indicates that sentences for perpetrators in queer cases are definitely not milder than those of most other defendants and quite probably are a little harsher than the average. Still, these observations are not conclusive. The same can be said about aggravated murder, in which the average term of 18.1 years edges towards the higher end, but the number itself is even less convincing than the manslaughter calculations. Firstly, it is based on only 20 observations. Secondly, the overwhelming majority of cases in this category include multiple murders (where more than one person was killed), but not all victims were killed because of their sexuality.

Simple murder offers the clearest statistical conclusion, firstly because it is the most numerous category in my sample with 67 victims in total, and secondly because the sentences in queer cases most obviously lie at the higher end in comparison with the sentences overall from the

Supreme Court data. In all years, judges across Russia generally sentenced defendants in simple murder cases to 5–8 years of imprisonment slightly more often than 8–10 years. Considering this, the average of 8.8 years in queer cases (and median 9) is definitely at the higher end of these terms of imprisonment: it falls into a less common category in all years and the category is of longer terms. What this signifies is that, for some reason, judges tend to award longer terms of imprisonment in queer cases than on average. This observation is clear in simple murder cases and somewhat supported by estimates in the two other types of homicide. Does this mean that judges try to unofficially recognise the vulnerable position of queer victims and restore justice at least in the case of serious crimes by giving longer sentences, despite the fact that they avoid applying the hate crime legislation?

The social hierarchies

The analysis of sentencing shows that, on the one hand, judges tend to award mild verdicts in queer cases when they decide relatively minor crimes, although there are exceptions. They use suspended sentences and amnesties, and they reclassify charges to less harsh ones. On the other hand, when they deal with serious crimes such as homicide, judges more commonly award longer terms of imprisonment than the average. Do they draw a line beyond which crimes – 'even' anti-queer ones – cannot be tolerated? If so, such behaviour would mirror law enforcement practices: mild cases of violence against queer people are hardly ever recorded, while homicides are investigated (sometimes properly, as in the case of Misha and Sergey that opens this Part) and perpetrators are made to answer for their actions. This conjecture is confirmed by the charges that make it to court, which grow significantly in number as the crimes become more appalling. Judicial practice adds a further layer to this, as judges seem to unofficially take into account the hatred motive by giving perpetrators in anti-queer crimes slightly longer terms of imprisonment than on average.

So, if judges seek to confirm societal values and hierarchies with their decisions, then they seem to be saying that killing people for who they 'are' is a worse crime than the average murder. They seem to communicate the idea that one can punch a queer, steal from them or even extort money without major consequences. However, once perpetrators cross the line of the permissible they are subject to harsher than average punishments, suggesting that there are limits to judges' tolerance of anti-queer crime. Such a conclusion may seem logical when hierarchies involving queerness are taken in isolation, without taking into account the intersection of other dimensions of inequality. As the example of the Central Asian gay man above shows, though, social hierarchies are complex. Perhaps judges uphold social hierarchies regardless of the presence of sexuality in the complex composition of society. In other words, judges may construct their version of justice, as reflected in sentencing practice, based exclusively, say, on economic inequality or race and pay no attention to other social markers. While the information that supports such a complex analysis is scarce, let me gesture towards some of the conclusions that my collection of rulings prompts in this respect.

The contexts of the crimes described in the rulings and the professional status of victims and perpetrators, which is sometimes revealed, suggests that many of the criminal incidents occurred in deprived settings: poor neighbourhoods, towns and villages across Russia. A common pastime in such places is to gather in someone's flat to drink strong liquor – a consumption pattern associated with poverty (Shtorn 2018; Kondakov and Shtorn 2021) – and as the drinking progresses, sexual tensions may develop, which may result in violence. Such everyday crimes would commonly result in average sentences. However, once social hierarchies come into play, judges' biases drive their decisions in significant ways. Consider a case of manslaughter in Magnitogorsk (1-10/2012, Magnitogorsk, Chelyabinsk Region). Three men were drinking port in a flat. As the evening wore on, one of the men began alluding to possible sexual contact, and the other two men beat him up. They used a kitchen hammer in their attack and the man died as a result. The homicide was classified as manslaughter (Article 111, para. 4): at the time the most common sentence for this was 5–8 years, with the average among queer cases being 7.25 years. In this case, however, the defendants received 11 years, a term considerably longer than usual – even longer than the average sentence for murder in my sample. One of the possible explanations for this is that the victim was in a relatable social position to the judge. He was a pensioner and had previously worked in the prison system as a guard. Perhaps this explains why the sentence in this quite 'standard' case stands out.

In the events and crimes described in the rulings, people signal various environments, but the descriptions incline towards poorer places. For example, victims' monthly salaries ranged from RUB 10,000 to RUB 120,000 (from roughly EUR 225 to EUR 2,900), yet only a few such indicators were found in the files and most of them were much closer to

Table 2.3 Social structure as reflected in cases of anti-queer violence in Russia, 2010–16

Victim's profession/social status	No.	Total in class
Person with disability	19	74
Former convict	16	
Unemployed	12	
Industrial worker	13	42
Doctor	8	
Student	8	
Pensioner	7	
Minor	7	
Occasional labourer	5	
Business person	5	14
CEO/director	3	
Artist	3	
Hairdresser	3	
Salesperson	3	
Homeless	3	
Janitor	3	
Specialist	3	
Law enforcement	2	
Farmer	2	
Sex worker	2	
Cook	2	
War veteran	1	

Key

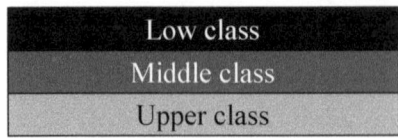

Perpetrator's profession/social status	No.	Total in class
Former convict	106	214
Unemployed	65	
Industrial worker	25	60
Occasional labourer	24	
Student	24	
Person with disability	9	
Specialist	7	11
Minor	5	
Law enforcement	4	
War veteran	4	
CEO/director	3	
Pensioner	3	
Farmer	2	
Homeless	2	
Artist	1	
Doctor	1	

the lower end. In extortion cases perpetrators were taking up to almost a million roubles (EUR 23,000), but most commonly they were satisfied with much smaller sums of money, in the range of RUB 40–100,000. The value of stolen belongings also varied significantly, from cheap mobile phones to diamond rings, with losses varying hugely from less than RUB 1,000 to more than RUB 100,000. Among popular stolen goods were iPhones, iPads, MacBooks and Samsung smartphones, but there were also cheaper Nokia and Asus models. Victims drove vehicles including Land Rovers, Daewoo Leganza and Hyundai Solaris. And their living arrangements ranged from dormitory rooms to communal apartments, personal flats (including a 5-bedroom one) and houses. All this speaks of a high level of diversity among victimised queers in my sample, although skewed towards poorer strata.

Victims' social positions

A better indicator of social position that plays out in the courtroom is the employment status of both victims and perpetrators. This indicator is more reliable because more than 200 rulings refer to it in respect of victims or perpetrators or both. Besides, some of these indicators can be officially taken into account by a judge, in accordance with procedural law, which stipulates that employed defendants (including students) may be given milder punishments than unemployed ones. Table 2.3 shows the categories of employment status of the victims and perpetrators. They are categorised into three groups for the purposes of my analysis (low, middle and upper class): the darker the category, the less income the person has. The grid in many respects mirrors the class structure of contemporary Russian society. Nevertheless, the grid is reflective of my sample only.

Among the victims in the cases I analysed, the most numerous class includes people with disabilities, former convicts, pensioners, minors and sex workers. Most of them are either officially unemployed or have only occasional opportunities to earn money. This puts them into a category of victims whose hardships judges can easily disregard, according to my analysis. It might be surprising that people with disabilities and pensioners fall into the same category as the unemployed. However, in Russia, many people with disabilities live on very low welfare benefits that are barely enough to buy food. Given that they may also require costly medical assistance or pills, the majority of them live 'below the poverty line' (Iarskaia-Smirnova, Romanov and Yarskaya 2015; Slobodenyuk 2017; Kondakov 2018a, 82). The same is true for pensioners, who struggle to get by and also need money for medical needs in their old age (Grigoryeva et al. 2015). Although some of the people in both categories might be better off than others, in the cases I reviewed they all showed signs of severe financial difficulty. As for 'minors', this social category in Table 2.3 includes homeless kids who (as some cases suggest) ran away from home due to domestic violence because of their sexual orientation. Moreover, these categories may overlap (former convicts can also be unemployed or occasional labourers): in such cases I recorded only one of their statuses. The poorest class of victims comprises 74 people. This is the largest category in my sample, and it shows that anti-queer crime is widespread in environments and situations characterised by low income, poor conditions of living, disenfranchisement, marginalisation and exclusion. The statistics show that on the whole these people are attacked by people from the same environments, and they are all judged as social outcasts in the courtroom.

Russia's middle class is comprised of service and industrial workers, as well as people who work for the state. This is why hairdressers and doctors fall into the same category. In fact, in the rulings I reviewed, hairdressers reported higher salaries than doctors. Industrial workers are relatively well paid, too. This class of queer victims is also quite large, amounting to 42 people. Their social status is considered respectable by the judiciary, but as my reading suggests, it actually does not influence sentencing significantly. Take for example two cases where hairdressers were murdered for their queerness. In one case the perpetrator received 7 years' imprisonment, while the other perpetrator received 10 years. What played a crucial role in the sentencing decisions was the social affiliation of the defendants, *not* that of the victims. Another important note is that crimes against this middle group are much less severe (more beatings and robberies than homicides) and often occur publicly. Hence, this social environment is a little less violent than that of the lower class.

Finally, the smallest group in my sample of victims comprises owners of businesses, company directors, relatively famous artists and specialists (such as accountants or engineers). It is unclear whether their social positions influenced sentencing, because many of them were victims of economic crimes (such as robberies and extortions) with less clarity in sentencing patterns, further limited by the small size of this class in the sample. However, in one case the defendant was sentenced to 10 years' imprisonment for a robbery – a very long term even for a murder, which it was not. In two cases of murder, the perpetrators were put behind bars for 9 and 10 years respectively – again longer terms than the average. On the other hand, in one of the cases, a CEO himself was described as a sexual predator who used his power to harass his employee by forcing him to have sex with him. His advances went on for years and culminated in a self-defence murder. Thus, power relations may run in different directions and high social positions may yield a false sense of impunity.

Perpetrators' social positions

When perpetrators' professions and other social affiliations are considered, the situation looks similar. The overwhelming majority of defendants fall into the lower class category (214). However, it is important to note that many of them – almost half the total number of people in this category (106) – are former convicts who had served time in prison. Other categories in this class are very much intertwined: former convicts constitute the majority of the unemployed and occasional labourers. What we can take from this is that people released from prison in Russia find it difficult to find a place in society due to the stigma of being a criminal, and therefore remain in violent environments (Pallot 2012). Consequently, they are pushed to the margins and there they resort to criminal activities to make a living or do so because this is one of the very few things they know how to do. As procedural law stipulates and judges agree, continuous involvement in crimes adds to their sentences. Hence, this group is sentenced much more harshly than other classes.

In the middle-class category (60 people), industrial workers and students form the two largest subgroups. The very fact of employment or studying acts in their favour. It should be noted, though (and this is not discernible from the table itself), that many cases in which students were involved were collective crimes in which groups of assailants organised attacks on gay men, women and trans people to 'teach them a lesson', humiliate and terrorise them. These are the cases involving 'Occupy Paedophilia' gangs and the like, and students feature prominently because they are considered young and handsome bait to attract potential victims. They did more than act as bait in some cases: several engaged in violence, humiliation and robbery. However, notwithstanding the depth of their involvement, judges seem to dismiss charges against them more readily than cases involving older people. Even where a criminal group consisted of both students and older men, the older ones tended to end up in prison, while the students would often be released with suspended sentences. Another case of group attacks on gay people was perpetrated by police officers who used their professional position to extort money from their victims by threatening them with criminal prosecution for 'homosexuality' (which is not criminalised in Russia). These defendants received little support from the judge: they got hard time and were prohibited from working in law enforcement.

The smallest group – consisting of the wealthiest perpetrators – comprises only 11 people. Moreover, even though they are referred to as 'CEOs', 'directors' and 'specialists', these perpetrators were involved in quite shady businesses. One case in particular offers a good example of this (2-37/2010, Krasnogorsk, Moscow Region). The victim was a young gay man. He was an orphan, and in the state-run dormitory where he lived as a child he was bullied for his sexuality. When he was old enough to live independently, he decided to move out and went to a real estate agency that could arrange to purchase a flat for him using a state voucher to which he was entitled. The director of the agency agreed to provide this service. However, instead of arranging the housing for the young man, he decided to take the new flat for himself. The director tricked the young man into signing a contract that gave right of ownership to the director himself. In order to make sure nobody would ever know about the fraud, he hired a hitman to kill the young man. The hitman took him to a forest under the pretext of possible intimacy, where he then strangled him and burnt his body. When the whole scheme was revealed, the real estate agency director was sentenced to 14 years in a high-security facility and the hitman got 16 years.

The sense of indifference

What follows from the discussion in this chapter is that biases in judges' decisions are conditioned by the legal field and procedural law, which presume that economically disenfranchised populations deserve severer punishments. Youth and the employed look somewhat better to judges than older people and, especially, the unemployed. However, unemployment is also very much associated with the status of previously convicted criminals. Economically deprived environments appear to contain more violence; this in turn results in the further criminalisation of those people who inhabit these environments and, consequently, in the compounding of these environments as violent spaces. When judges see defendants and victims in front of them who are exhausted by poverty and exclusion, they appear to feel no pity, no remorse. Rather, they look at these people with indifference, unsurprisingly concluding that criminals will remain criminals and formalising this sentiment with a harsh punishment.

I argue that this feeling of deep indifference is the main feature that characterises judicial decision making in the cases of violence against queers. The judges in these cases do not hate queer victims, nor do they think these victims deserve better protection as a historically marginalised 'social group'. They simply do not care about them at all. They care about following the letter of the procedural law, satisfying the concerns of their law enforcement colleagues, and punishing the poor – in other words, they care about anything but the victims' sexuality. Perhaps, counter-intuitively, this indifference is evidence not of judicial impartiality, but of violent affections. I argue that indifference is an emotion and, moreover, it perpetuates violence – it is a violent affection – when it drives sentencing in anti-queer violence cases. If hate crime legislation is supposed to send a message to potential perpetrators that their actions are unacceptable given the social position of the targeted population as marginalised, these indifferent decisions send the opposite message. They say that one can do whatever one wants, there is no way this violence can end, there is no way criminals will stop being criminals and there is no way the marginalised can be included in society with improved standing. The message that judges send is clear: no one cares.

While Russia is seen as an inherently homophobic society by both the popular press and many scholars (Gulevich et al. 2018), my conclusion diverges from this vision to some extent. There is homophobia in Russia, to be sure. Indeed, the Russian government has recently legalised homophobia through the gay propaganda law and the like. But I argue that the most prominent feeling that characterises approaches to queerness in Russia is this permissive indifference. The practice of law – when it is used to protect certain vulnerable groups from violence that stems from their vulnerability (such as hate crime legislation) – can be advanced from a place of care, from a feeling that stimulates attentive engagement with vulnerability and yields a desire to remedy current injustices. But when the law is used to condemn vulnerable populations further, it is practised out of violent affections of varying degrees: from open and unequivocal political hate to the simple indifference of a bystander. As I have argued previously (Kondakov 2013a), Russian society shows that queerness is of little concern to it. In opinion polls, people demonstrate inconsistency and a lack of any relevant knowledge in relation to LGBT+ issues. Judges seem to be perfect representatives of this societal position toward queerness, and in this sense they do convey the standards of societal justice. It is not that they seek to either protect or condemn LGBT+ people, it is that they know nothing and feel nothing about them. They will not step in if the government advances discriminatory legislation, they will simply implement it. They will not punish perpetrators of hate crime more harshly, they will instead apply procedural norms that they are more comfortable with. They could not care less about LGBT+ people. As my discussion in the following chapters demonstrates, this indifference offers a perfect environment for the political circulation of violent affections that ignites attacks on queers.

Notes

1. The official database, *Pravosudie* (Justice), can be accessed at http://bsr.sudrf.ru/bigs/portal.html. The second database, *Rospravosudie* (RusJustice), was accessible at http://rospravosudie.com.
2. I used more keywords, but they did not return unique results.
3. The categorisation of crimes based on gravity is taken from Article 15, which classifies four types of felony: particularly grave crimes (punishment of more than 10 years); grave crimes (less than 10 years); moderate crimes (less than 5 years); and minor crimes (less than 3 years).
4. The Russian LGBT Network publishes regular reports on LGBT+ victimisation across the country. The reports are based on an analysis of survey data from more than 5,000 respondents. In 2017, it showed that around 2,500 people reported psychological violence, more than 500 reported targeted robberies and another 500 reported physical violence. In addition, almost 300 queer people were evicted from their homes, more than 150 were unlawfully arrested by the police and 135 people experienced sexual violence (Kondakov and Subbotina 2017, 9). These figures are significantly higher than the numbers generated from the pool of officially recorded crimes.
5. I do not include cases where the judge believed the victim expressed sexual desire toward children: these cases deserve separate discussion, especially in the context of Russia, which offers such fertile ground for many prejudices even without controversial analytical decisions. Thus, I include only cases where the judge explicitly identified the victim as *not* a paedophile if such was at all alleged. For example: 'this message exchange does not objectively refute the victim's claim about the absence of intention to engage in sexual intercourse with a minor and about reasonable doubt in the shown age of his interlocutor due to the requirement of being at least 18 years old to register on the website' (1-2/2016, Stariy Oskol, Belgorod Region).
6. 'Occupy Paedophilia' was set up by a young neo-Nazi ideologue, Maksim Martsinkevich, whose projects usually aimed at cleansing the 'Russian nation' of things he considered vices. It was not only vigilantism, but also a business opportunity for Martsinkevich, who profited from his group's YouTube channel and ticket sales for 'safari hunting' events (Favarel-Garrigues 2021, 236). Despite sharing similar values, Martsinkevich did not support the current political regime in Russia. He was targeted by law enforcement and was imprisoned multiple times for hate speech and violent assaults. He died in jail in 2020 under suspicious circumstances, which were officially interpreted as suicide.
7. Legal education hardly solves this issue (Hendley 2018b; 2018a; Bogdanova 2019), firstly because many law schools are law enforcement-centred, and secondly because of the poor quality of legal education in Russia.
8. Throughout the book, when I convert Russian roubles into euros, I use the exchange rate at the time of the crime.
9. This line of enquiry is, unfortunately, impossible to pursue in more detail due to the lack of available data given that cases are anonymised: victims' names, citizenship and ethic identifiers are erased from the texts of rulings if mentioned. Some indications of ethnicity remain in a few cases, where perpetrators themselves refer to their victims in derogatory racial terms. These terms were used to refer to both foreign nationals and ethnic minorities within Russia: Asian (referring to Uzbek, Tadjik, Vietnamese nationals, and people from the currently Russian

Republics of Tuva, Buryatia, Yakutia and Tatarstan), Caucasians (peoples from the Caucasus), and Roma, Belarusians and Ukrainians. In all but two cases, the sentences seemed to be quite harsh, including murder and manslaughter sentences that went above the average. However, in the two cases of crimes against labour migrants, the sentences were mild: in addition to the case above, a Tadjik person was murdered, and the killer received the lower limit of 6 years' imprisonment under Article 105.

10 These were amnesties due to the 70th anniversary of Victory in the Great Patriotic War, where the mechanism was used to free a few defendants. Among the seven cases where this was used, five instances involved only a partial amnesty, where some charges were dismissed due to the Anniversary but others remained intact.

11 Of all the cases, in 12 instances the accused entered into a pre-trial agreement admitting guilt and consenting to any verdict. These cases were therefore decided under a 'special procedure' whereby the judge does not review evidence but simply confirms the prosecutor's version of events and issues a ruling. Of these, five defendants were given suspended terms of 0.5–3.5 years, another five defendants were given custodial terms (up to 5 years in a high-security colony), one was given community labour and the final one had to pay a fine. In such cases the interference of the judge is usually minimal.

Part II
Unruly sexuality

A Moscow tragedy

The district of Vykhino lies on the edge of Moscow. It stretches to and even beyond Moscow's third ring road that encircles the city. In 2011, the area around Vykhino metro station was the most vibrant place for sexual commerce in the Russian capital.[1] Svetlana – a transgender woman who was murdered there in the summer of that year – was part of the area's large sex-worker community. On the night of 22 June, she finished her shift too late to get the subway home, so she hung around and met a man called Dmitry. This man invited Svetlana to his home, which he shared with various other people. In fact, he was a homeless person, and his home was a self-made hut located in the woods in an urban area between a parking lot and the railway, close to the ring road. On the way, they bought alcohol – a common beginning to so many of these criminal stories. But here, I do not use the story to analyse its common narrative. Instead, I want to use it to start a conversation about how sexual and gender variance is expressed in Russia.

Svetlana and Dmitry reached the hut, only to discover that two other people, known as Grandpa Sasha and Altynbek, were already inside. As they were asleep, the newly arrived guests decided to chill outside for a while. Two more men, Slava and Albert, soon showed up, on their way to bed. However, upon meeting Svetlana they decided to keep her company. They all began drinking the alcohol that Dmitry and Svetlana had brought. The noise woke Grandpa Sasha and Altynbek and they left. They were not interested in joining this late-night gathering. The group relocated into the hut. Once inside, Svetlana started to 'orally satisfy' Slava, as the criminal court ruling put it. The narrative of the case file continues:

> When [Dmitry] approached and started to take off Svetlana's jeans, he found out that she was not a woman, but a man which fact he immediately reported to Slava and Albert. Slava reacted by punching this man in his shoulder so that he rushed out and towards a fence. [Dmitry] chased the man in anger. Slava and Albert followed. As they reached the man, Slava knocked the man off his feet. After that, [Dmitry], Slava and Albert started to beat this man's face and body with their fists and feet. [Dmitry] saw a wooden tray, took it and hit the man with it twice. Then, Albert took a shovel and hit the man's head roughly three or four times. [Dmitry] took the shovel from Albert's hands and hit the man's head two or three

times more. At this very same moment, Slava continued to kick the man. When they stopped, they checked the man's heartbeat and understood that they had killed him. (1-676/2011, Moscow)

Svetlana died at the hands of these men, but the violence against her did not end there, though it took a different form. As we witness in this short passage from the criminal court's ruling, the judge's narrative repeatedly reproduces a discursive mode of violence that transgender individuals are especially vulnerable to: the erasure of their experience through misgendering. Just like the murderers, the judge failed to grasp the gender and sexual identity of the victim in his ruling. The three defendants' violent affections surfaced the moment they realised Svetlana did not meet their expectations of female anatomy and feminine expression. They murdered her as a result. As for the judge, he struggled to shed light on Svetlana's gender identity, confusing and repeatedly hopping between terms to refer to the victim – gay man, woman, man, transexual . . . Consequently, the writing obscures who was killed in a ruthless act of violence in the Vykhino woods that summer night.

3
Russia in queer colours

Naming gender and sexuality in law

The beginning of the text of the homicide ruling, the full story of which I have presented above, indicates that we are witnessing a report of a gay man's murder. The text reads that the defendants committed the crime 'during a conflict with Gennady that emerged as a result of personal unpleasant feelings because of his non-traditional sexual orientation'. The formula 'non-traditional sexual orientation' appears frequently in Russian law as a euphemism for homosexuality. Judging from this short reference, then, originally provided by the prosecution, the victim is a gay male named Gennady. He is given a masculine pronoun in the text. This narrative is challenged, however, on page three when one of the defendants testifies that 'the conflict with Gennady erupted because he turned out to be not a woman'. In the text's narrative this complaint comes out of nowhere and makes very little sense alongside what up to that point appeared to be a very clear picture.

On the next page the narrative becomes even more confusing: 'that night they killed a homosexual man; [the defendant] learned that the girl was a man and immediately hit him with his fist to the chest and because of it he got out from the hut. Then Dmitry and Albert approached, started to shout and call this man names.' In these three lines, the victim is referred to as 'a homosexual man', 'the girl', 'this man' and 'he'. In the following paragraphs, the defendants continue to confuse gender and sexual categories, and use the victim's masculine and feminine names – 'Gennady' and 'Svetlana' – interchangeably. When they describe the events before discovering Svetlana's 'male genitals' and 'hairy legs', they refer to her in the feminine. As soon as the discovery is made, they shift to masculine pronouns, including a name change, and immediately start to categorise the victim as a homosexual male. How is homosexuality associated with changing one's gender, though?

An answer to this question is offered in another testimony. The handling of gender representation shifts again on page six as the case turns to Svetlana's custodial mother, Zoya. She refers to Svetlana by her masculine name at the beginning and then explains the period of transition using orientation terms:

> When he was 15, he changed his orientation, started to take girls' skirts and tops, and to run away from the orphanage. Zoya did not discuss this with him. When he was 17, Gennady ran away from the orphanage, came to her and said he felt himself as a girl, and asked to be called Svetlana. Subsequently, he dyed his hair blond and had breasts which he explained as the product of taking hormones although without a medical prescription. He introduced himself as Svetlana to everyone, but nobody perceived him as such.

If Svetlana had survived the summer, her hormone therapy and sex reassignment surgery would have been completed, and she would have 'looked like a girl', according to Zoya's testimony. Zoya reported Svetlana's disappearance to the police and soon received a phone call from them saying that they had 'found a young man in a skirt who looked like Gennady'.

The entire narrative is overshadowed by the spectre of silence. Zoya, for example, admits that the two of them did not often discuss Svetlana's gender and sexuality. This explains why she does not know any of the relevant ways to talk about her daughter's gender. Zoya's testimony stands somewhat in contrast to the testimony of Svetlana's sister: 'she mentioned the disappearance of her brother to her workmates who said that they saw a newspaper article about discovery of a body of a transsexual in the woods.' This testimony is short, but it introduces the term 'transsexual' into the text and this term is repeatedly used thereafter. In the very next witness testimony (of another homeless man), it is stated: 'he learned from Albert that in June 2011, near the hut in the woods . . . Albert beat up a transsexual.'

The linguistic confusion found here can be diagnosed as a lack of accurate vocabulary to describe gender and sexual variance. The judge who composed the ruling drew on all the sources presented in the courtroom, yet he simply could not seem to find the correct words and was generally ignorant about the details of transgender experience, despite the fact that he was presiding over the case of a murdered transgender person. As a result, 'girl', 'man', 'woman', 'not a woman', 'he', 'she', 'a cross-dressed man', 'a person with non-traditional sexual orientation' and 'a homosexual' are all used interchangeably and with little rhyme or reason. At the very least, the judge – or his clerk – could have consulted a dictionary for the benefit of their own writing. Doing so would probably also have pushed in the direction of a better judgment. As it stood, the murder was interpreted as manslaughter, Dmitry and Slava were sentenced to 10 years in a high-security facility, and Albert was never found.

But in fact what were the judge's options, given the story he had to tell? Another way to deal with this 'gender trouble' would have been to employ the category 'transgender' to refer to Svetlana. This move would have made the judge's writing less confusing, but it would also have introduced a term that is foreign to Russian law. The category forms part of a longer acronym 'LGBT' that may have structured some recent conversations about gender and sexuality in the US courts but has not been unproblematically adopted elsewhere.

Take, for example, Daniel Schluter's (2002) attempts to survey Soviet queerness at the beginning of the 1990s. As he reports, his respondents seemed to confuse homosexual and heterosexual as both applying to themselves, at least in the 'sexual' part of the words. He therefore modified his questionnaire and included local community terms (*goluboi*, 'our people', 'our theme'), and then translated the answers to 'Western' identity categories such as 'gay', 'lesbian' and 'bisexual' (Schluter 2002, 44), regardless of whether these different sexual vocabularies really matched. Even if they did match, though, some respondents failed to properly identify themselves by mixing up or appropriating all the categories and, therefore, turning out as simultaneously gay, straight and bisexual despite Schluter's efforts at rigid classification (Schluter 2002, 77). To this day, there are many people engaged in same-sex eroticism and desire in Russia[7] who are confused about identity categories or actively resist confining themselves to the rigid LGBT+ identities (Barchunova and Parfenova 2010; Kondakov 2012; Chernova 2016; Shtorn 2017). So perhaps, almost ironically, the above judge's contextual vocabulary of sexuality and gender actually mirrors what queer theory literature advances as a more accurate way to refer to sexualities, which are always fluid, changeable and unstable.

Queer theory

In this chapter, I discuss various approaches to making sense of sexual experiences with the goal of understanding which analytical tools I have at my disposal. Since I investigate questions of power relations and sexuality throughout the book, queer theory, which focuses on the critique of sexual identity as a product of power, offers important insights. Largely taking their starting point as Foucault's *History of Sexuality*, many queer theorists argue that when people identify with one of the letters of the LGBT+ acronym, they simultaneously expose themselves to the workings of disciplinary power (Halberstam 2018, 7–8). This power – enhanced through law and other kinds of expertise used to create the truth about oneself (Godwin Phelps 2016; Adler 2018) – significantly limits the many and changeable ways in which sexuality is practised (Halperin 2012). In other words, once identified, we begin to embody the discursive category we have chosen. Conversely, queer theory has sought an academic vocabulary to speak about sexuality without the confinement of identity, instead expressing its phenomenological fluidity, changeability and multiplicity.

The application of queer theory in Russia faces at least two major problems. First, as my discussion of Svetlana's case shows, the rigid categories of sexual and gender identity are not entirely relevant, as they are not fully grasped by the law and other vocabularies. Consequently, a theory that criticises those identities and the way law structures sexual experience by insisting on identity categories cannot be an appropriate analytic instrument here. Instead, Russia seems to find itself in a state of fluid and changeable sexualities that has only been envisioned in the West by queer theory (Baer 2002). Second, both LGBT+ identity language and queer theory may appear to be Western invasions (Healey 2006, 107) that only obscure what is actually going on by introducing a foreign discourse into local practices. This may have many social and political consequences. An obvious one is the description of any non-heteronormative sexual or gender experience as external to the Russian nation – an argument that appears all the more convincing once foreign identities and theories are there to evidence the imposition (Mole 2011; Edenborg 2021; Vorontsov 2017). Regardless of the possibility of political manipulation, a *generalised* application of epistemologies built on a *particular* example is a methodological trap: even when it creates the impression of explaining local experiences, it is still very much biased towards the place of its theoretical origins.

This chapter thus offers a rethinking of queer theory – by which, because of the lack of a better signifier, I simply mean to imply a poststructuralist enquiry into the multiple effects of power – in order ultimately to use some of its insights for the analysis of neo-disciplinary power relations that follows. To be honest, I do not think it is important to defend or dismantle queer theory per se. I actually do not really care about queer theory. Rather, I believe that we need an analytic language to communicate complex, unstable and messy power relations that we observe in our societies. Queer theory is a way to name such a language because as an intellectual endeavour it has worked with concepts of fluidity, complexity and messiness, especially in the sphere of sexuality (Browne and Nash 2010). Certainly, many other intellectual traditions have done similar jobs but have not been referred to as 'queer theory' or have been given other names (Plummer 1996; McRuer 2006). For the sake of consistency in my narrative, I mostly use the literature that in one way or another has close affinities to queer sexuality.

The following excerpt, offered by Judith Butler, encapsulates most of the ideas I associate with queer theory as a specific, US-centred intellectual and political venture. In *Bodies That Matter*, Butler explains what 'queer' could mean as a perspective for both academic and activist projects seeking to combat current inequalities. She helpfully defines queer theory and practice thus:

> If the term 'queer' is to be a site of collective contestation, the point of departure for a set of historical reflections and futural imaginings, it will have to remain that which is, in the present, never fully owned, but always and only redeployed, twisted, queered from a prior usage and in the direction of urgent and expanding political purposes. This also means that it will doubtless have to be yielded in favor of terms that do that political work more effectively. Such a yielding may well become necessary in order to accommodate—without domesticating—democratizing contestations that have and will redraw the contours of the movement in ways that can never be fully anticipated in advance. (Butler 1993, 228)

There are three elements in this definition that I want to highlight. First, the definition posits queer theory as a perspective ('point of departure') – a way of looking at things from a particular angle which facilitates both the methodological and political outcomes. Queer theory here is a *method* of reading with a queer eye (Sedgwick 1990). Second, this method is deployed with the particular purpose of 'futural imagining' or building a political project of a better, albeit never fully defined, future. Queer theory tends towards figuring out *a utopia* (Muñoz 2009). In the most Marxist of traditions, queer theory seeks to identify current unjust conditions of (sexual) inequality and propose a way of eradicating them in order to advance to a better situation. Third, queer theory prioritises fluidity, multiplicity and changeability – even of its own definition – to *subvert* the workings of power. Fluidity and multiplicity serve as a way to escape power relations: classifying practices into rigid categories is a technique of disciplinary power (Butler 1990, 43). If the power of, say, gender identity is based on how neatly we repeat previously given ways of being a woman, then the fluidity of one's practices from feminine to masculine and back again interrupts this repetition and breaks the cycle of the application of power. This is the utopian aspiration of queer theory, too: as a result of subversions, we are presented with the contours of a genderless society in which people are truly emancipated from the power that governs the external categorisation of their sexual embodiment.

I argue that while queer theory is uniquely useful as a method of reading and describing fluid, messy and unstable sexualities, it also misses many insights since it still centres on identity, its critique and utopian predictions. Could queer theory's obsession with identity and utopianism be an aspect of its US legacy that can be overcome with decolonised queer methodologies?[3] To begin this task of decolonising queer theory, I look at the Russian experience. In doing so, I introduce a more realist form of thinking into queer theory by rejecting its utopianism. While it is arguably admirable to imagine a future time when things get better – and I do not deny that this very imagining may prove performative and drive societies to progress – I nonetheless argue that this idea of progress may be an overestimation and, more importantly, that things may become much worse in the future. Thinking beyond this progressivist futurism may help us to focus on what is going on now.

The queer in Russia

Previous endeavours to apply queer theory to situations in Russia and Eastern Europe more generally have made use of its many insights about sexual fluidity, multiplicity and complexity (Kowalska 2011; Kulpa and Mizielinska 2011; Szulc 2018). In her groundbreaking work, Laurie Essig documented her encounters with uncommon uses of sexual identity vocabulary within Russian queer communities in 1991: 'their definition of transsexual was quite different from our own. We had expected women who wanted male bodies. Instead, we found girls who seemed like any other girls, except that they had female lovers' (Essig 1999, 39). This account does shed some light on the seemingly mistaken sexual orientation vocabulary used to refer to the transgender experience in the court case above. I mention it here for another reason: it is just one example of the many contestations of identity vocabulary found in Russia and the post-Soviet space (Channell-Justice 2020). Observers have pointed out that unlike in the 'West', where historically there has existed a sharp boundary between hetero- and homosexuality, in Russia 'sexuality is far more subtle than the rigid categories, the concrete bunkers, that we create to circumscribe it' (Tuller 1996, 290). Essig summarises this idea beautifully and coins the term 'queer subjectivity' to refer to the fluid sexuality she observed in Russia:

> Sexual otherness in Russia has not formed easily into the rigidity of identity. Instead, queerness is more a free-floating pick-up game than the codified rules and clearly defined players of identity. Identity demands the identifier to perform in ways that are consistent and coherent with its founding mythology that we *are* an identity, rather than that we act in identifiable ways . . . even without the safety of true identity, queerness represents itself, signifies itself, in a system of signs that speaks in both recognizable and unrecognizable tongues . . . Queer subjectivities utilize the dominant language for their own purposes in ways that are sometimes incomprehensible to others. Queers gather secretly in public places—secret because their queerness is unacknowledged. Sometimes queerness is seen. Queerness can speak loud enough to get public's attention . . . queer exists as both subculture and culture, particular and popular. (Essig 1999, 83)

As a queer person who was born and raised in a small Russian industrial town in the middle of the Ural Mountains, Essig's vision of queerness hits very close to home, despite my decolonial intentions here. When I came across her work, I felt that I had found someone who was able to shape into words what I sensed and experienced. However, I also recognise that precisely because of the urgency of the project to decolonise knowledge, the application of queer theory outside its place of origin requires critique and careful revision – and Essig's work has certainly met with a lot of criticism (Healey 2006; Baer 2009; Amico 2014; Stella 2015). I see the point of critical dialogue as the refining and advancement of an idea rather than the destruction of one. It means asking proper questions in relation to the concepts that are up for rethinking. Have Essig's critics asked the right questions when trying to rethink it?

One way to reject the applicability of queer theory in Russia and elsewhere outside the English-speaking world is to argue that it cannot logically be subversive because the word 'queer' does not exist there or does not mean the same thing as in English. Indeed, 'queer' appeared as an English-language slur that was later reclaimed by political and academic communities in the US (de Lauretis 1991; Patton 1993, 146). The very act of reclaiming its usage was considered subversive. But in Russian there is nothing to reclaim: 'queer' or the localised *kvir* will strike most as nothing but a simple loan transliteration from English (cf. Hartblay 2014). In fact the word 'gay', which has been domesticated in Russia for at least half a century (Kozlovsky 1986), is a much more provocative term to 'reclaim' if there is any need for reclaiming (Sozayev 2012). Consequently, 'queer' in Russia forms part of an inner-circle vocabulary: it is a secret word that allows one to hide one's sexuality rather than subvert and disturb the workings of power that created it. This is why Stephen Amico's (2014, 8) Russian interviewees dismissed the term 'as "nonsense" ("*erunda*"), or indicative of a man's "complexes" (i.e., the inability to admit to a homosexual orientation)'. Amico thus opted for more common terms among the Russian gay male community in the mid-2000s: 'the terms gay and homosexual (rather than queer)' (Amico 2014, 11). Similarly, Francesca Stella stated in relation to the Russian women interviewed in the second half of the 2000s and early 2010s: 'I deliberately avoid collectively naming the subjects of the research as queer'; she chose to use 'lesbian' instead because it 'is empirically grounded' (Stella 2015, 6). One thing this shows is that sexual identity categories appear to have taken root in the Russian language and among LGBT+ communities, which clearly use them to refer to themselves (Bingham 2017; Weaver 2019; Nartova 2008).

Furthermore, critics ironically suggested that if Russian sexuality is queer – which is understood by queer theory as a subversive post-identitarian sexuality – then Russia is exceptional and even superior to the West, in which post-identitarian queerness is only hoped for. Thus, Brian Baer doubted: if Russia was indeed queer, then it 'perhaps skipped a stage in its sexual history, moving directly from premodern polymorphous sexuality to queer' (Baer 2009, 33). This just could not be true. The conclusion was reached that Russian fluid sexuality was not queer; it was a different kind of fluidity. It was more similar to sexuality in the UK and US back in the 1950s, where sexuality was not confined to rigid categories of orientation and people switched between heterosexual and homosexual behaviour (Stella 2015, 58). Hence, rather than post-identitarian, it is some sort of *pre*-identitarian sexuality – a form of sexual fluidity not only prior to queerness, but also temporally prior to the strictures of LGBT+ identities appearing.

To my mind, this conversation reaches a dead-end by asking all the wrong questions and suggesting all the wrong answers. The discussion circles around comparisons of Russia and the West by implying either Russian sexual superiority, or its submission and inferiority to the uninvited Western 'standard'. Is Russia just like the US? Or is it better than the US? Or is Russia like the US, only a few decades earlier, and thus worse? On this narrative, Russia is almost-the-US-but-not-quite-the-US; it is catching up with the West only to be late to the party every time (Kulpa and Mizielinska 2011; Tlostanova 2018). These kinds of narrative fuel questions that lead nowhere and do not illuminate our understanding of either Russian or Western sexualities. They simply reproduce the well-rehearsed spatial temporalities of Cold War rhetoric (Davison 2019; Essig and Kondakov 2019; Serykh 2017; Wiedlack 2017): while the US continues to progress, nothing ever changes in Russia; it reproduces the 'premodern polymorphous sexuality' that gives the impression of queer fluidity, but actually it is the same old thing.

Asking the right questions

The rejection of queer approaches to Russia is based on a very clear understanding that queer is a set of practices and even an identity. A skeleton then begins to appear in queer theory's closet: despite all its critique of identity, the term 'queer' has been reified into yet another identity category added to the LGBT+ spectrum (Floyd 2009; Levy and Johnson 2012; Buist and Lenning 2016). And so it might seem advisable not to use the term at all, since so many interviewees have rejected the category: as if queer theory will only be applicable once the 'locals' catch up and end up identifying as queers in a few decades' time. But of course relying exclusively on a set of interviewees necessarily cuts off the degrees of diversity that they fail to represent. It is not the task of qualitative methods to argue over which word is generally used in a given population. Today, for instance, 'queer' is finding momentum in Russia as a category of analysis, as an identity category in the Russian language and as a practice of reclaiming local slurs (Mozzhegorov 2014; Suyarkulova 2019; Garstenauer 2018; Gorbachev 2019). It may not resemble the 'original' queer, as it is appropriated, domesticated and reinterpreted for new uses outside its initial context. Paraphrasing the words of Gloria Anzaldúa (1999), 'queer' resonates as a form of *mestiza* – a mixture of various cultures and contexts. Using inspiration from scholars and activists in India and Uganda, Rahul Rao points this out by suggesting that as an inherently open-ended term, 'queer' makes itself available to various appropriations, to melding with other processes and ideas, and to innovative functionalities, regardless of its US American history (Rao 2020, 27). In a similar way, Mohira Suyarkulova concludes her analysis of the use of the term 'queer' in Kyrgyz Russian by claiming: 'The multiple uses of "queer" across languages bear a "family resemblance", but are not in a relationship of one-to-one correspondence of equivalence and identity. Each utterance and translation of "queer" hides a particular story of political and ideological resistance and struggle' (Suyarkulova 2019, 52).

Hence, it seems that queer comes in many contradictory forms at once and, therefore, its rejection or acceptance may mean different things to different people. For Amico and Stella, queer meant an identity category that was not found among the people they interviewed. For Baer it meant a stage of US sexual history that is still to come in Russia. For Essig it meant a method of analysis drawn from the US queer literature to help make sense of the unruly sexual subjectivities she encountered in post-Soviet Russia. For Rao and Suyarkulova, 'queer' refers to a category of practice that is simultaneously a form of knowledge created from many different sources, of which US literature forms only a part among a great variety of others. In this latter version, US queer theory becomes provincialised by expanding its sources and reinterpreting certain questions of queer theory that have been thought of as central to it for the sake of other pressing issues. I join the voices that argue for such a provincialisation of queer theory and for the co-authorship of a truly global framework that addresses power relations in their full complexity rather than taken separately in different localities. Petrus Liu describes this global queer theory in relation to his focus on Chinese sexualities:

> . . . we must take Chinese materials seriously as intellectual resources rather than local illustrations of theoretical paradigms already developed by the canon of queer theory. Doing so also means that we must adamantly reject the common division of intellectual labor in area studies programs between the production of paradigms (queer theory) and the gathering of raw materials (Chinese examples). Hence, we should not assume that queer theory automatically refers to the distinct body of theoretical works

produced in 1990s' United States and later translated into Chinese. In my study, queer theory refers to a global discourse that was simultaneously developed by English, Chinese, and other academic traditions. Queer theory is a transnational and transcultural practice of which its US instantiation is only part. (Liu 2015, 15)

The task I am performing in this book is similar. Queer theory in Russia is not a search for a specific identity or set of practices. It is not a method developed exclusively in US universities and then referred to as queer theory in other localities. It is not just the application of an already known perspective to Russian material. Rather, queer theory is an analysis of power relations in which Russia and the US, the East and the West, the global South and North each reflect one important facet of a complex story. I endeavour in this analysis not to compare Russia and the US. I do not want to even imply such a comparison because it results in all the wrong questions and conclusions. Hence, I ask not how queer theory can help us understand sexuality and anti-queer violence in Russia, but, following Liu's insight (2015, 21–2), how studies of Russian cases can help queer theory.

I argue that in its contribution to global queer theory, Russian experiences advance at least two sets of ideas. First, they displace questions of sexual identity from its central role in queer theory and instead ask how disciplinary power works without necessarily producing identities. Second, the Russian experience of pursuing utopias demonstrates that things do not necessarily get better, even though they do change. Hence, I also propose that we should not expect a queer utopia as resulting from subversions of power because this argument implies a certain progressivism without acknowledging it. Instead, a more realist version of temporality and a more cautious attitude towards the future may posit the possibilities of dystopian times ahead of us as a direct result of the subversions that will reconfigure power relations.

The rest of this chapter turns to the history of sexuality in Russia in order to figure out how disciplinary power constituted it without overwhelmingly relying on identity vocabulary. I then show how the promise of utopia stemming from the fluidity and multiplicity of sexual practices as assumed in some queer theorisations has resulted in the queer dystopia that is currently unfolding in Russia.

The birth of the homosexual species

According to Foucault's foundational-for-queer-theory account, medical expertise enhanced by legal authority produced the modern homosexual in late nineteenth-century Europe (Foucault 1978b, 105). While what 'Europe' consisted of can be a matter of many interpretations, as Liu points out (2015, 27), the term 'homosexual' was coined somewhere in the middle of it by a Hungarian author in correspondence with a German sexual science enthusiast and activist (Takács, Kuhar and Tóth 2017, 1945; Janssen 2021). At about the same time, the term was making its way through legal and medical expert circles in puritanical Britain (Weeks 2002; 2017). But homosexuality is not simply a term; it is an entire discursive constellation that invites disciplinary power as soon as someone is classified as homosexual. More contemporary categories of sexual identification such as those abbreviated in the LGBT+ acronym are understood as sharing a genealogy with this medical term, but also as reinterpretations in new contexts of grassroots politics and community (Seidman 2013). These new meanings for queer sexuality relate directly to the Stonewall events in the US and the emergence of the LGBT+ social movement that has managed to globalise these identities (Massad 2002; D'Emilio 2012). My point is that we should not regard any of these 'stages' of sexual history as necessary or as universal, and we can do this by looking beyond identity criticisms.

Historians of Russia have argued that before modernity, religion organised knowledge about sexuality and condemned all non-procreative sexual behaviour, including homosexuality (Levin 1989; Kon 2006, 321; Muravyeva 2013b; Mayhew 2020). However, the Orthodox Church did not keep a record of its many persecutions for same-sex attraction, nor did it enforce capital punishment or other strict penances, limiting sanctions to lengthy periods of prayer and fasting, if anything (Levin 1989, 197; Muravyeva 2012, 207; Mayhew 2020). In general, what religious law seems to have sought to prohibit was the sin of 'sodomy' (*sodomsky blud*, *sodomstvo*): a set of sexual practices vaguely related to non-procreational sex, from masturbation and adultery to same-sex intercourse (Levin 1989; Muravyeva 2012, 209). Late seventeenth- and early eighteenth-century reforms replaced the biblical language with more physical vocabulary: male homosexual intercourse got its own category – *muzhelozhstvo* (buggery), which for men literally meant the situation of lying together with another man (Kondakov 2013b, 406; 2020a). This category travelled to Article 995 of the nineteenth-century Penal Code and then to Soviet law (Engelstein 1992, 60; Healey 2001, 94). Yet, a 'premodern' understanding of *muzhelozhstvo* remained in legal practice. Sometimes the article was used just like 'sodomy' once had been: *muzhelozhstvo* was interpreted widely as any practice outside conventional heterosexual intercourse (Muravyeva 2014; Mayhew 2020). In any case the article was rarely adjudicated and so had little legal impact (Engelstein 1992, 69; Petri 2019).

As a reader of Foucault would predict, it was medical science, especially Krafft-Ebing's theory of degeneration, that made the Russian homosexual a species. The law enhanced this medical knowledge with regulatory overtones. Dan Healey cites several sources of forensic medical expertise in the late nineteenth century and then Soviet Russia which actively discussed ways of identifying homosexuals for the purpose of applying criminal law (Healey 2009). After the 1917 Socialist Revolution, the Bolsheviks reinforced the medical vocabulary of sexuality, making 'a homosexual' a totally legitimate medical category (Engelstein 1995). Male homosexuality was initially decriminalised, but, as part of a larger attempt to introduce more control in the USSR, same-sex intercourse between men returned to the Criminal Code in 1934 in the form of a ban on buggery, *muzhelozhstvo* (Essig 1999, 6; Healey 2001, 186). This move is interpreted by scholars as a biopolitical attempt on the part of the Soviet government to discipline sexual bodies towards sexual reproduction for the dawning of the Soviet nation (Zdravomyslova and Temkina 2003; Healey 2014, 176). However, the re-criminalisation of male homosexuality also marks a considerable departure from the usual Foucauldian history of sexuality. Instead of a proliferation of sexual discourse as an act of resistance to the pressure of prohibition and resulting in the fortification of sexual identities, the Soviet totalitarian approach ensured the silencing of all sexual topics and the production of alternative fragmented vocabularies of sexuality (Naiman 1997; Rotkirch 2000; Zdravomyslova and Temkina 2003; Kondakov 2013b; 2019b).

The extent to which this silencing worked can be illustrated by the almost complete erasure of the medical definition of homosexuality. Indeed, only the legal category *muzhelozhstvo* made it into the Big Soviet Encyclopaedia until the 1960s, when the category *gomoseksualizm* (homosexuality) was reinstated there (Essig 1999, 7). Thus, in a matter of years, the USSR went from encouraging rich and diverse expert discussion of sexuality in general and queerness in particular, beginning in the 1920s (Engelstein 1995), to an almost complete suppression of expert knowledge about queer sexualities over the next three decades (Naiman 1997; Kon 2010; 2011; Kondakov 2019b). The Soviet Union eventually followed other socialist countries in allowing certain changes in the sexual discourse in the 1960s and 1970s, including more discussion of various forms of sex (Ingbrant 2020; Gradskova, Kondakov and Shevtsova 2020, 363; Davison 2021; Takács and Tóth 2021), but not until then. In the USSR, discussions mostly circled around the criminal law and the question of whether or not voluntary same-sex intercourse should be decriminalised again (Alexander 2018b; 2018a).

The very fact of silencing queerness speaks to attempts to regulate sex rather than leave it as is. Sexuality indeed appears to be central for Russian politics (Swader and Obelene 2015). But while silencing may be understood as very poor ground for the production of strong identities, it does not mean that it did not yield disciplinary power productive of differently organised forms of knowledge about queerness. All it means is that there was no major principle of organisation of this knowledge beyond silencing. As Arthur Clech puts it (2019, 33), 'homosexual identity is only one of the possible forms through which individuals in their experience of homosexual desire can render themselves the subject of their homosexuality'. As attempts to stop all conversations about queer sex in the USSR made these conversations unstructured, diverse and fragmented, multiple vocabularies for referring to queerness got their chance to establish themselves as valid and legitimate for various segments of society: criminal law vocabulary for legal actors; criminal subculture vocabulary for prison inmates; vague literature references for the educated; foreign vocabularies for sex-workers looking for international clients, and so on (Kondakov 2014a). These vocabularies were claimed and owned – not unlike 'queer' – and the resulting subversion led to a reconfiguration of power relations. In being silenced, Soviet queer bodies were disciplined as outcasts – people whose actions constituted a crime. As a result, alternative spaces were produced that allowed for queerness – spaces in a fragmented underground in which various communities circulated their own vocabularies and knowledges about sexuality. I argue that this must be seen as a modern disciplinary regime of power (not 'premodern polymorphous sexuality'), even though it produced multiple competing truths instead of one truth as understood in a discourse organised by sexual identity.

The queer of one's own

In this climate of silencing and the prioritisation of criminal solutions, the law on *muzhelozhstvo* was one of very few official enunciations regarding homosexuality. As researchers have shown, the Soviet concept of *muzhelozhstvo* was defined very narrowly and strictly as anal penetration between men (Jong 1982). Hence, determining whether or not this 'criminal' act had actually occurred usually required a relatively straightforward medical examination of a person's anus, where forensic experts would look for signs of intrusion (Aripova 2020, 107–8). This concerned the penetrated partner, who seemed to assume all the criminal guilt in such cases. Or was he interpreted as the victim (Jong 1982, 347)? The criminal and legal dimensions of the sexual discourse were centred on a firm distinction between 'active' and 'passive' roles in same-sex activities, in which the active party was somehow exonerated from any wrongdoing, on the one hand, as performing a legitimate version of masculinity (Kuntsman 2009; Healey 2018, 35–6, 111; Vincent 2020, 83). On the other hand, however, criminal article 121 comprised two sections: voluntary (up to 5 years in prison) and forced (up to 8 years in prison) sex.[4] The second section applied to the 'active' partner and could be used especially in cases against prison inmates, where same-sex practices are regarded as violations of the internal rules. While this law was commonly applied in all Soviet republics, we do not know whether these two sections of criminal article 121 were applied evenly, or how the law was used more generally. What we do know is that from the 1960s until the collapse of the USSR, on average 1,000 men a year were sentenced under one or other section of the criminal article (Gessen 1994, 24–5; Valodzin 2020). At the same time, the use of this article in relation to gay men is inconclusive. For instance, those who could be prosecuted under the voluntary section of the criminal article believed it could not apply to them because only violent incidents and public sex were regulated (Kondakov 2019b, 409). The article was also used in cases which did not even involve sex between men at all: for example, against political opposition and women who clearly fell outside the category *muzhelozhstvo* – translated as men-lying-with-men (Gessen 1994; Clech 2019; Valodzin 2020). In summary, this official form of enunciating queerness was quite messy from the beginning.

Alongside the legal discourse, queerness manifested itself in the medical field too, especially in the late Soviet period (Alexander 2018a). Lesbian desire and transgender experience became the domain of psychiatric practice (Gessen 1994; Essig 1999; Stella 2015; Clech 2017). Sex reassignment surgery was known in the USSR from 1968, but probably was not very common (Turovsky 2018). Moreover, both expert and lay accounts suggest that homosexual orientation was sometimes interpreted as 'transsexuality' and sex reassignment surgery was prescribed as 'treatment' (Essig 1999, 36–40; Stella 2015, 47–8). Psychiatrists would also deal with lesbian (and in some cases with gay male) desire without resorting to invasive surgery, using methods ranging from counselling to electroshock (Gessen 1994; Clech 2017). In other cases, where medical experts were not involved and queer practices were regarded as a mere 'temporary' confusion, Soviet citizens could be referred to their peers at comrades' courts and hearings at Komsomol assemblies (gatherings of the youth division of the Communist Party). Francesca Stella describes many stories where queer sexual behaviour was subjected to moral assessment by young Communist Party members at these gatherings. Such 'matters of personal relationships . . . were understood to fall under the broad definition of "antisocial behaviour" which did not constitute a criminal liability but was considered to be against accepted social norms' (Stella 2015, 50). Comrades' courts could revoke one's membership of the Party for queerness or offer advice on how to conduct a 'decent' sexual life. Their vocabulary tended to be colloquial and centred on morality.

Alongside the legal term 'buggery' and the medical term 'homosexuality', many other definitions of queer desire circulated in Soviet society, acquiring various levels of popularity. These were the colloquial vocabularies of diverse communities, from queer Soviets gathered on cruising strips in big cities to prison inmates inventing rigid hierarchies for their sexual practices (Healey 2001; 2018; Kondakov 2019b; Fiks 2020; Vincent 2020; Mielke 2017). Starting in the nineteenth century, some gay men referred to themselves as 'aunties' (*tyotki*), a word still popular among Russian drag artists as well as used to mean older gay men (Kozlovsky 1986, 69; Healey 2002). The term *goluboi* (colloquial Russian for 'gay' and literally translated as 'light blue')[5] was used as a local community category of identification up until the 2000s (Schluter 2002; Shtorn 2020a). The same is true of *tema* (literally 'the theme'), *nashi* ('ours' or 'us'), and *rozovaya* ('pink' for lesbian). All are local terms that are losing their currency (Sarajeva 2011; Stella 2015).[6]

Vladimir Kozlovsky (1986) documented Soviet urban queer vocabulary in the 1960s and 1970s. Aside from those mentioned above, terms included: *seksual'nye menshinstva* (sexual minorities), *gei* (gay), *lesbiyanka* (lesbian), *tribadizm* and *sapfizm* (lesbianism), *pidor* and *pedik* (fag and queer), *dyatel* (woodpecker for a 'top'), *aktiv* (top), *passiv* (bottom), *universalka*, *sintetika* and *kombain* (versatile), *baba* (sissy), *devka* or *pidovka* (fairy), *dochka* (daughter for a twink), *mamochka* (mommy for a sugar daddy), *Don Pedro*, *pedagog* and *pederastita* (a homosexual man), *streit* and *natural* (heterosexual), *shalava* (sex worker) and many others. These terms stem from both a specific urban queer subculture and an offensive prison vocabulary, mixed up and developed through continuous reappropriation, subversion and use. Most of these terms form a particular type of community vocabulary united under the umbrella of *khabal'stvo*, a specific queer idiom employed at cruising sites and underground bars which is similar to 'camp': a combination of jokes and irony with references to same-sex practices balancing on the edge of politesse and recognisability (Sedgwick 2011, 66; Sarajeva 2011, 130; Cassiday, Goscilo and Platt 2019).

This vocabulary does not just provide an alternative to the medical and legal definitions of homosexuality, it opens up a fresh reservoir of queer community knowledge available to those seeking truths about their sexuality. All of this taken together reveals why the forms of queerness in the USSR were so diverse: various communities engaged in producing fragmentally legitimate knowledges about queer desire and practice under the general veil of silence. The resulting constellation reveals a deep plurality of truths about sexuality that promotes vulnerability and openness to its fluidity, multiplicity and contestability. I argue that, according to the Foucauldian theory of disciplinary power, the search for truth need not be accomplished for the discipline to work, nor does it need to end in 'finding' oneself in a particular form of sexual identity. The very availability of knowledges and the will to know the 'truth' provide ground for the discipline to function (Foucault 1978b). Perhaps in situations of silencing – the concealment of knowledge – the will to know actually intensifies. As a result, what we witness in the Soviet condition is an inconsistent collection of competing knowledges on queerness. Hence, instead of an arrangement of the true self structured predominantly by sexual identity, we deal with contradictory accounts amalgamated in an assemblage under the cover of silencing.

Queer dystopia

This was the state of sexual history in Russia at the end of the Soviet epoch in the 1980s: queer sexuality was subversively inconsistent, fluid and changeable in a context of coexisting contradictory forms of knowledge pulled together by the workings of silence. And just like certain interpretations of queer theory, the feeling was that things could only get better, leading the way to a utopian genderless future. The gay and lesbian interviewees in my previous studies were all hopeful about future prospects as they saw the Soviet Union crumbling (Kondakov

2014b, 165–6). By the beginning of the 1990s, queerness had become more visible in big Russian cities: 'Queer subjectivities bubble to the surface of the Russian public sphere in the form of discos, publishing houses, cruising strips, theaters, and even restaurants' (Essig 1999, 82). As the USSR crashed, signs of improvement indeed appeared elsewhere. First, voluntary male homosexual intercourse was once more decriminalised in 1993 (Healey 2018, 106). Second, in December that same year a new constitution was adopted by popular vote, and it emphasised equality and human rights. The first wave of Russian LGBT+ activism crested at this point (Kondakov 2013b; Buyantueva 2018; Buyantueva and Shevtsova 2019). Not only were independent media and show venues featuring a lot of unrestricted sexual content (Borenstein 2008), but most importantly LGBT+ topics were being discussed from various angles, including in a positive light (Omelchenko 1999; Cassiday 2014; Gradskova 2020). Religion started to play a greater role in society and managed to both alienate and attract LGBT+ Russians (Stähle 2015; Kislitsyna 2020). In all these developments, legal and medical authority was shaken and eventually overshadowed by the mediated political vocabularies, including that of queer communities.

At this time, queer theory's goal of subversion leading towards utopia was apparent in Russia. Reflecting her interviewees' euphoric sense of drastic societal changes unfolding imminently, Laurie Essig enthusiastically emphasised how fluid sexual desires were producing a different kind of sociality and politics (Essig 1999, 81). Amidst these long-hoped-for changes, visions of what was coming next were still very opaque. Liberation meant being free from embodied constraints and limits. It was that kind of moment when one could feel the freedom in the air, touch it with one's hands, taste its bittersweet scent on one's tongue. If Butler's 'futural imaginings' (1993) were to be envisioned at the beginning of 1990s Russia, only utopian pictures would have been drawn. The collapse of the USSR and the track taken by post-Soviet countries immediately afterwards somehow inscribed them all into the Western progressivist imagination (Tlostanova 2018). After decades of diversion, Russia was returning to a path that ensured (capitalist) growth, development and advancement in all aspects of life.

While queer theory does not necessarily form part of this progressivist rhetoric by virtue of its critical stance towards ideologies of capitalist progress, some writers who work on queer temporalities do tend to emphasise a version of the future that structures time in a linear progression. Within US queer theory, the critique of the progressivist timeline gained prominence as a response to the assimilationist politics of the LGBT+ movement (Duggan 2003; Halberstam 2005; Eng 2010). As a result of the inclusion of some LGBT+ people exclusions were produced for all those already marginalised among queer communities: the poor, the racialised, the gendered and so on. In his *Cruising Utopia*, José Esteban Muñoz offers an alternative for all the excluded – the queer utopia. His version of the queer future does not entail assimilation to 'traditional straight rationality' as exemplified by same-sex marriage (Muñoz 2009, 21). To get to the future, Muñoz proposes a clear process of becoming queerer and eventually ending up in a better place, even though he explicitly rejects the realisability of his utopia (Kondakov 2021c). This line of thinking is important in queer theory because it engages with the idea of performativity: the very image of queer utopia works to produce changes today (Muñoz 2009, 19, 97). In reality, however, things can go sideways since no one is in full control and there are more powerful actors pushing their (not so queer) agendas. Consider, for example, the insights of distributed agency discussed earlier (Bennett 2005). More importantly, if utopias are realised, they may give way to unpredictable and even unwanted outcomes (Cooper 2013). In short, queer does not necessarily mean good, in this sense. A queer utopia is, then, a cultural belief that things always get better. A more realistic analysis would rather engage with change as it is, acknowledging that the quality of the change might be unknown.

In Russia there is a cultural belief that things will always get worse. I do not want to fully adopt it or to sound alarmist, but I do want to set it in opposition to the idea of a queer utopia, because clearly a utopia can turn into a queer dystopia. In this vein, what I want to suggest is that fluid sexualities and changes in the ways sexuality is known and dealt with *reconfigure* power relations, even though they may not result in a genderless queer utopia. This reconfiguration does not necessarily lead to a better situation, or a worse one. But it does mean that things have changed. The subversion of power that queer theory hopes will result in its eradication may actually lead to the adaptation of power relations to new circumstances. The 1990s first witnessed this rush of elusive flows of sexual uncertainty and ambiguity, quickly followed by a popular demand to bring it back under control. In other words, sexual fluidity, avoidance of identity constraints and a more complex definition of the sexual self than a rigid classification can provide do not necessarily result in the eradication of inequalities, misogyny and other forms of violence. As this book further shows, despite elusive forms of sexual expression, queer people are still targeted in Russia as queers. Hence, I do not see how the implied marriage between queerness and utopianism is an unshakable one. If anything, it should be understood as uncertain. It is far more helpful to recognise that we do not know the future and we do not know if it will be better.

The reconfiguration of power

After the collapse of the USSR, not only could queer (and straight) sexualities finally be discussed freely on TV, in newspapers, film, theatre, music and elsewhere, but this discussion also found an eager audience (Essig 1999; Horne et al. 2009; Heller 2007; Amico 2014; Cassiday 2014; Andreevskikh 2020). After decades of silence, post-Soviet consumers longed for sexually explicit content in diverse forms and, consequently, sex literally cascaded down on the Russian people (Borenstein 2008). Instead of hiding in shadowy, fragmented places where diverse definitions of queerness circulated, sex became a central topic in the marketplace of common discussion.

This impressive lava flow of sex could not but provoke a demand for order to return. While in the early 2000s, when Putin's government was beginning to really build state control, sexuality was of very little concern to the Kremlin, it soon took centre stage precisely because power is so intimately connected to gender and sexuality (Borozdina et al. 2016; Kondakov 2020a; Suchland 2018; Swader and Obelene 2015). Politicians once again returned to the idea of a ban on *muzhelozhstvo* and proposed the re-inclusion of criminal articles against voluntary same-sex intercourse as well as a ban on 'homosexual propaganda' (Healey 2008). These initiatives had been rejected until a time when the reimagining of queerness became primarily a question of foreign policy for the government. Expressions of queerness, the public visibility of which coincided with the opening of borders and the collapse of the USSR, were soon construed as brought from abroad by foreign powers with dark intentions (Wilkinson 2014; Borenstein 2019; Edenborg 2021; Chandler 2021). A discourse of Russian sexual 'traditions' took shape in response.

The concept of 'gay propaganda' is one of the earliest products of the reconfigured power relations. The idea behind the propaganda bill is that the law should stop the influences that supposedly make people queer: foreign cultural products, LGBT+ activism and other forms of outside informational threats. As a meme, this idea resonated in the 2010s, although the first regional 'propaganda' regulation was silently adopted as early as 2006 in Ryazan Region. The connection between opposition to homosexuality and Russian national traditions was further discussed by the Constitutional Court in 2006 and 2010. In the 2006 decision, the Court established a definition of family that centres exclusively on heterosexual procreation as, it was argued, one of Russia's central national traditions. As for the 2010 decision, the Court defined 'homosexual propaganda' as harmful to children, because exposure to it upsets their morals. These morals must be based in 'family, maternity and childhood in their traditional, passed from ancestors, understanding' (Constitutional Court 2010), which together comprise 'traditional values'.

The full definition of 'gay propaganda' given by the Constitutional Court eventually resurfaced in one of the widely discussed regional 'propaganda' bills[7] adopted in 2012 in St Petersburg:

> In this article, by public actions directed at propaganda of *muzhelozhstvo* [buggery], lesbianism, bisexuality, and transgenderism to minors, the following is understood: intentional activity that involves uncontrolled dissemination of information in open sources that can harm the health, morals and spiritual development of minors, including if they can form deviant ideas about the social equality of traditional and non-traditional marital relationships. (Law of St Petersburg 2012)

The text applies and appropriates the LGBT+ identity categories by listing sexual and gender classification in a very particular manner: *muzhelozhstvo*, lesbian sexuality, bisexuality and transgender experiences. This text is a 'hybrid' of the history of queer sexuality in Russia, applying its various current definitions and transforming foreign identity categories in odd ways (Dorogov 2017). The federal 'propaganda' ban in 2013 departed from this approach in favour of the less clear umbrella term 'non-traditional sexual relationships'. The federal law essentially put an end to regional laws, which were rendered unnecessary by the higher-level legislation. The bill for the most part repeats the wording of the St Petersburg law and forms part of the overarching administrative legal system in Russia that regulates misdemeanours and other minor offences (Kondakov 2019b; Utkin 2021a). Russia's major censorship state agency, *Roskomnadzor* (the Federal Service for Supervision of Communications, Information Technology and Mass Media), enforces this law by ordering the withdrawal of information rendered 'propaganda of non-traditional sexual relationships' from public access. But its effects go further than mere law enforcement, as this book and other studies show (Shtorn 2018; Novitskaya 2021; Utkin 2021b; Soboleva and Bakhmetjev 2015; Kondakov 2017b).

The propaganda law shifted attention from homosexuality per se to information: the law targeted queer expression and queer exposure. It shows how the regulatory functions of law – stimulated by the drive to re-establish order after the lawless freedoms of the 1990s – can enact new configurations of disciplinary power. This power builds on existing categories of queerness (local and international) and adds to the field a generalising push using umbrella terminology ('non-traditional sexual relationships'). This umbrella term captures very well the turn away from a queer utopia – it is literally opposed to queer; it is its antonym. It has a similar meaning but casts an opposite, negative quality on the defined phenomena. In this very sense, the terms are similar as they encapsulate and cover the complex variety, multiplicity and fluidity of things by offering one overarching category. They are two resonances of the same global process (albeit they take somewhat different shapes in local contexts).

Hence, considering the context of the Russian experience of sexual history outlined above, I argue that fluid queer sexualities may indeed be inspirational, but they may also invite regulatory power. In this way, queer utopia transforms into queer dystopia as a more probable – and unfortunate – outcome. One way or another, power relations are reconfigured. No matter what kind of future is promised, however, the important thing is that a change occurs. I argue that the non-progressive development of sexual history in Russia demonstrates that power relations in this sphere are being reconfigured and that the place of application of power has shifted from bodily policing of identity to the governance of information.

Ultimately, my point here is to say that sexuality in Russia is complex, contradictory and inconsistent. It encompasses a great variety of sexual experiences and sexual expressions, not necessarily confined by the boundaries of identity categories, although sometimes they fall quite strictly inside them or remain framed by local histories. This sexuality embraces a complex time flow that leaves traces of legal, medical, criminal, community-based and globalised vocabularies. As a result, both easily identifiable and elusive forms of sexual expression comprise the current form of what sexuality is in Russia. This current form is not the same as it was centuries ago, because it is built upon experiences that have run through the sexual history of modern Russia: cruising, legal prosecution, medical treatment, prison culture, art, literature, silencing, urban subculture, commercialisation and so on. In fact, sexualities in Russia resonate with more general global trends in their own ways, such as the drive to unify multiplicity and complexity under the roof of one umbrella term. Queer theory as an intellectual endeavour offers an idiom to communicate this fluidity, inconsistency and diversity, once it is enhanced by a global perspective. This enhanced version of queer theory nudges one to doubt, however, that sexual fluidity is subversive to power to the point of promising a utopian future. Rather, when power is subverted, its relations are simply reconfigured. Perhaps, then, the classifying of various sexualities is not a mechanism of power itself but a snapshot of power's current configuration. In the next chapter, I take this snapshot of sexual expression as it is given in court rulings on anti-queer violence cases across Russia. In doing so, I continue my analysis of disciplinary power.

Notes

1 For example, see estimations made by mapping telephone area codes corresponding to city districts onto urban geographical locations in Gdeetotdom 2011.
2 This book deals with contemporary materials from Russia and historical developments in the larger territories colonised by the Russian Empire and the USSR. I draw mostly on literature about Russia, but note that queer studies of other places that were emancipated from its rule are maturing, too: the former Soviet republics Armenia (Shirinian 2018); Azerbaijan (Moon and Helbıg 2018); Belarus (Solomatina and Shchurko 2014); Estonia (Kadri 2019); Georgia (Mestvirishvili et al. 2017; Tolkachev and Tolordava 2020); Kazakhstan (Shoshanova 2021; Sekerbayeva 2020); Kyrgyzstan (Wilkinson and Kirey 2010; von Boemcken, Boboyorov and Bagdasarova 2018; Sultanalieva 2020); Latvia (Vērdiņš and Ozoliņš 2019; Aripova 2020); Lithuania (Mažylis, Rakutienė and Unikaitė-Jakuntavičienė 2015); Moldova (Mitrofanova 2020); Tajikistan (Hall et al. 2020); Turkmenistan (Latypov, Rhodes and Reynolds 2013; Wirtz et al. 2013); Ukraine (Bonacker and Zimmer 2019; Martsenyuk 2012); Uzbekistan (Latypov, Rhodes and Reynolds 2013; Wirtz et al. 2013); as well as Mongolia (Billé 2010) and the former Socialist bloc in Europe (Darakchi 2021; Sweet 1995; Takács 2015; Fejes and Balogh 2012; Ayoub 2016; Štulhofer and Sandfort 2005; Slootmaeckers, Touquet and Vermeersch 2016; Takács and Tóth 2021).
3 In postcolonial debates, Russia is positioned as both an empire and a periphery, as Madina Tlostanova puts it: 'The most doomed situation is in Russia itself, which has suffered under the imperial difference syndrome for several centuries . . . Russia strove to fit into the logic of catching up and tried to build a separate Socialist modernity, with its own coloniality sharing the main premises of modernity at large, such as racism, Orientalism, progressivism, the rhetoric of salvation, a fixation on newness, asymmetrical divisions of labor—that is, generally the coloniality of being, gender, knowledge, and sensibility. The Russian empire was dominated culturally, technologically, intellectually, and in other ways by the core European countries, yet it subsumed other peripheral spaces, making it a clear case of semiperiphery' (Tlostanova 2018, 6). Thus, my rhetoric of decolonisation should be interpreted in a context in which Russia is both colony and empire, the oppressed and the oppressor. Hence, I do not intend to exonerate Russian colonialism past or present by pointing to the US or the 'West' as current oppressors.
4 Each Soviet republic had their own criminal code. Article 121 was in the criminal code of the Russian Soviet Federative Socialist Republic (it was Article 154 in the first version of the criminal code). Similar criminal articles were introduced in other republics and they sometimes varied as to terms of imprisonment or pertinence to particular chapters of the criminal code (Healey 2001, 186). Uzbekistan and Turkmenistan still retain their respective Soviet anti-homosexuality articles in their current criminal codes (Latypov, Rhodes and Reynolds 2013).
5 Kozlovsky reports that the word originated in the 1940s in the Gulag, where it meant a homosexual man involved in sexual intercourse as a 'passive' partner or a raped male (Kozlovsky 1986, 44). It

appears to have been claimed by the gay male community later, only to become a derogatory term again today.

6   The word *tema* is interesting because, even though there is nothing sexual about it as such, it belongs to queer sexual vocabulary more generally as it is also used among the BDSM communities (Kondakov 2017e, 176). It can be interpreted as a 'fashioned' sexuality – secretive sexual practices which are somehow special or peculiar. As for *nashi*, it is simply a word that refers to any inner circle ('our people'): for example, it is currently used by a pro-government youth organisation that is acquiring nationalist overtones.

7   The regions that adopted the 'propaganda' legislation include Arkhangelsk, Vladimir, Irkutsk, Kaliningrad, Kostroma, Krasnodar, Magadan, Novosibirsk, Ryazan, Samara, St Petersburg and Ufa (Kirichenko and Sozayev 2013, 12; Fedorovich, Yoursky, and Djuma 2020).

4
The sexual subject of law

Queering the language of law

In the previous chapter I argued that the coexistence of various vocabularies can be understood as a working of discursive power relations – namely discipline – even though some of these vocabularies may not centre on a clear definition of the self, such as identity. Furthermore, I also suggested that while elusive sexual vocabularies communicate the fluidity, multiplicity and messiness of sexuality, they can result in greater webs of discipline rather than subvert power and achieve a genderless utopian freedom. In this chapter I analyse manifestations of these elusive vocabularies through the 314 criminal instances of anti-queer violence in my sample.

The purpose of this analysis is twofold. First, it provides empirical evidence and additional knowledge regarding the diversity of queer sexuality in Russia, as theorised in the previous chapter. Second, my study shows which configuration of power manifests in court decisions: in other words, how exactly sexual difference is conceptualised as a line between queerness and heterosexuality. As I argued in the Introduction, in order to work disciplinary power requires the production of asymmetries. The differences between the various sexualities described in these rulings are meant to lay the ground for this asymmetry, which later gets used in the mechanics of power relations – which I scrutinise in the next part of the book. In sum, this chapter reviews the techniques of classification of desire used in courtrooms, but, rather than showing how this classification works as disciplinary power, I demonstrate how it is only one element in a more complex machinery of power.

To analyse power, it is necessary to figure out the various methods of classification; that is, how 'gays' are sorted from 'straights' (not necessarily by articulating their different identities). However, despite Foucault's own argument to the contrary, I show that this is not how power is applied. Rather, this classification sets the conditions for power to start working by introducing the idea of difference between subjects. Into what relationships and engagements these now differentiated subjects enter depends on the affective mechanisms of bonds between them. In other words, it is widely believed – and I said the same at the beginning of my analysis of Svetlana's case in the previous chapter – that employing 'correct' language categories not only shows some respect for the people in question, but also directly translates into 'good' practices. Svetlana's murder was portrayed by the court using inconsistent and improper vocabulary that amounted to a re-victimisation of the transgender body by rendering it invisible, even non-existent. Similarly, the homeless people who killed Svetlana, when they discovered that her body did not meet their expectations of female anatomy, also expressed an inability to comprehend sexual diversity, which they reacted to in the extreme by physically eliminating her body. However, the case file also showed that sheer ignorance of a proper vocabulary did not translate inevitably into violence. Indeed, the way Svetlana's gender and sexuality were classified did not dictate her fate, as the following elaboration of the story demonstrates.

Svetlana's custodial mother, Zoya, exhibited little difference from the judge and the murderers in terms of her understanding of transgender experience. She too employed a tactic of silencing and erasure, yet this did not translate into physical violence. Rather she offered care and respect. Zoya had two jobs, as a kindergarten director and social worker. She met Svetlana when visiting a troubled family. At that time, Svetlana was 12 and lived with her grandparents, who were alcoholics. Zoya decided to place her in an orphanage to save her from domestic violence. There, Svetlana spent a few more years under the supervision of Zoya. Eventually she ran away from the orphanage and started to live with Zoya, who adopted her and, despite having little understanding of Svetlana's transgender aspirations, worked to ensure her transitioning:

> In the Institute of Human Reproduction, she was told that Gennady needed sex-change surgery because he had the female nature. This operation would cost 10 000 US dollars; authorities of the North-Western Administrative District [of Moscow] agreed to pay a half of this sum; the Institute would cut the other half. Also, in the Institute

named after Alekseev, she was told that Gennady had 'children's schizophrenia' that, as she believed, was connected to his non-traditional orientation which he had had since 15. (1-676/2011, Moscow)

The text is written in a way that indicates no understanding of or respect for Svetlana's identity; it is not just authored by the court clerk: Zoya also contributed to it with her vocabulary. It is full of questionable medical theories and exhibits signs of misunderstanding many details of the sexuality that Svetlana lived every day. However, Zoya clearly expressed compassion when she used her power as a state official to adopt the girl and to facilitate sex reassignment surgery free of charge with the help of state funding. In other words, Zoya's language does not reflect her feelings towards Svetlana.

I will return to the analysis of feelings and affects in the next chapter when I interpret affect as a mechanism of power. Here, it is important to keep in mind that the classification of gender and sexuality does not work as a mechanism of power without affectual bonds or without feelings that structure relationships between the classified subjects.

In this chapter, I scrutinise the ways in which queer sexualities are classified by actors in the legal field. As I argued in Chapter 2, these actors are driven by feelings of indifference towards queerness. What matters to them is following procedural norms, not engaging in any kind of sexual politics. This indifference manifests as a form of violence – albeit non-physical – because it is directed towards victims belonging to historically disadvantaged communities who deserve remedies. Furthermore, the judges in the cases reviewed generally do not care about queerness; they simply have the very pragmatic goal of delivering a judgment within a limited timeframe. But they still have to make some sense of the sexual and gender diversity they encounter.

Vocabulary of multitude

Let me first catalogue all the different references to queerness that I found in the cases under review. I classified all articulations of queerness, starting with subject categories (expressed in nouns and other forms) and then moving on to actions that people do to appear queer or that signal their queerness to others. As will become clear, the texts of the criminal court rulings do not employ just one kind of vocabulary to communicate queerness – they contain many different forms. This is because the rulings are compilations of various accounts of alleged criminal incidents presented in the courtroom and then pulled together in judges' decisions. Notably, the umbrella term 'non-traditional sexual relationships' is becoming increasingly prevalent and absorbing other forms of queer enunciations.

Among the categories found in the court decisions referring to queer subjects, there is a collection of community terms that merges both the oblique Soviet vocabulary and contemporary in-your-face identity-based expression. Vague references such as *nashi* (ours), *takoy* (like that) and *ne takoy* (not like that) were discovered in the rulings. For example, when referring to a gay man, one witness stated that he was 'not like everybody else' (*ne takoy kak vse*) to indicate his homosexuality without any further explanation (1-70/2016, Penza). Another term was *goluboi*, which was even used on one occasion to insinuate an association between queerness and the decadent privilege and luxury of a capital city in contrast to the wholesomeness and sexual innocence of the Russian provinces: this was at a time when it was believed that all gay men came from Moscow ('gays from Moscow', *golubye iz Moskvy*). A more colloquial noun was also used to refer to someone in a queer relationship, transliterating a word from English: *boifrend*.

Identity-based vocabulary was also widely used in the court rulings and included 'bisexual', 'lesbian' and 'homosexual' (referring to men only).[1] Interestingly, the word *gei* (gay) showed signs of being only in the process of gaining familiarity, and in several rulings it was given in forms that estranged it: either written with a capital letter (Gay) or in quotation marks ('gay'). This indicates that the word seemed to be new or foreign to the authors of the court decisions and, therefore, less real. They knew what it meant but marked its novelty and foreign origin through punctuation or capitalisation. This is not the case with 'lesbian' or 'bisexual', which were both already considered to be rooted in the Russian language and used without any special markers. Notably, little reference was given to transgender experiences in the texts apart from the already mentioned use of 'transsexual'; there was also the use of 'transvestite' (*transvestit*). Otherwise, confusing phrases such as 'either woman, or man', 'not a woman' and 'a cross-dressed man' (*pereodetyi muzhchina*) proliferated when referring to transgender women.

Collective nouns were also used in the court rulings, for example 'LGBT', 'gay community' (*gey-soobshchestvo*) and 'LGBT society' (*obshchestvo LGBT*). This points at the imagined institutional structure of LGBT+ communities as a kind of association of people with formal membership. This is probably partly a feature of official Russian language, which requires one to indicate one's formal status in relation to a group. Either you are a member of the LGBT+ community (or a representative of it) or you are not:

> On [a date] at [o'clock], [the defendant] was outside chatting with his associate. An unknown drunk young man approached them with the aim of making friends and offered them a drink, but they refused. During a short conversation, this young man specified his sexual orientation. [The defendant] asked him if he was a member of LGBT society and the young man answered that he was [*sostoit li on v obshchestve LGBT, na chto tot otvetil, chto sostoit*]. [The defendant] replied that he did not want to talk and make friends with him, because they were not acquaintances and it was late. (1-6-2/2016, Rostov-on-Don)

Regardless of how such words sound, they appear to be deployed as neutral categories and, therefore, are not supposed to convey additional meanings. Hence, 'a homosexual' is just a gay man, as well as 'a representative of LGBT society'. Officially. On this view, variations and diversity within these larger categories do not matter either. The terms are used to state a matter of fact. Yet as we will see, facts – just as much as opinions – can trigger violent affections.

Inmates' sexual positions

Vocabulary of the prison subculture was used not only where former inmates were involved but in other contexts as well. This evidences the spread of this vocabulary to the wider population. Specific to this subculture are terms like *opushchennyi* (the untouchable), *obizhennyi* (the offended), *petukh* (a cockerel), *Annushka* (diminutive of Anna) and *dyryavyi* (the holed). All these terms are meant to signify a category of prison inmates who are raped by other inmates and as such occupy the lowest position in the prison community: 'He was surprised because he had never encountered before a man who would caress another man; in prison, people with such orientation are referred to as "cockerels" – the lowest prison caste' (1-309/2015, Kyzyl, Tuva Republic). At times, the terms were clearly defined: '[they] considered him an *opushchennyi* (i.e. a homosexual person) because he associated with people of non-traditional orientation' (1-4/2011, Velikiy Novgorod). If the terms above are more specific to the prison subculture, other terms belonging to this vocabulary are more widespread and include *pidor* (faggot), *pedik* (queer) and *gomosek* (homo). All of these terms are considered very offensive both within and outside the prison subculture.

Prison vocabulary focuses primarily on one's position in sexual intercourse, to differentiate between 'degrading' homosexual conduct and reputable heterosexual behaviour with some homosexual implications. The former is associated with a 'passive' role in intercourse and is stressed using such terms as 'passive homosexual' and 'passive gay' in the court rulings. The latter is linked to the 'active' role and is not considered damaging to heterosexual masculinity. Instead, it is believed to be an expression of heterosexuality despite manifesting as same-sex intercourse. This distinction is important for many victims and defendants and confusions around it may lead to violent reactions, such as when an 'active' (hence, self-identifying heterosexual) partner is asked to switch his role in sex:

> He maintained friendly, including intimate, relationship with [the victim]. On [a date] at 23.50 o'clock, [the victim] visited him at home. In the flat, they drank alcohol – vodka and beer, and after that voluntarily entered into a sexual intercourse, in which he performed an active role. Then, [the victim] offered him sexual intercourse, where [the defendant] would perform a passive role. He replied that he would be back soon, went to the kitchen, took a knife from the windowsill, exited the kitchen, came to the room where [the victim] lay naked on a bed and stabbed him 8–9 times to his neck and chest. (1-239/2013, Engels, Saratov region)

There are also many instances of offensive vocabulary without a particular subcultural origin. Here, I include 'a man of wrong orientation' (*chelovek ne toy orientatsii*), 'a queer/weird lad' (*strannyi paren'*), 'a pervert' (*izvrashchenets*) and 'an HIV infected' (an HIV-positive person, which was seen as a sign of victims' homosexuality in several cases). These references are rare but not one-off occurrences.

Legal queer dictionary

While the court rulings use the language of those who present their testimonies in the courtroom, in most cases this language is translated into an official legal dialect that is characterised by a supposedly neutral vocabulary and peculiarly formal terminology. One of the categories that gained popularity as a neutral reference to queers was 'sexual minority' and the subsequent framing of a victim of anti-queer violence as 'a representative of sexual minorities' (*predstavitel' seksual'nykh men'shinstv*). This phrase has stuck to LGBT+ people in Russia – so much so that, in the court rulings, it is used even without specific denotation, using just 'the minorities' to imply sexual ones.

Among the most important legal terms is 'social group'. This category is used in law to guarantee protection under hate crime and hate speech legislation in the absence of explicit references to 'sexual orientation'. The term has been used when applying relevant Criminal Code articles to argue that violence has been carried out against 'a social group of sexual minorities' or 'a social group of persons with non-traditional sexual orientation'. In a case in which an elderly lady was charged with dissemination of hateful materials during a public rally, the ruling held:

> [The defendant] committed . . . actions directed to incitement of hatred and enmity, as well as to humiliation, against a group of persons based on ethnicity and affiliation with a social group . . . According to the expert opinion of GUP 'TsIAT' No. e/2 dated 00.00.0000, the brochure of [the defendant] contains manifestations of incitement of conflict (enmity, hatred) against a group of people based on sexual orientation – the homosexuals [*gomoseksualisty*]; against a group of people based on ethnic and religious affiliation – the Judaists (the Jews), as well as against members of masonic organisations – the Masons. (1-2/2013, Moscow)

One of the most common terms in the sample is 'non-traditional sexual orientation' (*netraditsionnaya seksual'naya orientatsiya*), and the nouns belonging to it vary from the extremely formal *litso* (a natural person) to the neutral but gendered 'a man, an individual / a woman of non-traditional sexual orientation' to informal 'a lad [*paren'*] with non-traditional sexual orientation'. One can be 'of' or 'with' this orientation. Again, when the formal language of law is employed here, this belonging to a population is considered to be membership and representation of the entire community – that is, a formal status: he 'is a person of non-traditional sexual orientation, which he is not ashamed of and which status he openly claims' (1-1045/2016, Krasnoyarsk).

As an umbrella term, 'non-traditional sexual orientation' is used to signify all the various queer sexualities that judges encounter: 'bisexual, that is an individual with non-traditional sexual orientation' (1-3/2013,

Moscow); '*goluboi*, that is [a person] of non-traditional orientation' (1-1009/2011, Yoshkar-Ola, Mari El Republic); '*pidor*, that is [a person] of non-traditional orientation' (1-105/2012, Konakovo, Tver Region). Yet, more critically, the term is sometimes understood as too broad and all-inclusive, and therefore in need of specification: 'he might be a person of non-traditional sexual orientation, namely a homosexual' (1-131/2014, Moscow); 'he called him and [the defendant] persons of non-traditional sexual orientation – *golubymi* [gays]' (1-104/2016, Dolgoprudny, Moscow Region). Or consider the following passage, where a sequence of definitions specifies how a community euphemism translates into an identity-based category and into a legal classification that shows kinship between all these words:

> He got acquainted with [the victim] through his associate [witness] who invited him to visit a friend, namely he said: 'let's visit one of ours.' By the word 'ours' he meant 'gays', that is, persons with non-traditional sexual orientation. (1-376/2016, Izhevsk, Udmurt Republic)

All these categories point at a subject that is contextualised in various settings as non-heterosexual (in a very broad definition of heterosexuality that sometimes includes homosexual practices). This subject reflects a long and diverse sexual history in Russia, embracing various vocabularies and, consequently, expressing colloquial, subcultural and formal classifications of queerness almost simultaneously. Most importantly, these different classifications do not stand on their own, but are intertwined. What is more interesting is how these multiple vocabularies coexist, compete and cooperate.

Queer as a verb

The court rulings also catalogue *practices* relating to queerness. These words attempt to portray what people consider to be queer behaviour. Again, the language used to enunciate such practices is varied; as with the categories discussed above, the words here comprise a melange of subcultural vocabularies and official terminology. People are described as performing 'the role of passive partner' and even engaging in 'gay debauchery' (*goluboi bespredel*), signalling prison language. Interestingly, the queer community term '*tema*' (theme) was only mentioned in relation to same-sex BDSM practices: 'a citizen whose non-traditional orientation was based on erotic dominance and submission' explained his 'bruises by thematic entertainment' (1-34/2014, Novosibirsk).

Medical and pathological language is rather diverse in the analysed texts. Queer sexualities are regarded as 'deviations' and 'abnormal sexual orientation'. Individuals may have an 'inclination to homosexuality' (*sklonnost' k gomoseksualizmu*) or just have a 'sexual orientation'. Interestingly, sexual orientation comes in two distinct forms in the court decisions: *seksual'naya* and *polovaya* orientation (*orientatsiya*). The latter is part of a more dated Soviet vocabulary (sex in terms of gender is *pol* in Russian, whereas sex in terms of intercourse is *seks*). Therefore, one may orient one's desire either to the same gender as in the older Soviet terminology, or to certain sexual practices. At times, sexual orientation as a practice may be understood as 'wrong' (*nepravil'naya*) or 'undefined' (*neopredelennaya*) – meaning the unintelligible negative of heterosexuality.

Specific legal terms include references to 'non-traditional' actions: 'non-traditional signs of sexual advances' and 'non-traditional contacts'. There are some more charged terms that may have legal consequences when they are introduced as mitigating circumstances for a defendant. Here victims are portrayed as provoking criminal actions against themselves in situations of sexual 'harassment' (*domogalsya*), 'amoral behaviour' (*amoral'noe povedenie*) or even an 'amoral way of life' (comprised not only of sexual activities, but in addition to other 'amoral' habits, such as alcoholism). 'Amoral' as a term may be attached to a variety of actions that judges regard as inappropriate. In the context of online dating, this is frequently seen as beginning with 'an amoral exchange of messages'. When 'amoral' actions grow into 'unlawful behaviour' (*protivopravnoe povedenie*) and are not simply a 'lewd offer' (*nepristoynoe predlozhenie*), they become the statutory ground for exoneration or extenuating circumstances, and so are cast as a defence strategy or an excuse to act violently against a queer person.

In their descriptions of queer activities, legal actors rely on the available legal vocabulary in cases where they see same-sex behaviour as unjustifiably intruding into otherwise innocent interactions between people. In these events, same-sex behaviour turns into the previously criminalised 'buggery' (*muzhelozhstvo*) or 'sexual homosexual intercourse, buggery' (*polovaya gomoseksual'naya svyaz, muzhelozhstvo*). Alternatively, they may cite 'actions of sexual character' (*deystviya seksual'nogo kharaktera*) – another legal phrase – which is a statutory term for sexual activities that do not involve genital penetration (used in many cases to refer to lesbian sexuality). Another way to signal the criminal nature of queerness is to refer to it as sex work, using the notion of 'homosexual services' (*uslugi*) – even when nothing points to any exchange of money for sex.²

On the flip side, law can also be mobilised to protect LGBT+ people from violations of rights, as in the cases that apply the notion of 'social group'. Many of these instances stem from the articulation of homosexuality as 'information that defames . . . honour and virtue' in cases where people seek to blackmail gay men using threats to 'out' them. So, clearly, judges are capable of discussing queer sexualities in a more respectful way and sometimes they do so by suggesting that people are just engaged in a 'homosexual relationship' or even 'same-sex love' (*odnopolaya lyubov'*). This classification, however, does not necessarily entail any positive treatment of queer victims, as we see in the following murder case:

> The Court agrees with the argument of the Defence and establishes the amoral actions of the victim as an extenuating circumstance when [the victim] offered same-sex love to [the defendant], because in our society, there are disagreements about acceptance and unacceptance of same-sex love; and, therefore, from the criminal law point of view, morality or amorality of such behaviour must be interpreted in favour of the defendant – that is it must be interpreted as he interpreted this behaviour in that moment, namely as amoral and offensive for him. (1-415/2015, Chelyabinsk)

In this narrative, vaguely positive descriptions of homosexual desire as love are deployed to speak about a shameful and ultimately amoral practice. The word 'love' is arguably used because more 'sexual' language was considered inappropriate to use in public. There are other examples like this. To escape more overt articulations of queerness, court rulings may indicate that a man had 'sympathy towards' another man or simply that he 'likes men'. At the same time, these very same practices can be interpreted as 'lust' (*pokhot'*) or 'a wrong lifestyle' (*nepravil'nyi obraz zhizni*).

Earrings, makeup and mannerisms

Legal actors sometimes rely on visual evidence of queerness. Defendants in the court cases frequently identified LGBT+ victims by interpreting their appearance as queer. They were not always correct in their assumptions. One of the regular features of a queer body is an earring. However, defendants confuse which of the ears should be pierced to signal that a person is gay.[3] While it does not really matter which ear is pierced, it does matter that the very fact of wearing an earring indicates a departure from conventional masculinity, according to some perpetrators' perspectives. Other signs that can evoke gender confusion are regarded as marks of queerness:

> The first lad looked like this: about 20 years old, Caucasian [from the Caucasus region] appearance, short, slim, hair was done like he was a girl, his behaviour was suspicious, and it seemed like he was of non-traditional sexual orientation, he even talked with intonations like a person with non-traditional sexual orientation. The second lad was about 20 years old, Slavic appearance, medium height, also slim, hair was done in 'crew cut' style. He was dressed analogously to the first boy, manners and behaviour were like he was a person with non-traditional sexual orientation. (1-339/2014, Astrakhan)

In this case, the full constellation signalled queerness: not just stylish hairdos, but also two similar and questionably male bodies in physical proximity to each other. Hence, haircut, body type and manners may all betray male heterosexuality. In the reviewed cases, 'long curly hair', 'women's habits' (*povadki*), 'mannerisms' (*manery, manerniy*), 'high voice' and 'squealing' (*tonkiy golos, vizg*) led perpetrators to question men's masculinity and heterosexual orientation, and, eventually, to become 'irritated by their body type and outlook', culminating in violence (1-245/2014, Tomsk).

A person's appearance is usually taken as a whole, not in separate parts, to establish queerness:

> In the queue near them, there were three young people, one of whom had an unusual, ridiculous look that evidenced, as he believed, this individual's belonging to persons of non-traditional sexual orientation. He had black round objects in his ears that in addition to his haircut, clothes and shoes, as well as mannerisms, prompted laughs and smiles. (5-304/2016, Volgodonsk, Rostov region)

As for women, markers of masculinity were often interpreted as queer. For example, a 'man's hairy legs' discovered on a transgender female body led to an outburst of violence, as the unfortunate Svetlana discovered. When defendants encountered cross-dressing, they were immediately convinced that they were observing queerness. The 'blurring' of genders and paying special attention to one's body were cited by both defendants and witnesses as signalling something unmistakably queer:

> In the courtroom, it was established that [the victim] was a person of non-traditional sexual orientation. Thus, all defence witnesses testified in court that it was an obvious fact: the deceased person used decorative makeup, had a pedicure and covered his toes and fingernails with polish, went to the gym and solarium, i.e., he paid a lot of attention to his look, spoke with mannerisms and gesticulations, as well as dressed in the appropriate fashion for this category of people, namely, womanly. He had never hidden his sexuality, on the contrary he was flashing it. (1-15/2014, Moscow)

In another testimony, the mother of a murdered man assumed that, since he had 'lately started to pay more attention to his look, used perfume and skin cream', it meant he had 'begun to stick to non-traditional sexual orientation', although she never discussed it with him directly (1-121/2012, Severskaya, Krasnodar Territory). One final instance of queer appearance is the expression of an intimate relationship between people of the same gender in public. For example, two teenagers were attacked for holding hands on a bridge while gazing at the flowing river.

Evidence, witnesses and facts

I have already started to discuss what counts as evidence of someone's sexuality in the courtroom. As the above examples show, judges may rely on witness testimonies to determine sexuality. But why bother proving it in the first place if no hate crime legislation is to be applied? To begin with, defendants are usually the ones to bring up the queer element. It was not uncommon for the defendants in the reviewed cases to use so-called 'homosexual panic' as a defence strategy.[4] According to this strategy, the perpetrator argues that the sexual advances of their victim provoked panic which, in turn, justified their acts of murder and violence. I stated above that sexual advances may fall into the legal category of 'amoral behaviour', which is an extenuating circumstance in Russian criminal law. This means that a successful argument about unwelcome sexual advances towards a defendant may result in reduced prison time, or no prison time at all. However, it is worth mentioning that Russian judges do not see 'amoral behaviour' as automatically coming from someone's homosexuality:

> The defence's argument that the [defendant's] case should fall under Article 107 para. 1 CC RF as homicide in a state of strong emotional agitation (affect) because of [the victim's] non-traditional sexual orientation and her advances towards [the defendant] continuing for an hour and resulting in affect, the court found unsubstantiated. A strong emotional agitation (affect) emerges suddenly as a reaction to the unlawful or amoral behaviour of a victim. Yet, [the defendant] knew very well about the sexual orientation of [the victim], as she confirmed in the courtroom. [The defendant] testified that she did not approve of this, that she avoided encounters with the victim, but they still had a friendly relationship, and it was [the defendant] who invited [the witness] to visit her friend's [the victim] flat, where they drank alcohol. In the courtroom, it was established that [the victim] and [the defendant] argued for an hour, [the defendant] freaked out, threw things, they moved from kitchen to the room, then [the victim] fell to the floor, while [the defendant] straddled her, squeezed her mouth and nose shut, and hit her with her right hand. (1-122/2010, Kargapolye, Kurgan Region)

In other words, as another case illustrates, 'there is no ground for qualifying the amoral behaviour of the victim as an extenuating circumstance, because [the victim's] belonging to persons of non-traditional sexual orientation alone does not evidence by itself the unlawfulness of his behaviour' (1-173/2015, Tyumen). Certainly, not all judges are of the same opinion and not all cases have similar facts. Nonetheless, legal actors' jobs are made easier when defendants themselves bring up the motive of their crime – their violent reaction to sexual offers or advances. Hence, in trying to evade justice, perpetrators may provide one of the elements that ensures the successful processing of a criminal case, namely a testimony with their motives. Furthermore, they also invite an investigation into the victim's sexuality. In such cases, it is necessary to verify the victim's queerness or disprove it to clear the criminal file. In my initial sample, which I narrowed down to 314 relevant cases, there were many instances of the 'homosexual panic' defence failing. Here is an example:

> The Court denies the version of the Defence that [the victim] threatened to commit actions of sexual character to [the defendant], because, according to witness testimonies by MP and VV, [the victim] did not have any expressions of non-traditional sexual orientation, he was characterised positively, enjoyed authority and respect among his colleagues and sportsmen, he was married and had children, and when drinking alcohol, he acted calmly. (1-27/2015, Zabaykalsk)

Given the judge's scepticism as to the victim's alleged homosexuality, I excluded this case and similar ones from my file of court rulings on anti-queer violence. Note, however, the arguments that were put forward to classify someone as heterosexual: peer respect, authority, family and sports. It is implied that homosexuality, in turn, is characterised by their opposites.

Witnesses, surviving victims and defendants all testified in the courtroom as to their own definitions of queerness when they were asked. These definitions relied heavily on existing prejudices in society, but also sometimes challenged common assumptions. One of the most frequent ideas that haunts these testimonies – as I mentioned already – is the association of queer sexuality with confused gender. This means that queer men are believed to express feminine traits, and queer women are expected to exhibit signs of masculinity: 'they went to the café "Vegas" where they saw the previously unknown to them [male victim] who looked and danced not like a man' (1-41/2015, Shchekino, Tula Region); 'he was interestingly dressed and he had a strange bag in his hand that looked like a woman's purse. They took him as a person of non-traditional sexual orientation' (1-83/2014, Saratov). Consider this testimony by a victim's mother: 'her daughter [the victim] was an active lesbian and hid details of her personal life from her. [The victim] was fond of fishing and on [a date] she bought a knife' (1-108/2011, Orekhovo-Zuevo, Moscow Region). This account articulates the association of lesbian sexuality with 'manly' leisure activities such as fishing, as well as with being active and in possession of weapons.

Similarly, male homosexuality in the testimonies is associated with passiveness and weakness: 'they assumed that a man with non-traditional sexual orientation should be weak' (1-12/2014, Zheleznogorsk, Kursk Region); '[the defendant] argued that they stood up for [the victim] like for a girl because he couldn't stand up for himself' (1-2/2016, Mil'kovo, Kamchatka Territory); 'he was a hard-working, funny and reserved man who did not have military training' (1-193/2014, Vladivostok, Primorsky

Territory); 'the victim . . . stated that he had been a person of non-traditional sexual orientation since he was 20, he had entered into sexual intercourse with other men as a passive partner. He did this voluntarily' (1-25/2011, Likino-Dulevo, Moscow Region). These characterisations of men as 'passive' and the speakers' definitions of femininity led to the conclusion that the men should be classified as queer. As for women, the opposite argument seems convincing in the Russian courtroom. Generally, witness testimonies construct the world as sharply divided by gender:

> When they met, she told him that she closely socialised with girls, because she did not like guys, and that she had a girlfriend in the town of . . . in Moscow Region . . . She also knew [Name], who was acquainted with [the defendant] and [victim-1] and [victim-2], who were persons of non-traditional sexual orientation and lived together as a man and a woman. She did not know if [the defendant] knew [victim-1] and [victim-2] . . . In the flat No. [ ], his neighbours lived, [victim-1] and [victim-2], they drank alcohol together if they invited. They told him during drinking that they were persons of non-traditional sexual orientation, because they liked only other women. They had some friends, all of them females. (2-93/2013, Krasnogorsk, Moscow region)

These witness testimonies refer to a strict distinction between femininity and masculinity, homosexuality and heterosexuality, the female and the male worlds. If women were understood as lesbians, they were believed to socialise only with other women, despite the fact that one of the witnesses who occasionally drank with the women above was a man. This idea was strengthened through the notion of gender division of labour in women's same-sex families where one of them was supposed to perform 'masculine' functions as opposed to the 'feminine' functions of the other woman. However, these opinions were sometimes challenged by the victims themselves and did not constitute the only form of queerness that was circulating in Russian courtrooms:

> She knew that [the victim] abused alcohol and drugs, wore women's clothes, was a person of non-traditional sexual orientation . . . [The victim] also said that he found a woman, who he wanted to marry. This surprised her very much, because she knew that he was a person of non-traditional sexual orientation, he often wore women's dresses and walked in them. (1-15/2016, Perm)

There is no word in Russian that can fully grasp sexual or gender fluidity. 'Queer' is not used by witnesses and in any case pertains more to the academic domain as an analytic category. Consequently, the testimonies under review all struggle to articulate unspecified or changing sexualities. Indeed, they inscribe this fluidity into their rigid taxonomy of sexuality by classifying the various desires separately. In this universe, queerness is secondary to heterosexuality. As a secondary phenomenon, it has its debut when the subject of desire turns towards unexpected fare. Queerness is also carefully kept separate from the concept of family, which is assumed to be exclusively and fundamentally heterosexual. I discuss these two arguments further below.

The age of becoming

Heterosexuality is assumed by default. Hence, people whose desires lead them elsewhere are believed to be able to pinpoint an exact moment in time when they stopped being heterosexual. In one of the quotes above, a victim explained that he had been a gay man since he was 20 years old. This age is important: it is above 18, when a person legally becomes an adult in Russia and is thus capable of making free choices. Queerness is something one can opt for (even under the influence of 'propaganda') after turning 18 without suspicion from the state. Notably, though, this framing demands that there be a point in time when this choice is made. This is why one man was asked how long he had been of 'this kind':

> Questioned as a witness, [witness 2] testified during investigation that for the last five years he had adhered to non-traditional sexual orientation, upheld sexual liaisons with persons of his own sex. With the purpose of dating, he periodically visits various websites on the Internet, where he finds individuals who also adhere to non-traditional sexual orientation. (1-255/2013, Vladimir)

In this testimony, the mention of five years establishes the necessary moment of decision. Note also the language used in this and some other rulings, where sexual orientation is regarded as something one 'adheres to' or 'sticks to'. It is a matter of mood or 'inclination' – a choice that one makes:

> They greeted each other, bought bottles of beer and strolled to the park in front of [a monument to] Ordzhonikidze. During their chat,

> [the victim] said that he previously dated girls, but a year ago he tried to maintain relations with a guy, and he liked it, because there were no obligations in relationships with guys ... Then they bought more beer and continued their conversation. As he understood, [the victim] was a proponent of one-night stands with guys. (1-50/2014, Ufa, Republic of Bashkortostan)

Again and again, the fluidity and instability of queerness is stressed in these accounts through references to the temporal character of 'non-traditional sexual orientation' and through a vocabulary that signals ideological rather than biological affiliation with this kind of sexuality. It appears that queerness must leave open opportunities for change and this language supports such openness. Whether or not one uses these opportunities to 'return' to heterosexuality under social pressure is also an open question and may point to the darker anti-emancipative possibilities that these terms and vocabularies generate and maintain.

The modern family

It is usually assumed that queer sexuality stands in opposition to the idea of the heterosexual family. For example, the case from Zabaykalsk above that I excluded from my sample clearly draws the line between family and 'non-traditional sexual relationships', making the family an exclusively heterosexual affair. However, as fluid sexuality, queerness may seep into and flow through the heterosexual family, too: 'She does not think that she should discuss her husband's sexual inclinations, because it is a private matter' (1-124/2015, Zlatoust, Chelyabinsk Region). In such testimonies a boundary is established, suggesting that individuals within the family would like to deal with their sexual matters privately: 'Two years ago, as she read her husband's phone messages, she, [the witness], learned that her husband participates in homosexual relations with men. [The victim] did not deny this fact, but they decided not to divorce because of their children' (1-636/2014, Moscow). While such family secrets may be shared between intimate partners, they may become a Pulcinella secret in the family:

> Given that [the victim] was born and grew up in the Caucasus and worked a lot in Asian countries, he got along very well with people of Asian and Caucasian ethnicities. He, [the witness], guessed that perhaps his father [the victim] was a person with non-traditional

sexual orientation, because he often invited unknown men to his house. (1-439/2011, St Petersburg)

Not all family members are aware of the queer sexuality flowing around them. The testimonies I reviewed suggest that local police officers (*uchastkovyi*), neighbours, co-workers and associates may be more reliable sources of information as they form part of the local peer surveillance apparatus: 'Witness-1 clarified that Victim-1 is his neighbour. He knows that Victim-1 is an individual with non-traditional sexual orientation, everyday Victim-1 receives visits from men' (1-130/2016, Blagoveshchensk, Amur Region); 'She worked as a cleaning lady in the gym . . . [the victim], who was a homosexual, worked there as a janitor' (1-172/2015, Makhachkala, Dagestan Republic).

Queer places

Judges, perpetrators and witnesses rely on queer places to identify queer bodies too. Queer places frequently appear in rulings on anti-queer violence, especially when the perpetrators choose known locations of queer exposure to organise their attacks. Hence gay bars, clubs, parlours and other 'thematic' places constitute the list of crime scenes in the reviewed court documents:

> He was with [Defendant-1] and [Defendant-2], when he learned that there is a club for sexual minorities in Tomsk. They felt they wanted to beat up some customers of this club. After this, they went to this club in a taxi, and [Defendant-1] took a chair leg with him. He looked around and saw that the club was situated in [Street,] Tomsk. Then he saw two lads coming from the direction of the club. He approached them and asked where they were coming from. The lads answered that they were coming from a garage. He did not believe this and that's why he hit the guy who answered with his fist. (1-224/2012, Tomsk)

Some queer places are closed environments that mainly cater to the sexual desires of their clientele: '[the victim] frequented this venue once a week, most commonly maintained relations with men, but talked to girls, too. He could enter into sexual intercourse with men' (20-04/2012, Moscow). But there are also places that are less visibly queer, which may thus shock unprepared people who fall victim to their ignorance and then seek to victimise others to remedy it. For example:

> The sauna is mostly frequented by men of non-traditional sexual orientation, although it welcomes anyone. In the sauna [redacted], clients can get professional massage services, health and spa sessions, there is also a gym. The masseuses are all men, but their orientation does not play any role when considering them for the job. (20-04/2012, Moscow)

These witness testimonies account for the many ways in which queer sexuality is expressed in the language of perpetrators, victims and lawyers. The texts also evidence a certain level of diversity in definitions of queerness, reliance on rigid gender and sexual categories, and, conversely, on the unstable, fluid vocabularies of sexualities.

Material evidence

The criminal justice system relies on evidence in various forms: alongside oral testimonies collected via interrogation or interviews, it uses forensic science and material evidence to support cases. As noted above, Soviet law enforcement had a very particular vision of queerness that was shaped around the passive/active distinction between male sexual partners engaged in *muzhelozhstvo*. Today, in some cases prosecutors follow this Soviet logic to identify and prove victims' queer sexuality by collecting 'a sample from the penis and a swab from the anus area' (1-239/2013, Engels, Saratov Region). What they are looking for are two signs of sexual intercourse: traces of faeces on the glans penis and remains of spermatozoa in the anus. But rarely do they find what they are after: 'forensic examination of swabs with the content of the dead body's rectum discovered no sperm'. So they have to be satisfied with the more subjective fact that the dead body's anus 'yawns' (1-50/2014, Ufa, Republic of Bashkortostan). Sometimes 'no changes in the area of [the victim's] anus that would prove his non-traditional sexual orientation were discovered' (1-62/2015, Kaluga). Still, even if no other material proof is found, the very physical availability of the body may be interpreted as evidence enough of queerness: '[the victim] had his pants pulled down and his genitals exposed'.

Other material clues may count as evidence of queer sexuality: 'condoms, lubricant for sexual intercourse, DVD disks with pornographic content involving men of non-traditional sexual orientation' (1-50/2014, Ufa, Republic of Bashkortostan). The combination of condoms with lubricants is treated as strong evidence of a person's queer sexuality. This is why these pieces of material evidence are taken seriously and treated with great care:

> They also saw that a plastic tube of lube and a pack of condoms lay on the ground near [the victim] and this surprised them . . . In the crime scene, the following was found and collected: swab with a brown substance resembling blood, fat traces; a vessel with lubricant and condoms accounting for 3 pieces . . . during examination of the crime scene, a vessel with gel-like substance and 3 'CONTEX' condoms were inspected. (1-175/2013, Pyatigorsk, Stavropol Territory)

In the digital era, investigators also take advantage of victims' computer habits. Some people tend to store 'files of photos and videos depicting sexual acts between men, as well as messages exchanged with persons of non-traditional sexual orientation' (1-497/2012, Ekaterinburg). Photos are not necessarily stored in digital formats. A person with a disability who was deaf and did not use oral language to communicate kept pictures of naked men in his bag to reference same-sex eroticism in his conversations with able-bodied people:

> During drinking, [the victim] took a blue notebook of a 10–20 cm size from his bag, where he kept pictures of naked men. At first, [the defendant] did not understand why he showed these pictures to him . . . [The defendant] called the victim by a derogatory term, which meant a man of non-traditional sexual orientation, who enjoyed sex with men, he said that the victim showed him pornographic photos, then pulled down his pants and offered to engage in sexual intercourse. (1-124/2015, Zlatoust, Chelyabinsk region)

The victim survived the attack and testified that he simply had a 'platonic interest in men' and had been misunderstood by the perpetrator.

Other items that prosecutors bring to the courtroom straight from victims' bags or their dead bodies include 'women's tights of red colour and blue panties' (1-1009/2011, Yoshkar-Ola, Mari El Republic), women's dresses preferred by men, dildoes and various additional signs of gender and sexual transgression.

Finally, material evidence can also include contact details shared online or in physical spaces:

> The record of examination of men's public toilet situated in the building of a railway station in St Petersburg [address redacted] showed that the inspection of one of the toilet stalls found [the victim's] phone number . . . written with a pen; besides, inspection of the stalls identified that virtually every stall contained handwritten phone numbers on the walls. (2-72/2015, St Petersburg)

Just like other evidence, material evidence bears witness to a variety of queer expressions across Russia. It demonstrates physical manifestations of queerness related to sexual intercourse and objects used to have sex. It both draws on the continued existence of pre-online dating practices such as sexual solicitation in public toilets and also attests to the migration of queerness to the internet as well. I treat these testimonies as both elements of criminal procedure and anthropological observations on shades of queerness in current Russia.

Noted silences

Oral testimonies and material traces of queerness are articulations that classify and more or less clearly define the queer subjects. However, the reviewed cases also taught me that queer sexuality is still frequently silenced in court rulings. The silencing works on three different levels.

First, queer sexuality is noted across the rulings, but never fully accounted for. That is, it is never taken seriously as part of the crime scene context. Rather, legal actors tend to ignore it. An illustrative case summarises this:

> In mid-February, [the defendant] was driving a car with registration No. 000000, which he used to provide taxi services, and he met [the victim] to whom he gave his phone number. [The victim] occasionally texted [the defendant] and informed him about his non-traditional sexual orientation because of which [the defendant] developed unpleasant feelings for [the victim]. On [DATE] at 6pm, [the defendant] was in his apartment where he acted on these unpleasant feelings [toward the victim] and plotted his criminal plan to openly steal [the victim's] money . . . [I]n order to realise this criminal plan, he took [the victim] to a parking lot . . . opened the

back door of his car and, while standing beside that door and holding a metal stick, he demanded that [the victim] give him all his money. (1-505/2014, Krasnoyarsk)

Despite the fact that queer sexuality was noted in this text, it was overlooked by the judge in the case. Importantly, the defendant only began to develop criminal intent once he learned about the victim's sexuality. Yet the judge just notes this without discussing the motive further. At least queer sexuality was kept in the text, with a short reference to 'non-traditional sexual orientation'.

In the second category of cases, a more thorough process of silencing occurs: 'he knows that his mother was [. . .] after serving her time in prison. Village dwellers complained to him that his mother was [. . .]' (1-229/2015, Nizhniy Taghil, Sverdlovsk region). The silencing in this excerpt is literal: the relevant nouns are simply redacted. Thanks to a mistake by a court clerk who forgot to remove 'non-traditional' references in some other parts of the ruling, I was able to identify this case file as having something to do with anti-queer violence. This case of literal silencing concerned lesbian sexuality, but similar redactions can be found in cases about queer men.

In Russian law, sex practices that do not involve genital penetration are referred to as 'other actions of sexual character'. This category is so broad that it incorporates many heterosexual and queer activities, including – most importantly for this research – lesbian experiences. Hence, if a judge decided to refer to lesbian sex as 'actions of sexual character' without specifying that these actions were 'non-traditional', the case may have been missed by my search due to the impossibility of processing all accounts of 'actions of sexual character'. This is an important limitation of the study that should be acknowledged. More generally, whenever queerness was totally silenced, those rulings necessarily escaped my scrutiny too.[5] Underreporting is another limitation. Perpetrators are well aware of this and often use it to their criminal advantage: 'they expected that homosexuals whom they chose to attack would not report to the police, because they would be ashamed to admit to their sexual orientation' (1-3/2013, Moscow).

Finally, the third level on which silencing operates involves the use of euphemisms to refer to queer sexualities. One of the most frequent euphemisms in this respect is the idea of 'a conversation' or 'a talk' (*obshchenie*), for example: 'in the intimate sense, her brother preferred conversations with men' (1-254/2016, Kirovo-Chepetsk, Kirov region). Some more articulate accounts in the same case file eventually reveal with greater precision that the 'conversations with men' meant not just using their tongues but getting naked and engaging with their genitals too.

Classifications without meaning

In this chapter I have argued that queer sexuality is expressed in a greater variety of forms than any categorical taxonomy can allow. However, in order to express it, one must perform an operation of classification, defining the subject by drawing a line to delineate queerness from heterosexuality. This is done in a variety of ways and with varying degrees of success. Analysing this process helps to reveal the configuration of power relations – or, simply put, who is considered secondary in a relationship. I traced queer as a subject category ('noun'), queer as a verb or a set of practices and actions, queer as appearance, queer as a place, queer as a thing, queer as silence and other forms of queerness as it bubbles up into and haunts the legal field. In the analysed rulings, queerness exists as confined by identity categories and, when liberated from them, becomes ensconced all the more in strict gender divisions. The cases above make it clear that once people start talking about queerness, they are bound to categorise various sexualities and produce queerness in their speech as something distinct from heterosexuality.

If sexual identities were applicable in every case I studied, I would say that of all 314 victims of anti-queer violence from 2010 to 2016, the overwhelming majority could be referred to as gay men (294), 10 people could be identified as lesbian women, six could be identified as bisexuals, and four as transgender persons. However, I feel I would be betraying the very nature of queerness if I classified the victims in this way. These figures do say something, but they also fail to convey the fluid and open form queerness takes in criminal court rulings. It can more accurately be said that the cases include violence against 314 people targeted for exhibiting signs of queerness. Something in the encounter between the victim and the perpetrator communicated a difference between them and, once the difference was understood, it resulted in the construction of a hierarchy in which the queer victim was made subordinate to the perpetrator.

Throughout the chapter I have noted that the mere fact of classifying various desires as queer or as heterosexual does not necessarily entail violence (although of course my materials are focused on violent encounters). What matters is the context in which such classifications are actualised. Sometimes the difference between sexual subjects may entail indifference, and sometimes care. At other times, the difference is responded to with violence. Thus, the classification itself seems to be meaningless without further work of interpreting the established difference as inequality by the subjects. This is work of meaning production and interpretation and it can function as a central mechanism of power relations. In the next chapter I argue that emotions, feelings and affects give meaning to these encounters, and explain how mere classifications are followed by the exercise of power leading to violence.

Notes

1. The most common category was *gomoseksualist*, not *gomoseksual*. Both academics and activists highlight a stark difference between these ostensibly similar words, which is also relevant for the difference between *gomoseksualizm* and *gomoseksual'nost'* (homosexualism and homosexuality). According to them, the term 'homosexualist' is offensive and it is inappropriate because there is no such thing as a 'heterosexualist'; because the suffixes '-ist' and '-ism' are used to refer to ideologies, not genuine desires; because people may confuse it with the Soviet pathological terminology; and because it tries to impose too much stability on sexuality, which is naturally fluid (Kon 2006; Sozayev 2011, 6).
2. Sex work or, officially, 'prostitution' is an administrative offence (misdemeanor) in Russia, but many activities associated with it are banned by the Criminal Code, including organisation of a venue for prostitution, involvement of other people in sexual commerce and sex trafficking (McCarthy 2015; Kondakov 2018b).
3. In my childhood, if the right ear was pierced, it meant that the person was queer.
4. The 'homosexual panic' defence is a very common criminal court strategy. It was used by the defendant in the Matthew Shepard case in the US, a ground-breaking case for American hate crime legislation (Zylan 2011, 153–5).
5. The events in the Republic of Chechnya in 2017 attest to a case of erasure of queerness that made visible both the very fact of violent repression and the linguistic manipulations meant to conceal it (Kondakov 2019a). The Chechen authorities denied that there were any gay men in the Republic, making the claim of repression of 'those who do not exist' a logical impossibility (Brock and Edenborg 2020). The Chechen police targeted gay men and arrested more than 100 of them in the first round of the purge, even though the arrests were never registered, and the people's queer sexuality was ignored in all official comments.

Part III
Affects, emotions and law

A cannibal rising

It was a February night on the outskirts of Volgograd, a city renowned for its furious battles during World War II as Stalingrad. A woman – I will call her Lyudmila – went to her neighbour's house to ask her partner to come home. He was having a party there with his pals, a 40-year-old local resident, Ivan, and a young heterosexual couple, who were hosting the drinking event. Lyudmila's partner Anton was a young lad, just over 20. They already had two kids together, although they had not officially registered their relationship. When Lyudmila entered the neighbour's house, she saw people having a lot of fun. They were drinking vodka and beer. Anton was enthusiastically taking pictures on his new phone. Lyudmila did not want to join them so she returned home alone. The clock struck midnight and she went to bed.

The next morning, Lyudmila woke up early and found Anton sleeping in the bed. She got up and went to the kitchen to prepare some breakfast. There, Lyudmila 'spotted a frying pan with the remains of fried meat and onion' on the stove (2-4/2015, Volgograd). She smelled the meat and decided that it had gone off due to its bad odour. Lyudmila threw the contents of the pan into the bin. Suddenly, her morning routine was interrupted by the police, who broke into the house and arrested Anton. Ivan's body had been found that morning in the front yard of the house that Anton had been partying in the previous night. A blood trail in the snow marked the way from Ivan's dead body to Anton and Lyudmila's residence. As both neighbours clearly remembered, Anton and Ivan left the house at around 3am, but Anton came back alone half an hour later. He drank two more shots of vodka and then left.

In May of the next year, the judge on the case established:

> On the 16th of February 2014, at night, in [address], Anton waited for Ivan to come out from the house of [the witnesses], where they all had been drinking alcohol together, and because of personal unpleasant feelings to Ivan caused by his offer to engage in buggery, he hit his head 4 times with a nail puller, then with a knife cut out his heart, which he fried and ate at home; he shot this process on his phone camera with comments. He had previously taken the nail puller and knife from his house and after the murder of Ivan brought them back home.

The video recording of cutting out the heart, frying it with onion and eating it was presented in the courtroom. Reasonable concerns about Anton's mental state were rejected by a psychiatrist, who concluded that the murder was rather caused by the defendant's 'drive to assert himself, to show his "rawness" to others'. The victim's alleged homosexuality was barely discussed in court; it seemed to matter very little to the judge. What is also striking is that this brutal act of cannibalism was explained only by a brief reference to an awkward notion of 'personal unpleasant feelings', a mild phrase so distant from this outburst of violent emotions.

The murder was an exceptionally cruel one. However, I highlight this case not for its gore, but to analyse the emotions at play, which, in the ruling, are relayed in a particularly subtle form.

5
Power's affectual mechanisms

Pleased or hated

'Personal unpleasant feelings' (*lichnye nepriyaznennye otnosheniya, lichnaya nepriyazn'*) – on which the motive to murder and eat an individual was based in the case above – account for the motives of violent attacks on 138 queer victims of the 314 in my sample. It is the most frequent emotional motive identified in the cases. Personal unpleasant feelings have explained not just cannibalism, but also why people have tortured and stabbed others to death, as well as committing acts of extreme violence with less fatal consequences. In all of these 138 narratives, as soon as the defendant learns that someone nearby is queer, they report feeling displeased. And once they are not 'pleased', they kill or strike. This emotion is like a trigger mechanism for violence. The phrase rationalises motivations for violent actions, such as when one judge explained that an assault derived 'from the fact of unexpectedly emerged personal unpleasant feelings because of the victim's sexual orientation confirmed by the defendant, [a witness] and partly by the victim himself' (1-113/2015, Kuybyshev, Novosibirsk Region).

    An emotion as the motivation for a crime? An emotion, more to the point, that is deeply connected to the soon-to-be-victim's sexuality? In many jurisdictions, such a crime-manufacturing feeling is referred to as 'hate' in criminal law (Lawrence 1999, 9). Queer criminologist Gail Mason analysed a variety of hate crime statutes and arrived at the idea that all the legislation involved three elements: emotion, causation and difference. The emotional element requires evidence of negative feelings towards 'a presumed attribute of the victim' (Mason 2014b, 299). The second element links this feeling to the offence. And the difference element points to otherness, or presumable attributes of the victim that differentiate them from the perpetrator. It is this difference that ultimately evokes the negative emotions, which lead to an assault. Classic examples include sexual orientation, race, gender and ethnicity. According to this doctrine, a combination of negative emotions towards otherness and difference as well as the violence that these emotions cause results in an enhancement of the status of these crimes to 'hate' crimes (Mason 2014a, 61). As I showed in Chapter 1, Russian law follows this doctrine, with its well-developed hate crime legislation.

In the case of the cannibal, he was sentenced to 25 years in a maximum-security correctional colony with 10 years in prison confinement and 2 additional years of probation after release. In 2015, only 179 of 1,877 people received comparable sentences for the same type of crime – aggravated murder under Article 105, para. 2 (Court Department 2015). However, I cannot draw any clear conclusions from this: after his arrest, the cannibal confessed to two more murders committed a few months earlier and the sentence was punishment for them all. The investigation into the crimes revealed that he had been planning to kill two police officers but had murdered two random passers-by instead, that he illegally possessed a Kalashnikov rifle, and that he was preparing to steal a car. Given these facts, it is impossible to establish whether the sentence was indeed 'enhanced' due to the expressed hate, or whether the ruling was harsh because the crimes were so numerous and ghastly. One fact remains clear, though: the notion of 'hate' (*nenavist'*) was not even mentioned by the judge, who opted for the awkward phrase 'personal unpleasant feelings' in his ruling.

In this chapter I investigate the place of emotions in violent criminal encounters. I previously established that power is involved in constructing the difference between queer and heterosexual subjects. I also argued, however, that this difference alone does not matter without the interpretative constellation that arranges differentiated subjects into asymmetrical hierarchies. In contrast, this part of the book deals with the question of what makes difference a matter of inequality. I argue that the mechanism that turns difference into inequality is affect. In other words, affect is a mechanism of power relations and indeed a central one in the emerging neo-disciplinary regime. I first review the literature on law, emotions and affect to highlight how affect operates as a mechanism of power. This literature ranges from theoretical legal studies to queer theory. My aim in this chapter is to make sense of affect in relation to disciplinary power. In the next chapter, I catalogue all the affectual encounters reported in the 314 cases of anti-queer violence that I work with throughout this book. These are, simply put, violent affections. The criminal rulings attest to this.

Emotional law

Classical ideas regard the law as emotionless, but this view has been challenged in many accounts (Bandes 1999; Blix et al. 2019; Karstedt 2002).[1] Legal theories offered doctrinal interpretations of emotions, because, as one of the major contributors to this field, Richard Posner, argues, '[m]uch of the behavior that law regulates is emotional' (Posner 1999, 309). In such accounts of emotions in law, scholars start with a challenge to the dichotomy between emotion and reason, exemplified by the suggestion that '[i]n the legal realm, the term [emotions] has long functioned as a catchall category for much of what law aspires to avoid or counteract: that which is subjective, irrational, prejudicial, intangible, partial, and impervious to reason' (Bandes and Blumenthal 2012, 162). Instead, legal research contends that emotions are rational, because they are subject to the cognitive process (Posner 1999, 310). In contrast, folk knowledge and some classic psychological theories tend to see emotions as opposed to reason – as mere reactions to external stimuli that obscure context and, consequently, result in bad judgement-making. This is why many assailants use emotions in the courtroom as an excuse for their actions. Posner's contesting of the dichotomy between reason and emotions instead characterises actions resulting from external triggers as a conscious process that can often be rationally controlled.

What this literature does demonstrate unequivocally is that it does not make sense to talk about acting in the absence of emotions. In order to act, one has to be touched, one has to be entertained by an idea to start thinking about it and acting upon it. Emotions do exactly this – they touch and entertain. This is how emotions motivate us to do something. In other words, it is not that we are making good or bad decisions when emotions interfere, it is that we are not making any decision without involving emotions in the process (Goodwin, Jasper and Polletta 2001, 10). Moreover, these decisions are conditioned by a larger societal context, because as a cognitive process, emotions are social phenomena too and must be learned (Bandes and Blumenthal 2012, 171). From my point of view, this argument reinforces and revolves around one of the central dichotomies that the debate reproduces: social versus natural. I argue in contrast that taking the social and the natural together really offers an innovative perspective.[2] Let me first deal with the two domains separately and then review what comes up when they are combined.

Martha Nussbaum has dedicated much of her career to investigating the role of emotions in law, emphasising the social aspect (Nussbaum 2010; 2013; 2016). In her book on disgust and shame, she convincingly shows that strong emotions like 'disgust' are routinely taught by societies. Nussbaum points out that, according to relevant studies, children, for example, do not distinguish disgusting from non-disgusting objects until they learn (by the age of three, she claims) to use the toilet (a common practice that can explain the spread of a recognisable form of disgust cross-culturally). At this point in development, the routine fact of producing human waste becomes connected to a feeling of strong rejection and by association many similar things are designated disgusting, too: 'Disgust, then, is taught by parents and society,' she concludes (Nussbaum 2004, 94). In other words, there is nothing per se disgusting about faeces, but we learn to be disgusted by such substances early in our lives and come to believe that they are disgusting by their very nature.

Yet this rather banal process of toilet training has further societal repercussions. What we learn is not simply to be disgusted by faeces, but to interpret the value of things as nice things or bad things. The cognitive structure of disgust is composed of several features, according to Nussbaum's review of the research (Nussbaum 2004, 74–93). First, the object of disgust is connected with human 'animality' – a reminder that our bodies are biological entities that produce waste, which signals that we are still animals and, therefore, mortal. Disgust helps us cope with this fact of bodily vulnerability by distancing us from the waste products. Second, disgust establishes borders between the human body and the rest of the world, including those things that were part of us but are now pushed outside. Luckily, disgust does not attach to all outside things – only those things that are assessed as contagious. This means that, third, for a thing to be disgusting, it should be understood as capable of making everything it touches like itself (for example, putting faeces in a glass of milk makes the milk unusable). In this sense, the incorporation of a disgusting object infests the entire body that has incorporated it and, consequently, turns it into an animal – vulnerable – mortal. Now, all these elements play out not only at the individual level, but on a societal level as well:

> So powerful is the desire to cordon ourselves off from our animality that we often don't stop at feces, cockroaches, and slimy animals.

> We need a group of humans to bound ourselves against, who will come to exemplify the boundary line between the truly human and the basely animal . . . One sure way of putting a group down is to cause it to occupy a status between the fully human and the merely animal. (Nussbaum 2004, 107, 110)

Hence, not only are emotions social products, because they are learned, but they are also social in the sense that they function in different ways in a society. Emotions like disgust are used to draw boundaries between social groups, according to Nussbaum, as they are 'frequently hooked up with various forms of shady social practice, in which the discomfort people feel over the fact of having an animal body is projected outwards onto vulnerable people and groups' (Nussbaum 2004, 74). In my analysis of Russian court cases, in Nussbaum's own study of similar cases in the US and in a lot of other research (Raj 2020), homosexuality is an example of one such projection:

> . . . disgust is ultimately disgust at one's own imagined penetrability and ooziness, and this is why the male homosexual is both regarded with disgust and viewed with fear as a predator who might make everyone else disgusting. The very look of such a male is itself contaminating . . . The gaze of a homosexual male is seen as contaminating because it says, 'You can be penetrated.' And this means that you can be made of feces and semen and blood, not clean plastic flesh. (And this means: you will soon be dead.) (Nussbaum 2004, 113–4)

I argue, however, that, as scary as Nussbaum's account makes it sound, the fear of being penetrated very much depends on one's perspective. In other words, defining certain emotions as 'social' puts a lot of emphasis on the social as common or average, meaning that, if not everyone, then the majority of us feel the same, implying that those who do not are abnormal. While Nussbaum creates a general legal theory of disgust and other emotions, she has a very particular subject in mind. Her emotions work for an 'average' person – an imaginary figure that functions as a gatekeeper to exclude everyone who fails to meet the standard. Needless to say, this usually accounts for a very small number of people: in this particular case, it is those presumably heterosexual males who fear penetration. This sets in motion a paradox. On the one hand, the disgusted perpetrators seem to be part of the population of 'average' or 'normal' people insofar as they feel exactly what they are supposed to feel once they face a homosexual: disgust. On the other hand, they are excluded from the population of average people when their actions turn criminal and, therefore, abnormal. An average 'reasonable man' – although disgusted – would surely walk away from the object of disgust rather than eradicate it. As a result, we find a pair of odd, outcast bedfellows united by their exclusion: queers excluded for their lack of disgust and perpetrators of anti-queer violence excluded for the unreasonable actions that the very normal feeling of disgust instigated.

Critical legal view on emotions

Legal theories of emotions like Posner's and Nussbaum's have a number of logical flaws and limitations that, ultimately, may be misleading and confusing for the analysis I am conducting here. I have pointed out that despite offering all-encompassing explanations, they focus on specific – real or imagined – groups and even unconsciously support power structures that privilege the male heterosexual standard as the norm. If perpetrators feel disgusted by a homosexual person and kill because of that feeling, then how do we account for the emotion of that victim who by definition seems to be attracted to the same sex? Certainly, many gay people may also feel disgusted by homosexuality and beat themselves up in acts of self-hatred. However, I argue that this alone is not a good foundation for explanatory theories in which disgust is presented as such a fundamental emotion that delineates humans from animals, reminds us of our bodily mortality and signals dangerous contagions. Are gay people so different from the 'average' person that they do not distance themselves from the animal kingdom, do not fear death, do not dread contagion? If so, how does this theory of emotions make sense of gay feelings? Are these feelings somehow different from the rest of the world? In this way theory can reinforce inequalities and ideas of normality which have historically played crucial roles in the reproduction of anti-queer sentiment.

By explaining emotions as felt by an 'average' person, this type of thinking further alienates everything considered unaverage and abnormal. The idea of an 'average' person is such that it claims a norm, a regime of normality that seeks conformism and subjection. Failure to be disgusted at a 'normal' moment – when one is expected to – indicates failure to be an acceptable element of society more generally. It becomes a criterion of social inclusion and exclusion. Therefore, instead of explaining perpetrators' brutal reactions to sexual diversity, this theory further reinforces a marginalised position of queerness that has already been established prior to analytical efforts.

I argue against this legal theory of emotions because it also has internal inconsistencies. Let's take disgust again, as an example of an emotion that reminds us of 'ooziness', mortality and other similar things. It is supposed to keep us away from dead bodies, because we are afraid to become one – there is a cultural belief that even touching a dead body might be contagious and, consequently, fatal. Nonetheless, as my and Nussbaum's discussions of criminal cases show, the murderers seem to have a different logic: instead of staying away from death they produce it. But when asked in a courtroom, they explain that they killed precisely because they were disgusted. This does not make a lot of sense within this legal theory of emotions: the murderers are both attuned to disgust in regarding homosexuality as a sign of their own animalistic mortality and – at the same time – completely unaware of disgust as they look forward to approximation to death by killing someone.

In sum, the theory explains fully why we are disgusted by faeces but tells us very little about emotions. First, it is partial, because it accounts for the emotions of a particular group of people, although that group is never defined, but just assumed under the banner of 'average' normality. Second, the theory presumes a universal reaction to an emotional stimulus in the form of a cognitive process that connects deep thoughts (for example, about death) with mundane objects (for example, gay men). Certainly, an 'object' such as a gay man can ignite various emotions, including love rather than disgust, and – as some cases that are analysed in the next chapter will show – may even simultaneously 'provoke' opposite emotions (both love and disgust). Third, theories like this tend to be described within subject–object relations, thereby universalising in a very particular manner not only emotional reactions, but also emotional stimuli (in Nussbaum's universe, faeces, homosexuals, other animals). Hence, instead of emotional exchange, flow or intercourse, we are led to believe that the 'objects' of emotions are passive irritants that must somehow be removed from sight to end the unbearable awareness of mortality that they enflame.

How bodies feel

This framing of emotional processes as merely social cognitive processes contributes to another outcome that explains Nussbaum's confusion. As cognitive processes, emotions are analysed as pure products of our thoughts about an object. This in turn results in both a reproduction of the existing discourse and a disregard for the entire process, which would include the physical, embodied encounter. It is as if what we analyse is only the process of rationalisation of an emotional state experienced at a certain moment, rather than the full experience itself. In short, we focus on how people explain their actions, justify violent reactions and treat a stimulus as a pure object. Indeed, an account of how the thought process clarifies feelings might be helpful and very useful for social science instruments. In such an analysis, though, we may confuse various linguistic forms that are used to signify what we feel (say, 'disgust' to mean strong disapproval) as actual representations of our felt experiences. But what if we feel the same, but express it in different forms? What if we express in one form something that is felt differently? Does a language category used to describe what we feel capture enough to give an accurate, sufficiently textured picture of that experience? Are there other ways to do a fuller analysis of emotions that would include both the discursive and physical forms of people's relations involving feelings? I argue that uniting the social and the natural may offer sensible answers to all these questions.

The questions stem from my empirical observations of the cases of anti-queer violence studied in this book. For example, many perpetrators claimed that they felt something uncontrollable (let it be 'disgust' again), which resulted in the emergence of emotions that segued into a physical attack. If we trust them in their assessment of their emotional state, why do we not trust them in the part of their story where they claim to lack control? In theories of emotions like Nussbaum's, this initial phase is understood in terms of the 'encounter' and initiates the cognitive emotional process *but* is distinct from it. Once its role has been played, it fades away into the history of experience and does no more work apart from serving as this initiation. The theory does not offer an understanding of how the initial encounter impresses on us. Instead, it only seeks to account for how we then rationalise what has touched us. This helps us to distinguish not only between emotions and other feelings, but also between the subject and object of emotions: the subject thinks (*cogito, ergo sum*) and in this sense is interesting to a social analytic, whereas the object is passive and does little – it is claimed – to help illuminate this process analytically. But this results in seeing only one perspective (for instance, how 'normal', average people are disgusted by 'abnormal' ones). I show now that there is a way to bring some agential power to other participants in this process, not just the subject who allegedly 'feels'.

Martha Nussbaum explicitly claims that 'emotions are not mindless surges of affect, but, instead, intelligent responses that are attuned both to events in the world and to the person's important values and goals' (Nussbaum 2004, 37). She opposes any understanding of emotions that would include 'mindless surges of affect' in its structure or otherwise fully embrace the emotional process by analysing both intuitive anticipation and rationalisation of this intuition (Ahmed 2004). But what if it is precisely this 'affect' that holds the various perspectives together? This approaches the claims of recent work in affect theory: 'affect is found in those intensities that pass body to body (human, non-human, part-body, and otherwise), in those resonances that circulate about, between, and sometimes stick to bodies and worlds, *and* in the very passages or variations between these intensities and resonances themselves' (Gregg and Seigworth 2010, 1). I turn now to this recent scholarship in affect theory.

Affect theory

Affect theory is a term used to refer to various explanations for why and how we feel what we feel. I am interested in the ways affect works as power relations. What I am looking for here is thus routes of cross-pollination for the queer approaches that I outlined in previous chapters, which some of these emerging strands of affect theory take (Berlant 2011; Brinkema 2014; Chen 2012; Sedgwick 2003). For example, Judith Butler suggests that affect is part of the process of subject formation (*sentio, ergo sum*). She contends that prior to saying and rationalising, a subject is already affected to be able to utter and in uttering to appear as a subject. Butler envisions a network of connections between everything in the world that functions via mutual impressions on each other: 'I am affected not just by this one other or a set of others, but by a world in which humans, institutions, and organic and inorganic processes all impress themselves upon this me who is, at the outset, susceptible in ways that are radically involuntary' (Butler 2015a, 6–7).

These involuntary connections seem to be beyond any one person's control, on the one hand, because the connections are dependent on the very openness of our bodies to the possibilities of connecting: since bodies are entities present in the world together with other entities, they are open to multiple impressions. However, on the other hand, this does not suggest that such physical connections are separate from cognition. As I have argued from the outset, this dichotomy should be challenged, because drawing a line between affect and thinking, the physical and the discursive, body and language, is to split something that is a single whole:

> Just as philosophy founders time and again on the question of the body, it tends to separate what is called thinking from what is called sensing, from desire, passion, sexuality, and relations of dependency. It is one of the great contributions of feminist philosophy to call those dichotomies into question and so to ask as well whether in sensing, something called thinking is already at work, whether in acting, we are also acted upon, and whether in coming into the zone of the thinking and speaking I, we are at once radically formed and also bringing something about. (Butler 2015a, 15)

Viewed in this way, affect theory scrutinises both physical and discursive forms, nature and society, things and words – bringing all this together in a comprehensive embrace that attempts to give a fuller account of the subject than that found in the likes of Nussbaum's theory. While it does focus on the processes that run before an emotion's articulation, it does not reject either of these parts as irrelevant or uninteresting:

> Affect theory is an approach to history, politics, culture, and all other aspects of embodied life that emphasizes the role of nonlinguistic and non- or paracognitive forces. As a method, affect theory asks what bodies do—what they want, where they go, what they think, how they decide—and especially how bodies are impelled by forces other than language and reason. It is, therefore, also a theory of power. For affect theory, feelings, emotions, affects, moods, and sensations are not cosmetic but rather the substance of subjectivity. (Schaefer 2019, 1)

Importantly, I believe, affect theory can help to show ways of answering some of the questions I have asked above, as well as help to clarify my overall aim in this book of scrutinising power relations by understanding how feelings may impress upon people to make them kill others. In his overview of affect theory, Donovan Schaefer indicates that affects are understood either as chaotic, individual sensation, or as a mechanism of 'structuring our embodied experience' (Schaefer 2019, 1). In my view, the first version addresses affect in the way Nussbaum does – as simply a fact of physical feeling that entails little relevance for social questions or law. Yet the second version emphasises social power relations at the expense of material and embodied dimensions. What does it mean to bring these dimensions together?

Affect or emotion?

One of the ways to seek connectivity between the natural and the social is to question the difference between affect and emotions. Like the legal theorists above, Brian Massumi, one of the major contributors to affect theory, argues that affect has no place in 'mind'; its location is solely in the 'body' (Massumi 2002, 28–9). Following insights from a selection of psychological studies mixed with philosophical illustrations, Massumi suggests that affect is trivialised, because it is part of everything the body feels or does every day. For Massumi, the environment signals its presence and our presence in it by impressing on our bodies in various ways as we also impress on the environment. Hence, affect is present at the start of any action we take, decision we make or thought we muse over, and it remains an integral part of all these processes. What we can do, however, is block certain socially undesirable actions that stem from affect and divert our actions in different directions. Thus, agency is concentrated in the conscious decision to act in a certain way, but this decision – as well as the effort required to stick to it – is conditioned by the affective impressions that impress themselves upon our bodies.

This idea matches the definition of emotions analysed earlier, but it has several very important repercussions that are different. First of all, instead of assuming subject–object relations (where the subject feels and the object is simply felt), affect theorists like Massumi advance an account of network-like relationships, where everything is connected through mutual impressions on each other. Following Spinoza, Massumi suggests the relational character of affect by the formula 'to affect and to be affected' (Massumi 2015, viii). Thus, he explores the events before the subject is formed by looking at encounters that mutually affect bodies to condition them towards certain actions. Such an affective network is surely a network of power relations.

Second, this change of focus also allows us to concentrate on power relations beyond the subject, which presumably expresses or manifests the effects of power in their thoughts, words or actions. As Massumi puts it, '[a]ffect holds a key to rethinking postmodern power after ideology' (Massumi 2002, 42), or, for my purposes, affect is key to understanding neo-disciplinary power relations. Thus, affect hints at a Foucauldian network of relations between forces that constitute power and are located in these encounters between bodies (S. Hunter 2015; Schaefer 2015). As I argue, the 'neo-' part of 'neo-disciplinary' is precisely Massumi's suggestion that current power relies less on the Panopticon-like knowledge expressed in expert vocabularies ('ideology' in Massumi's approach) and more on random circulations of seemingly disorganised information.

Third, although Massumi is looking for a clear-cut separation between bodily affect and the workings of the conscious mind (emotions), it nonetheless appears that 'affect and cognition are never fully separable' (Gregg and Seigworth 2010, 1) in the sense that affect is structurally embedded in conscious processes, albeit not defined as in Posner's account. Indeed, an affected body is stimulated to think and decide how to act in response to an impression, but may choose to act in various ways, especially in instances that are not routine and, therefore, not automatic. In this sense, affect can actually mean more than bodily encounters and include a variety of impressions that touch us and move us and that are simultaneously touched and moved in response. Therefore, a boundary line between affect and emotions, physicality and discourse is ultimately an illusory one that offers little heuristic insight.

Hence, Massumi's focus on encounter as necessarily pre-subjective and, in this sense, de-contextualised (assumed as encompassing no history of experience) is misleading. In his interpretation, the encounter is the moment of becoming a subject by feeling one's body (Massumi 2002, 35). But, as Schaefer shows (2015, 26), only by separating body from mind can Massumi theorise this operation, whereas the very separation seems unfounded. Furthermore, the separation does not account for a variety of affects that are repetitive and remembered by the body and at least in this sense are both cognitive and physical. In sum, it is another unnecessary dichotomy that obscures rather than enlightens the connections between bodily experiences and social relations that affective encounters produce. Schaefer contends that this pushes Massumi's theory away from many others that seek to queer approaches to binary logics, especially to those logics that work politically to hierarchise genders such as the dichotomy of body and mind considered here (Schaefer 2019).

The Matrix

What I have presented so far is an account of affect theory that challenges the boundary between body and mind by suggesting that the two are inseparable and that feeling requires physicality and discourse to intertwine. Think of the Wachowskis' *The Matrix*, the motion picture from 1999. It is based on the premise that the human world is controlled by powerful AI machines that captured people, connected them to virtual reality and made them believe that they still lived normal lives in cities, towns and villages, whereas in fact their bodies have been dumped in reservoirs that process the energy those bodies produce for use by the machines. When the protagonist Neo takes the red pill from the resistance leader Morpheus and awakes from the illusion, he finds himself in a pod of sticky liquid and is attached to wires via holes in his body. In order to produce a realistic illusion of life, the matrix has to immerse entire human bodies in this liquid so that every step, encounter or movement can be impressed on the body to create an accurate feeling. Furthermore, all human vessels are connected through a network that feeds mutual impressions.

If the technology were created based on Nussbaum's or Posner's theory, then it would only be required to connect to the human mind and simply upload the necessary information. Massumi's theory would not work at all, because the technology based on it could create only bodily impressions without clearly accounting for the further cognitive process they enact. But if we think of affect as an essential part of an overall structure of both sensing and making sense, then we come to an understanding that to be active in the world and to believe that it is real, we need our body to be open to impressions from the physical world and we need to process and interpret information about the world, as well as to articulate our impressions of the world. We also need to be connected to others to ensure mutual impressions. *The Matrix*'s use of total body immersion with multiple flows in and out helps capture this in ways that Nussbaum, Posner and Massumi all fail to do.

Ultimately, this system is a network of power relations inasmuch as it is capable of producing various kinds of knowledge (the illusory matrix in the Wachowskis' film or the reality we are immersed in). Given that impressions affect our bodies, we process impressions to come up with explanations for what has been done. Under the Panopticon model, these explanations may take only certain forms depending on the currently enacted discourse formation and its legitimate knowledge (epistemology). Within neo-disciplinary power relations, these explanations are shaped by various knowledges and are more fluid, fragmented and messy because of it. In any case, meanings originate in both affect (as corporeal impressionability) and discourse (as a set of available interpretations of impressions). In this sense, it is unhelpful or negatable to distinguish between emotions and affects, body and mind, nature and society, since all of these dichotomies appear to work not simply in concert, but inseparably from each other.

Powerful affects

A queerer version of affect theory is Sara Ahmed's interpretation, which explicitly rejects Massumi's dichotomies. My reading of her work perhaps adjusts many of her arguments to what I argue is a queer theory of affect that can account for the mechanisms of power relations that enable power to operate regardless of the many contradictory forms of expression of affect. Ahmed suggests that while the experience of emotion and affect may be interpreted differently, 'this model creates a distinction between conscious recognition and "direct" feeling, which itself negates how that which is not consciously experienced may itself be mediated by past experiences' (Ahmed 2004, 40). She therefore advances the idea that affects 'evoke past histories, and . . . this process bypasses consciousness, through bodily memories' (Ahmed 2004, 40). This connects her theory to the idea of performativity ensured through repetitive acts (Bourdieu 2013; Butler 1997; Sedgwick 2003). She convincingly argues that there is no original action that has no history at all; on the contrary, all actions are somehow reactions connected through a never-ending chain of fluctuating repetitions (Ahmed 2004, 162).

Ahmed's theory offers ways to conceptualise affects or emotions (without distinction) as a process of radical interdependency, 'if we think of the skin surface itself, as that which appears to contain us, but where others *impress* upon us' (Ahmed 2004, 31). In this sense, affect is relational, and this is why it is always a set of mutual reactions. The work of these relations is that of power and the effect of these power relations is a delineation of various boundaries: between bodies, collections of bodies and different kinds of bodies (S. Hunter 2015, 30–1). Moreover, what I want to add, and what I argue, is that these relations work as power not because they simply delineate different bodies from each other (classify), but because together with this delineation they arrange them in an asymmetrical order. In other words, affect both performs a primary operation of classification – sorting objects into groups and coming up with category names for those groups (Foucault 1991, 195) – and simultaneously introduces a hierarchy between these groups that activates the power relations within this encounter. This latter operation of creating asymmetry is more important as a mechanism of power relations than the operation of naming the classified group.

A Foucauldian understanding of power relations is not pessimistic per se. Rather, Foucault contends that power is simply productive (Foucault 1978b), while the qualities of its products can be interpreted in many different ways. In this book, I am of course interested in the effects of power that are violent, as I analyse violent encounters resulting in murder and physical injury. I call the affects that give rise to these encounters *violent affections*. This means that while the asymmetries may result in a variety of products of power, I focus only on the violent ones among them. Following Ahmed, I understand the method of assigning different qualities to the products of power as *politics*. We all receive impressions. Ahmed argues that politics comes into play when people articulate particular emotional responses to the impressions they receive. In other words, we are all affected by others, but what we make of these affections is a matter of political interpretation. Take 'disgust' once more. Ahmed's analysis looks at disgust as a process. It is defined by her as an ambivalent feeling expressing both attraction and rejection (Ahmed 2004, 82–100). An articulation of a feeling as disgust creates a boundary between those who are disgusted and those who are considered disgusting. Contrary to Nussbaum's claim, disgust does not work universally. Rather, it generates various fragments of society, including 'a community of those who are bound together through the shared condemnation of a disgusting object' (Ahmed 2004, 94). This interpretation shows how affects operate politically to produce portions of society separated by the workings of disgust rather than assuming disgust as a common emotion for all people. I further complicate this view in the next chapter by demonstrating the multiplicity of articulations of affects that produce such communities.

A political interpretation of affects engages in already existing societal hierarchies. Thus, Ahmed demonstrates how the condition of vulnerability felt in an affectual encounter can turn to hatred, fear, danger, anxiety and other discursive forms of affect when it is processed. Ahmed reworks Wendy Brown's idea that a history of wounds experienced by a social collective (for example, the LGBT+ community) operates politically to constitute a grievance-based community out of this collective (Brown 1993; 1995; Kondakov 2012). Ahmed flips this argument and suggests that current redefinitions of nation and citizenship towards more inclusivity of various historically discriminated-against groups impresses upon those who have held dominant positions that their privileges are being taken away:

> the normative subject is often secured through narratives of injury: the white male subject, for example, has become an injured party in national discourse . . . as the one who has been 'hurt' by the opening up of the nation to others. Given that subjects have an unequal relation to entitlement, then more privileged subjects will have a greater recourse to narratives of injury. (Ahmed 2004, 31)

In Russia, this reinterpretation of privilege as under threat is taken in a global perspective (Edenborg 2021; Morris and Garibyan 2021; Chandler 2021). It is politically employed in the anticipation of the expansion of LGBT+ rights coming from abroad and penetrating Russian borders, ultimately undermining the masculine heterosexual position in society. This shows that as a performative discursive phenomenon, affect rests on readily available societal structures. However, it also deploys these structures in various ways for differently positioned groups of people in diverse contexts. Notably, when a subject harbours beliefs of privilege, they are much more at risk of also coming to believe that their privileges are being taken away from them.

I interpret the individual criminal encounters that I analyse as resonances of these more general power relations. The perpetrators in the cases reviewed throughout this book are impressed upon by their victims. This impression is a basic condition of being alive, on the one hand. On the other hand, such impressions can be interpreted in various ways to cause further reactions depending on the position that the subject assumes for itself. When the assumed position is that of privilege, and when this privilege is understood as being under threat, then affects are more likely to become violent. Even though these affects are ambiguous, I single out those among them that instigate violence: violent affections. Because my analysis is focused on the context of sexuality in contemporary Russia, I understand that, in a heteronormative society – which to various degrees describes all societies – the position of privilege is that of heterosexual masculinity. Consequently, the perpetrators I study feel a threat to their heterosexuality once queerness impresses upon them. In the courtroom, they retell their rationalisation of this encounter in different, contradictory forms, all of which violent affections often take: anger, camaraderie, danger, disgust, fear, hate, indignation, shock and many others. These violent affections create connections between bodies who share them (produce a community) and bodies who do not share them (delineate communities). Their effects are also seen inscribed on the bodies of the victims. And there are many more ways in which violent affections may produce a chain of impressions upon victimised bodies, other than criminalised forms of violence: discrimination, exclusion, denial, etc.

In sum, I interpret affects as the mechanism of power relations in the following way. Affects are both matters of fact and of interpretation that work together to produce an impression of an encounter. This encounter reveals to us not only that we have a body and that this body is different from other bodies, but also that as a mechanism of power relations, affects arrange these encountered bodies in an asymmetrical order that is perceived differently by different subjects of the encounter. These asymmetries do not necessarily result in violence, because power is productive of many other effects. In other words, different people are touched by the presence of others in different ways. Some may like it and develop a desire to be together. Others may follow up violently on their recognition that others exist and are not always exactly like them. These subjects nearly always exhibit a sense of privilege and are consequently led by violent affections to fear that their privileges are threatened by the presence of others. The next chapter catalogues all the affections that made the encounters violent in the 314 cases this book analyses. It shows that violent affections are articulated in multiple forms. Chapter 7 will return to the discussion of affects to uncover the technique of power that circulates violent affections.

Notes

1 In Chapter 2, I might seem to suggest that Russian law is indeed emotionless as long as judges apply it with 'indifference'. However, I argue that indifference is also an affect, and it helps to interpret relations in certain ways: indifference is the feeling of not caring what happens next and, therefore, giving way to other actors involved in the encounter to push their agenda.
2 Thinking the social and the natural together forms part of the rapidly developing field of new materialism (Alaimo and Hekman 2008; Barad 2007; Bennett 2010; Coole and Frost 2010; Latour 2005; Low Reyna 2020; Tuana and Morgen 2001; Timofeeva 2018; Zhaivoronok 2016). There is no space to review this literature in my book, which is already rich with many interconnected academic endeavours. I make references to this literature throughout the chapters where appropriate, but it is important to add that just like queer theory, new materialism forms an essential part of my argument and writing. This confirms to me that there is little sense in labelling a set of academic literature with this or that title such as 'queer theory', 'new materialism' and 'affect theory' when they all speak to each other and can hardly be taken separately.

6
A catalogue of violent affections

Reasoning hate

This chapter provides an analysis of all the various articulations of emotions and affects in the court rulings that I use throughout the book. This is done with two major purposes in mind. First, the analysis shows that the category in which an affect is articulated in the legal field depends on how that particular articulation plays out in the law. How an emotion is referred to – say, as 'hate' or 'unpleasantness' – is significant because the choice has an impact on sentencing. Moreover, the analysis will help us appreciate that what was actually felt at the time of the crime becomes irrelevant: it is the law that structures articulations of emotions, not accurate reporting of someone's feelings. My second aim is to figure out how, regardless of the many ways in which affects are articulated as emotions, they manifest as mechanisms of power relations that produce hierarchies between subjects and lead to violence. In this analysis, I argue that it does not matter what category is used to describe an emotion – 'hate', 'disgust' or 'love' – because they are still violent affections once this mechanism of power comes into play. Therefore, I depart from trying to name particular feelings in order to analyse them because to do so necessarily fails to fully reflect what actually happened, and moreover it misses the main point: what affects produce. Instead, I offer the overarching category of violent affections, which defines affects according to what they do as a mechanism of power relations.

I first demonstrate how the law structures certain articulations of emotions. Consider the case of the cannibal mentioned at the beginning of the Chapter 5. Even though the emotion that triggered extreme violence was a negative feeling towards the victim's sexuality, it was not termed 'hate' in court, which the hate crime doctrine would assume. The legal actors involved in the case referred to it as a 'personal unpleasant feeling'. I suggest that this was done for a reason. Indeed, the decision was dictated by the legal principles behind 'unpleasantness' and 'hate'. One is a legal nod to a negative emotion that may motivate personal quarrels. The other is a political message. 'Hate' as a part of special criminal legislation is not merely an emotion; it is a juridical term that signifies bias towards an entire group represented by a single victim (Wickes et al. 2016).

Frederick Lawrence offers a useful classification that explains the difference. He contends that there are three types of crime (Lawrence 1999, 9). The first are crimes with random victims who just happen to be in the wrong place at the wrong time. Their identity does not matter, because the perpetrator's goal has nothing to do with them: take, for example, a cashier who becomes a victim only because the perpetrator wants money that it is the cashier's responsibility to keep safe. The second type are crimes targeted personally against specific people. These include revenge crimes or any other act of victimisation directed at an individual person. The third type are crimes where the victims are selected as representatives of a larger social collective, such as the LGBT+ community. The victim's personal history does not matter and may not even be known to the perpetrator, but the very fact of identifying that individual victim with a hated population is what motivates the offender. According to this classification, use of the term 'hate' in a court ruling implies a deliberate and conscious message to the whole group that the perpetrator detests (Perry 2001, 10). The message is expressed in an act of violence. 'Hate' entails this collective dimension, or, in other words, it presumes recognition of the existence of the 'hated' group by law. Moreover, an enhanced sentence sends a signal to potential perpetrators that a group they might have considered targeting for a violent attack is purposely protected as a particularly vulnerable group. Thus, every time hate crime norms are applied, judges enact this entire doctrinal system of justice: the system that acknowledges the collective vulnerability of LGBT+ people and takes measures to reduce the effects of that vulnerability by threatening to punish perpetrators of this sort of violence more severely. This is what 'hate' as a juridical form of emotion does politically.

To be fair, Russian legal actors are perfectly capable of making this move. Consider this unambiguous narrative of a hate crime presented in a case where the relevant hate crime legislation was applied by the judge:

> [The defendant] committed battery, which caused pain, but did not involve consequences indicated in Art. 115 CC RF, motivated by hatred to a person belonging to a social group. The crime was committed in the following circumstances: on the 24th of February 2013, at about 19.00, [the defendant] was on the street [address] drunk and motivated by hatred of the social group of 'sexual minorities', where he hit previously known to him [victim], who belonged to this social group; he hit him twice with a fist to [the victim's] face that resulted in pain, while he commented on his actions using words of hatred for the social group of 'sexual minorities', namely: 'I hate people like you and I will do this every time I see you!' After the attack, [the victim] went back home, and [the defendant] stayed in the same spot. (1-16/2013, Likino-Dulyevo, Moscow Region)

In this passage, all the necessary boxes for hate crime are ticked. Given that sexual orientation is not explicitly included in Russia's criminal statutes, the judge applies a more general statutory term, 'social group', and expands its reach to include queer victims. Besides, she mentions that the defendant clearly expressed his hatred not simply through his criminal actions, but also in offensive and threatening utterances. Finally, the victim is described not merely as an individual, but as an embodiment of a larger collective, the social group of 'sexual minorities'. In this case, the conflict between victim and offender is not personal; it has greater social implications. As a result, the hate crime legislation was applied and the perpetrator received a harsher punishment (a suspended sentence with a year of probation).[1]

But it is too early to announce the triumph of the hate crime doctrine in Russia as protecting queer people. As I mentioned in Chapter 2, out of 314 victims, only five were involved in cases where hatred towards the social group LGBT+ was prosecuted. In three cases, the same judge presided, and she awarded a 1-year suspended sentence in each. In another case, heard in a neighbouring town, the defendants received a custodial term of 1.5 years. In the fifth ruling of this kind, the defendant was sent for compulsory psychiatric treatment. Three more cases mentioned hatred: one as a general – non-juridical – emotion (hence without legal consequences) and two more where the hate crime charges were dropped and the defendants were prosecuted without this aggravating circumstance. In one case the parties reconciled; in the other the judge did not find the evidence of hate convincing and sentenced for a general crime (1-721/2015, Novosibirsk).

Notably, once 'hate' is out, the defendants are motivated by 'personal unpleasant feelings': '[defendant-1] said that [victim-1] and [victim-2] were homosexuals. Because of this, [defendant-2] felt personal unpleasant feelings towards them. He took a fork in the kitchen and started to wake up [victim-1] and [victim-2] by poking their bodies' (1-800/2015, Tyumen). Like 'hate', 'personal unpleasant feelings' is a juridical category of emotions. It sounds awkward (in both Russian and English) precisely because of this. People do not use this phrase in everyday life. In contrast to 'hate', 'personal unpleasant feelings' has exactly the opposite effect: instead of indicating social conditions that victimise a group of people due to prevalent societal negative prejudices expressed by an individual offender in hatred and violence, 'unpleasant feelings' shifts attention to the personal level of interaction between particular individuals – this one perpetrator and that specific victim. In other words, it is not that there is homophobia or prejudice against LGBT+ people that has found its expression in violence and hate; there are simply two people who disagree with each other and one of them resorts to the application of force.

In Russian criminology the term 'unpleasant feelings' has not received much attention. It is largely assumed as self-evident given its Soviet heritage and continued use thereafter. As one criminal law textbook states, 'unpleasant feelings' are among the list of 'subjective motives' of crimes (*mens rea*), which includes particular states of mind of a delinquent individual leading towards damaging actions (Rarog 2015, 151). Although there is a lot of confusion between 'hate' and 'unpleasant feelings' among academic criminologists who use the words as synonyms (Rostokinsky 2007; Yavorskiy 2014), the judges in the cases I analysed seem to know very well when to apply a political term and when to employ an apolitical one. Once 'hate' is applied, not only does one have to cite an exact statute and enhance the sentence, one also has to convincingly demonstrate that the hatred motive is well established and proven in the courtroom to avoid the risk of the ruling being overturned. As for 'unpleasant feelings', the term is not mentioned anywhere in the Criminal Code. There are no protocols or procedures involved in arguing that they were what a defendant felt, for these are subjective feelings and the defendant's general comments about some sort of negative emotion towards the victim are enough. 'Unpleasant feelings' do not influence the sentence – they are neither aggravating nor extenuating circumstances (Rarog 2015, 93). Put another way, in comparison to 'hate', 'unpleasant feelings' cause less trouble in terms of legal procedure and are even helpful in terms of rhetorically indicating a defendant's motivations, which is a crucial element of a crime narrative.

The pragmatic, procedural dimension of the term is clear, but the choice to use 'unpleasant feelings' also does a political job of the kind I identified in Chapter 2, where I argued for judicial indifference as everyday politics. 'Unpleasant feelings' individualise responsibility for a crime by making particular perpetrators solely accountable and by ignoring the social system that manifests itself in the act of violence. In the 'hate' discourse, the single violent incident is a manifestation of oppression of an entire group of people represented by the victim. As for 'unpleasant feelings', the incident becomes an ordinary and unremarkable event where violence resulted from the individual psychological states of mind of offender and victim. There is no homophobia or vulnerable social positionality of queer victims as a disadvantaged group, but a mundane quarrel between average people who simply disagree with each other and fight – sometimes to the death.

The choice of words

A decision to cite 'unpleasant feelings' instead of 'hate' is, therefore, an act of erasure. By scaling a violent incident down from a manifestation of societal, systemic prejudice to a simple interpersonal encounter, judges reject the very existence of LGBT+ as a vulnerable group. Regardless of evidence concerning defendants' 'hatred' of queer people as a whole, judges routinely decide to assign 'unpleasant feelings' to their emotional state. Consider the following case. A group of three young men decided to organise a hunt for gay people in Chita, a regional capital of Zabaykalsky Territory. They registered a fake profile on a dating website and agreed to meet with a young guy who had responded to their sexual advances. During the meeting, which took place in a remote, abandoned part of the city, they beat up the gay man and stole his belongings. Only one of the offenders wound up in court, where he clearly stated that he and his associates 'beat up [the victim] because of unpleasant feelings to persons of non-traditional sexual orientation, who include [the victim] judging from his behaviour and discussed topics' (1-140/2016, Chita, Zabaykalsky Territory). The case describes the common business of gay bashers who specifically target gay men out of homophobic prejudice.

My sample accounts for 78 specifically targeted queer victims. Hate crime legislation is very well suited to dealing with such cases, and so whatever word the defendant uses to name the emotion that fuelled his violence, it should be translated to the juridical notion of 'hate'. Instead, though, the judge in the above case opted for 'unpleasant feelings'. As a result, two charges (light injuries, Article 115, and theft, Article 158) led to 1.5 years of community service and the defendant was immediately pardoned due to, ironically, an anti-fascist celebration, namely the 70th anniversary of Victory in the Great Patriotic War in 1945. In other words, the accused walked free instead of being given an enhanced sentence.

By replacing 'hate' with 'unpleasant feelings', the judge avoided discussion of 'persons of non-traditional sexual orientation' as a 'social group'. In fact, she also avoided the entire line of enquiry relating to the victim's sexuality. This was all irrelevant: it was simply a case where two people (the rest of the gay-bashing group were not even brought before the court) had argued over some personal issues. By ignoring this (substantial) part of the story, the judge erased the very existence of gay men and LGBT+ people as a whole with a simple, conscious choice between two legal terms that stand for different kinds of juridical emotions.

How intentional judges' choice of juridical terms is can be a matter of both analysis and speculation. Since the notions of 'hate' and 'unpleasant feelings' imply different legal consequences and different procedures, judges definitely use them distinctly and consciously. However, 'hate' sometimes turns up in a text by mistake, as in the following case of a targeted assault on a gay man chosen from a dating website. This entire ruling uses the term 'unpleasant feelings' except for just one moment, when the victim's point of view is mentioned: 'the victim testified that the motive of the assault on him was the defendant's hatred and misunderstanding of the sexual orientation to which he adhered' (1-674/2011, Tomsk). This argument is not taken further or developed into a proper hate crime case.

There are also social conditions that support the preference for 'unpleasant feelings'. As I showed in Chapter 1, hate crime legislation is a relatively new phenomenon in Russia. It first appeared in the 1996 Criminal Code and was refined in 2007. As part of a larger flow of foreign legal transplants into post-Soviet Russia (Ajani 1995; Borisova 2008; Kurkchiyan 2009; McCarthy 2015), hate crime law incorporates particular assumptions that may sometimes be barely intelligible in a local context. Most importantly, hate crime legislation in the US, Australia and some EU countries was developed on the basis of existing standards 'found in the anti-discrimination norms of identity politics' (Mason 2014b, 295; Schweppe and Walters 2016; Haynes, Schweppe and Taylor 2017). Little is known about both anti-discrimination norms and identity politics in Russia to date, although, as I showed in Chapter 3, there are various messy developments in the latter area. Russian law, however, remains quite reluctant to take a strong stand in these domains, especially in relation to sexuality.[2]

Queer sexualities receive inconsistent treatment in legal settings. Queerness can be silenced, criminalised, ignored or occasionally protected and supported through law, although the former strategies seem to be more common. In effect, silencing or even overt hostility to queerness dictates not protective measures (via the use of 'hate'), but disgusted indifference (looking the other way). 'Unpleasant feelings' fits this purpose very well, because such feelings clearly deny the existence of queerness in a social group form and reassert it as an occasional sexual practice. This assertion is not necessarily conscious for every judge, however. Rather, it is the unintelligibility of the LGBT+ community as a vulnerable societal faction that produces such an effect. Since sexuality expresses itself in fluid queer forms in Russia, as I showed in the previous part of the book, its rigid identity-based LGBT+ formation is rather difficult for the law to stomach. While some instances of this understanding of queerness do occur, the more common sense of queer sexuality in the courtroom is conditioned by unintelligibility, silencing and repression.

Overall, there is a mismatch between the forms of expression of queerness in Russia that are fluid and elusive, and the more rigid identity-based doctrine behind hate crime law. Both consciously and unconsciously, judges rarely regard the notion of 'hate' as a feasible one in cases of violence against queer people. In part, judges benefit from less work associated with 'unpleasant feelings' as a procedural legal category. They also mirror more general conditions whereby queerness in Russia finds itself under the banner of silencing and ignorance. Because of all this, hate crime law is a poor instrument of justice in cases of violence motivated by prejudice against victims' sexuality and gender in Russia. The everyday politics behind the choice of words to name emotions demonstrates that legal actors do not care whether LGBT+ victims are properly protected. Rather, they are interested in following procedural norms that guarantee the smooth flow of justice across their desks.

From dislike to disgust

Both 'hate' and 'unpleasant feelings' are juridical emotions. They are not necessarily the words used by defendants during an investigation or in court hearings; defendants' own explanations for their crimes are translated into legal language to legally categorise their emotions as one thing or another. Yet, as I showed in Part I, the texts of the cases under review are much more complicated than mere legal utterances. They comprise the language of many different people and retain traces of their own vocabulary of emotions, which I will now examine further.

This exploration of emotional vocabulary aims to provide a better sense of the many articulations of emotions that people use to explain their anti-queer attacks. The palette of emotions I have identified ranges from 'anger' to 'fun' and contains 25 categories of feelings, including the two discussed at length above. Aside from another juridical emotion, 'affect' (used by the defence or in the legal categorisation of four cases to describe an irresistible impulse to act violently without criminal liability or as an extenuating circumstance), these emotions include: aggression, anger, the feeling of camaraderie, danger, disgust, dislike, fear, frustration, fun, fury, humiliation, indignation, irritation, nervousness, the feeling of offence, pity, respect, sadness, shame, shock, tension and uncomfortableness. All these emotions were mentioned in connection with the attacks or as an explanation for why an attack occurred. I argue that, regardless of the various names, they communicate one and the same affect. My goal is to show how these violent affections signal a generative event in an encounter in which opposing subjects are produced and then arranged in hierarchical order.

A more colloquial term for 'unpleasant feelings' could be simple 'dislike', and this word is part of the vocabularies of the court rulings. Thus, perpetrators report that they simply do not like queerness and that is why they attack men who associate with it: 'they beat him up because they did not like his sexual orientation' (1-12/2014, Zheleznogorsk, Kursk Region); '[the victim] started a conversation about persons of non-traditional sexual orientation. [The defendant] did not like it and so he hit [the victim] with a fist to his face' (1-59/2016, Shadrinsk, Kurgan Region). This feeling of 'dislike' was acted upon in various ways, including by trying to distance oneself from queerness:

> He met [defendant-1] and they decided to go to the café-bar [name]. On arrival, they settled down at the bar counter and began to drink cognac. Sometime later, they saw [victim-1] sitting at a table with a young man who, as it turned out, was [victim-2]. [Defendant-2] did not like the fact that [victim-1] was present in the bar, because he was a person of non-traditional sexual orientation . . . They approached [the victims'] table and asked them to leave the bar. (1-81/2011, Ruza, Moscow Region)

This quarrel continued outside the premises and resulted in light injuries and theft of the victims' property. But 'dislike' can also lead to more serious outcomes for victims' health. In another case several people had gathered in a private flat to commemorate the death of a victim's mother. They drank alcohol the entire night, and as time passed, guests started to leave. The two victims and the defendant stayed overnight. The defendant recalled in court that he was sleeping in one of the bedrooms 'when he heard noises from the living room, went there and saw two men having sexual intercourse. As he said, he did not like it and because of it he started to beat up these men' (1-986/2012, Cherepovets). At one point the defendant grabbed a metal teapot and hit his victims with it. One of them died, and the other was injured to the point of mental disability.

Dislike may also evolve into disgust, without any connotations of ooziness, animality or mortality. Rather, in the legal lexicon disgust appears to be nothing more than a way of referring to a feeling of strong dislike for someone. On the one hand, this feeling can be a momentary reaction to proximity to a queer other: '[Witness-1] said that [the victim] was a passive homosexual. [The defendant] decided to kill [the victim], because he was disgusted by such persons' (1-17/2015, Ulan-Ude, Republic of Buryatia); '[the defendant] understood that [the victim] would like him to join in sexual intercourse and to engage in buggery, he was disgusted by his advances. These actions caused strong rejection, anger and aggression' (1-134/2014, Dolgoprudny, Moscow Region); 'He understood that [the victim] was of non-traditional sexual orientation. When [the victim] asked him to take a shower, he developed disgust to [the victim] and a plan to rob from him' (1-353/2011, Omsk). On the other hand, disgust can also be a long-harboured feeling:

> At 11pm, every day, on [a TV channel], [a show] is aired and during this show, various dating solicitations are broadcast for people of non-traditional sexual orientation. He is disgusted by these people; this is why he seeks to shame these people. He does so by calling to the persons of non-traditional sexual orientation on the phone numbers broadcast on the TV in [the show] and by making a date with them without intention to appear there. (1-579/2012, Taganrog, Rostov Region)

The feeling of disgust that this person cultivates is articulated through the everyday practice of annoying gay men with dates that fail to materialise. A weird hobby in itself, this affectual attachment not only speaks of an enduring emotion, but also questions the clear-cut boundary between hetero- and homosexuality. A Sedgwickian reading of this case (Sedgwick 1990) would show that the false calls to gay men and false dates with them are, to an extent, still conversations with and dating queerness. The presumably heterosexual man performs a strange form of his own same-sex desire by engaging in affectual intercourse with those other men. Disgust points to this ambiguous place of encounter where homo- and heterosexuality are simultaneously produced and mixed.

In contrast to this mixture, defendants also stress the importance of distancing themselves from queerness out of shame and embarrassment – another universally anti-queer feeling (Ahmed 2004, 101; Halperin and Traub 2009; Nussbaum 2004): 'Before filming, [defendant-1] and [defendant-2] put on facial medical masks, because they were ashamed to be in one frame with a person of [redacted]' (1-285/2015, Chita, Zabaykalsky Territory). An important mechanism is at work in these encounters when, instead of emotional intercourse with the queer victim, perpetrators develop an emotional intercourse between themselves through the collective sharing of emotions: '[defendant-1] said he knew a man of non-traditional sexual orientation. They all were disgusted by this fact and commenced to plan how to punish him' (1-378/2013, Chelyabinsk). As I pointed out earlier, Sara Ahmed (2004) identifies this mechanism of the production of a community as a result of such affectionate impulses.

Camaraderie and fun

Feelings of camaraderie and fun are also explicitly shared emotions that produce community and connection among perpetrators. These emotions do not immediately suggest violent intentions. On the contrary, they are seemingly positive emotions that should bring about memories of a good mood and relaxing times. However, regardless of how the emotions are named, it all boils down to the context of the encounter that they signal. Note, for example, how in the following case a feeling of camaraderie was shared between the perpetrators, making participation in a collective act of violence their communal purpose: two men were fighting when another man (the defendant) entered the room. One of them explained to the newcomer that the man he was beating up was homosexual. As a result, 'acting out of a feeling of camaraderie and suddenly emerged unpleasant feelings to [the victim], [the defendant] . . . hit, multiple times, his head, arms, legs and body' (1-259/2011, Anapa, Krasnodar Territory). Forensic experts counted 108 traces of blows on the victim's dead body. A brief reference to the victim's sexuality was enough to stir another assailant's emotions and ensure his participation in a collective violent slaughter.

A similar passionate bond between men may emerge from an intention to have fun in masculine company by inventing masculine leisure pursuits. In a case heard in 2013, as one of the defendants recalled and others in the courtroom confirmed, five flatmates 'wanted to have fun and laugh at [their victim] because of his non-traditional sexual orientation' (1-17/2013, Rostov-on-Don, Rostov Region). They had registered on a dating website and invited the man to their home. One of them opened the door to the guest and showed him to the living room. The other four were waiting there. One closed the door behind the victim, another chopped the door handle off with a hatchet in a threatening manner, and a third put a wooden bat in the victim's mouth. They kept the man in the room for a day, continuously issuing insults and threats. The next day, they took him to a bank where he was supposed to take out a loan to buy himself out of abduction, but he begged for help and was rescued. The defendants described the events as 'humorous' (*balovstvo*) and 'a joke' (*prikol*). It was funny only to the five defendants: the 'fun' had produced bonds among them but created a clear boundary between them and the queer victim.

It is common for defendants in collective cases to describe their feelings in terms of fun. Another abduction of a man lured to a meeting through a dating website occurred in Novosibirsk. When the man arrived at the agreed spot in his car, three men got into the car from all sides. He was immediately threatened with a gun filled with rubber bullets. The defendants claimed that '[the victim] began to talk about his sexual inclinations and they all laughed' (1-218/2015, Novosibirsk). In other cases, defendants echoed time and again that they just wanted to have fun – a phrase ambivalently signalling both occasional sexual intercourse and the mocking of defenceless victims. It is certainly a way to diminish criminal liability. But in addition to this, 'fun', as well as 'camaraderie' (*chuvstvo tovarishchestva*), belongs to masculine collective emotions and is always shared with someone else. Fun and camaraderie are shared by the spontaneously produced community of violent offenders; they are not shared by their victims, who are terrified rather than amused by the abduction, threats and beatings. Such encounters also cultivate the different versions of masculinity that victims and perpetrators come to represent.

Pity and respect

The defendant and victim in a case that occurred in a resort near Sorochinsk in Orenburg Region had known each other for 10 years. The defendant worked at a recreation centre and his victim lived nearby. They occasionally drank alcohol together but stopped socialising once the defendant learned from a taxi driver that the victim 'was a person with non-traditional sexual orientation, which caused unpleasant feelings towards [the victim]' (1-46/2014, Sorochinsk, Orenburg Region). They had not seen each other for three months when the defendant relented and hosted a reunion. He claimed 'he showed pity to [the victim], [and] gave him 100 roubles for spirits and food' that they shared together. The feeling of pity ended up as a violent affection when the defendant stabbed his homosexual friend during their soiree and threw his dead body into the street.

Alcohol features in many such stories and is connected with another feeling: that of respect. There is a tradition in Russia whereby when a male participant at a drinking gathering intends to leave the table, he is asked whether or not he respects his companions (Kondakov and Shtorn 2021). This rhetorical question forces him to stay, because the question 'Do you respect me?' is also the question 'Are you man enough to drink on a par with me?'. It is a question about equality between men and about sharing a common version of masculinity – tough enough to drink a lot. This respect signals the production of a community among those who are 'man enough'. However, what if one of the drinking-mates turns out to be queer? A queer version of masculinity is immediately – in the cases of violent affections that I reviewed – regarded by default as not meriting respect from the other men: '[the witness] said to [defendant-1] and [defendant-2] that they were drinking with a person of non-traditional sexual orientation. [Defendant-1] does not respect such people, this is why he grabbed [the victim] by his clothes and took him to the corridor, then to the public toilet to beat him up' (1-105/2012, Konakovo, Tver Region). In this case, the implied inequality or asymmetry between the subjects in the encounter is evidenced in the lack of respect that the defendant notes.

Just like in the case of 'fun', respect is connected with both masculinity and the male collective. It is productive both of the collective itself and of the boundary separating the collective and those who are excluded from it. As the defendants in the reviewed cases attest, once they feel respect is betrayed or lacking, they act violently. However, this feeling is not about individual respect. On the contrary, the lack of respect that they perceive is more like a betrayal of manhood as a whole. It is expressed as a collective emotion, a shared feeling, despite being accompanied by the juridical and very individualised notion of 'unpleasant feelings', as the examples above demonstrate. In short, what is defended with violence when respect withers away is heterosexual masculinity, not individual honour.

Shock and humiliation

The cases under review reveal the affectionate logic behind the feeling of betrayed heterosexual masculinity. Queerness per se does not threaten masculinity as such or any gender in particular; certainly, as other scholars have pointed out, there are many versions of masculinity that accommodate sexual diversity (Connell 1995; Kon 2009). However, in the cases that end in violence, a chain of emotions emerges, leading towards a dreadful conclusion: the offenders are shocked and hurt, and feel humiliated as queerness endangers their version of masculinity, which they regard as the only possible version. As a result, they seek to restore their previous emotional state through the violent disposal of the perceived stimulus of these feelings:

> [The victim] pulled his pants down, turned around and exposed his butt showing in this way that he wanted to engage in sexual intercourse with [the defendant]. Although [the defendant] had previous convictions, he had always kept relationships only with women, he did not have relationships with men, he had a normal orientation, so [the victim's] behaviour shocked him and to an extent that was humiliating . . . The behaviour of [the victim] hurt him and so he kicked [the victim] with his foot shod in sneakers in [the victim's] backside. (1-124/2015, Zlatoust, Chelyabinsk Region)

Encounters with the diversity of masculinity can provoke shocking reactions, as defendants report. They perceive queerness as something that touches them so deeply that they feel humiliated by the very fact of their proximity to it. Instead of retreating to calm their feelings, the defendants attack. Take this example. Two men were drinking wine in a flat belonging to one of them and they went out onto the balcony for a cigarette. Fortified by wine, the victim was overwhelmed with feelings and kissed his friend. In response, the defendant bent the victim over the balcony rail, pulled his legs up and threw him over. In the courtroom, he recognised: 'He killed the victim because he teased him with hugs and kisses, which offended [the defendant] as a man' (1-185/2016, Nazarovo, Krasnoyarsk Territory). The feeling of deceived masculinity was central to this 'offence'.

A range of emotions emerges at every affectual encounter that is productive of queer and heterosexual asymmetry: '[victim-1] offered to [the defendant] and [witness] his sexual services. He said he could do a blowjob. [The defendant] did not like this, it was obnoxious and offensive, because he was of normal sexual orientation . . . He took it as a personal offence and humiliation' (1-92/2011, Nizhny Novgorod). Not all feelings of offence are generated by sexual advances, though: 'they met two young people near the mall . . . these two young people were holding hands, which fact offended [the defendant]' (1-28/2015, Chaltyr', Rostov Region). In another case, the two defendants who were standing in front of a shop 'saw two lads kissing. This shocked them, so [defendant-1] approached them and struck one in the face without saying a word' (1-332/2015, Berdsk, Novosibirsk Region). Queerness can also be expressed in less obvious forms, but still touch the perpetrators and meet with violence in response. For example, '[the victim] mentioned something about gay clubs, which offended [the defendant] and so he hit him in the face' (1-59/2016, Shadrinsk, Kurgan Region). The perpetrators in the reviewed cases insist that someone else's sexual orientation is a personal attack on them:

> [the defendant], [witness-1], [victim-1], [witness-2] and [victim-2] were consuming alcoholic beverages, when [the victim's] homosexual orientation was revealed. Considering association with such people offensive to him and believing that [the victim] hid his homosexual orientation from him and by hiding it humiliated [the defendant's] personal dignity, [the defendant] hit multiple, not less than five, times to [the victim's] head and face. (2-13/2015, Ivanovo)

One of the men present stood up for the victim, but the humiliation was so strong that the defendant grabbed a fire log, smashed this man's head with it and then the first victim's head, too. In such encounters, the perpetrators of violence find themselves in a situation that is generative of different sexualities that they cannot tolerate precisely because they hold that associating with queerness 'downgrades' their own sexuality and heterosexual privilege. Furthermore, personal humiliation and offence are collective community-generating affects, too. They are easily transmittable from one body to another by word of mouth and are not confined to just one person's corporeality:

> On the internet, he met someone who he now knows as [the victim] and who initially introduced himself as a girl. During their message exchange, it became clear that he was not messaging with a girl, but with a citizen of non-traditional sexual orientation. He was shocked by the behaviour of [the victim]. In the evening [date], he visited [defendant-2] with whom he celebrated New Year 2016. He told [defendant-2] about his unpleasant feelings towards the citizen he had been messaging. [Defendant-2] was also shocked by the behaviour of this citizen and they decided to 'teach him a lesson', in other words to beat him up. (1-172/2016, Rostov-on-Don, Rostov Region)

As these two men share their shock at witnessing queerness, they not only plot their criminal assault, but also produce bonds between themselves, just like in the cases of fun and respect. They are engaging in homosocial emotional intercourse, although of course they do not realise this is what they are doing. It is neither conscious nor unconscious; it resists this binary. This intercourse brings the perpetrators together *and* tears them apart from queerness at the same time. In an ultimately violent way, their own queer proximity to each other requires them to somehow mark themselves out as non-queer, lest their masculine company and time-spending activities 'risk' being designated as homosexual, not homosocial (Sedgwick 1990; 2003). Since the boundary between queerness and non-queerness is generally unclear, these violent encounters come into play to draw that boundary instantaneously.

Furious anger

Sudden shock may also be expressed in terms of fury and anger – emotional states that are meant to signify a high level of sudden emotional heat. In the following case, three men each drank a litre of vodka and fell asleep:

> [The witness] lay on the floor, and [the defendant] and [the victim] occupied the bed laying head-to-toe. [The defendant] was already

falling asleep, when he felt that [the victim] touched his genitals. He demanded hands off, but five minutes later, [the victim] grabbed him by his genitals again. He shouted at him, but [the victim] grabbed his genitals for a third time sometime later. In fury, he stormed out and, knowing that there was an axe in the bathroom, took it and slightly hit [the victim] twice into the forehead to calm him down. (1-107/2013, Slyudyanka, Irkutsk Region)

The victim died, of course. In a different case, the fury was slow cooked as the perpetrator contacted the victim through the internet, scheduled a date and attacked there. In this case, 'the man of non-traditional sexual orientation, whom he met in an online chatroom, was writing to him SMS messages of weird content, offering sex and pleasure. [The defendant] was furious because of this' (1-175/2013, Pyatigorsk, Stavropol Territory). During the date, the defendant broke the victim's neck and 'manslaughtered' him.

Furious reactions may accompany both sex and violence. For instance, in Vladimir, a man who had recently been released from prison saw a young lad who he thought was a migrant and gay. He invited him to drink and relax under a bridge. There, first he raped him and then 'became furious, acted very aggressively and had a knife' (1-255/2013, Vladimir). He stabbed the young man 81 times with this knife. In this case, violence erupted from both queer sexual desire and the rejection of queer sexuality. Consider another case where the boundary between hetero- and homosexuality is again very much blurred but at the same time clearly drawn by the feeling of anger that marks the turning point where difference becomes inequality:

> [The victim] said that he was ready to pay 200 dollars for oral sex with [the defendant]. Since they had been drinking alcohol and he was drunk, [the defendant] agreed to [the victim's] offer, who showed him the way to the bedroom and sat him on a sofa. After the oral sex was performed by [the victim], [the victim] gave to [the defendant] 200 US dollars . . . [The victim] then offered him sexual intercourse and more money . . . the allusions to sexual intercourse made [the defendant] very angry. [The defendant] grabbed a knife in his left hand and stabbed [the victim] in his stomach and liver. (1-636/2014, Moscow)

In this encounter, the defendant's heterosexual masculinity was not threatened until the reference to anal intercourse, despite the fact that he had just engaged in same-sex activities. Note that oral sex was perceived by the perpetrator without much offence (and was not even considered 'sexual intercourse'). Yet the suggestion of intercourse involving anal penetration caused offence, resulting in 32 stab wounds. The boundary between hetero- and homosexuality seems to be drawn somewhere in between a blowjob and anal penetration. Moreover, border patrol on that boundary is fierce and usually shoots to kill. This kind of anger results from betrayed masculinity in various forms, not only sexually charged contexts:

> Under the table, [defendant-1] saw a plastic bag belonging to [the victim]. There were women's red tights and blue panties in the bag. He approached [the victim] who lay on the floor and asked what his sexual orientation was, to which [the victim] replied that he was a normal guy [*normal'ny muzhik*] . . . [Defendant-1] and [defendant-2] elevated [the victim] from the floor and sat him on a sofa . . . When they were sitting him on the sofa, his trousers fell down and they noticed that he wore women's black tights. This made them even angrier, they understood that he lied to them and started to beat him up. (1-1009/2011, Yoshkar-Ola, the Republic of Mari El)

There is sometimes a feeling of regret after the anger dissipates: 'He got angry with [the victim], because he understood his own orientation as normal and did not understand people of non-traditional sexual orientation . . . He did not want to kill [the victim], he was simply very angry at him' (1-19/2016, Leninsk-Kuznetsky, Kemerovo Region). The emotional outburst seems to be a sort of release valve which is used to relax nervous tension when sexual intercourse as a relaxation option is off the table. This tension is generated during the spontaneous drawing of the boundary between hetero- and homosexuality.

Tension and the fear of danger

Perpetrators also claim that they are 'annoyed and irritated by the imposition of non-traditional sexual relationships' (1-124/2015, Zlatoust, Chelyabinsk Region) and so they are ready to injure people who they think flaunt it. Hence, after an encounter with two young men who looked like 'people of non-traditional sexual orientation', the offenders decided to steal a backpack from one of them, because he 'irritated him with his body type and outfit' (1-245/2014, Tomsk). Tensions can also rise when an encounter turns intimate: '[the victim] touched his genitals through his trousers, this made him nervous and jump from his seat' (1-145/2016, Vladivostok, Primorsky Territory). This particular experience of nervousness resulted in the victim being stabbed to death with a broken glass bottle.

Another case of violence erupting due to feelings of irritation and annoyance occurred when two young lads were approached by another young man on the street:

> The young man made it clear during their conversation that he was of non-traditional sexual orientation. He did not say it straightforwardly, but it was obvious. They were standing there in the evening, and [the victim] said: 'What are such handsome boys doing here in the late evening?' It was immediately clear that the individual was of different orientation. We asked him whether he was a member of such a group? He said he was. The witness did not know how it was called properly, LGBT or something like that. It was about the victim's sexual orientation. [The witness] felt uncomfortable talking about it. It was not a long conversation. He and [the defendant] asked [the victim] to leave. But he insisted: 'Lads, let's drink alcoholic beverages together, I want to stay here with you.' Then during this conversation, [the victim] started to behave provocatively, [the witness] was not accustomed to talking to people like that, namely, when a homosexual approaches a normal person, this causes irritation. (1-6-2/2016, Rostov-on-Don, Rostov Region)

For these perpetrators of violence, the very fact of being close to a queer person made the situation uncomfortable, irritating, annoying and provocative. Such feelings are productive of the very difference between heterosexuality and queerness. This difference is understood as provocative, because it is unclear to the defendants whether their heterosexuality will stand the test of temptation. Tensions can boil over and erupt, as I have shown, in various forms of violence, from a few kicks to multiple stab wounds. The perpetrators may not fully know what they are dealing with in such an encounter, but judging from the emotions they describe, as recorded by the legal documents, they are dealing with their own fears.

I argue that this fear is crucial in understanding emotions in the cases I review. It appears that these emotions are always productive of a thin, sometimes permeable line between hetero- and homosexuality. Crossing the line is somehow scary to the perpetrators simply because what awaits them on the other side is not only different but also inferior when interpreted from their privileged heterosexual position. Thus, line-crossings do not occur without fear:

> . . . according to the testimony of the accused given during primary investigation with presence of his lawyer, he knows who homosexuals are. He himself is a person of traditional sexual orientation. He met [the victim] in more or less 2001 when they both studied in college . . . Sometime about the second academic year, he and [the victim] drank alcoholic beverages on the coast of lake Staritskoe in the town of Orekhovo-Zuevo. There, an unknown man approached them and offered to 'blow' [the victim]. He failed to figure out what this phrase meant. But after this phrase, [the victim] stood up and went away with this man, and he stayed. Sometime later, he was bored and decided to look for [the victim]. He wandered around and then saw how [the victim] had sexual intercourse with that man. He got scared, packed his things and left the lake. (1-25/2011, Likino-Dulyevo, Moscow Region)

Why would witnessing sex make someone scared? The feeling comes from the possibility of loss of heterosexuality that is evoked by these perpetrators. Fear arises from spatial proximity to queerness, on the one hand, and from the resulting fear that the perpetrator is only one step away from merging with the queerness himself, on the other. Hence, the encounter simultaneously produces both the difference and the possibility of eradicating this difference. As affects always do, they highlight the vulnerability of heterosexuality in these instances. Violence appears as a sort of reactive defence mechanism.

Many perpetrators believe that the very presence of a gay person means that they will engage in sexual intercourse. Homosexuality here gets reduced to sex. Judges do not always buy this: 'the threat that [the victim] will commit actions of sexual character was not real, but was only assumed by [the defendant], who testified in the courtroom that when [the victim] grabbed his hand, [the defendant] feared that he would commit an act of sexual character with him' (1-32/2010, Sergiev Posad, Moscow Region). In this case, the fear resulted in murder. Sometimes, this strategy works and then the fear transforms into a legal 'affect' that exempts the defendant from harsh punishment. In the following case, a medical expert testified that when the victim made sexual advances to the defendant, the latter felt:

> . . . a complex of strong emotions – from surprise to disgust to a bad feeling: 'my internal guardian worked and I started to worry, tension rose', and this was followed by emotional tension in the examined subject accompanied by anxiety and fright. Because of the subject's personality traits (his rigid orientation to traditional conventional norms, including sexual roles, and his unequivocal rejection of non-traditional forms of sexual relationships), this situation resulted in an acutely frustrating condition. (1-62/2015, Kaluga)

This condition led to him hitting the victim's head 47 times with his hands, feet and a chair, ultimately causing the victim's death. It also resulted in house arrest for 2 years and 10 months – a decision that was overturned in the appellate court as it pardoned the defendant due to the 70th anniversary of Victory in the Great Patriotic War. I am not claiming that the court decisions were wrong. Rather, I am interested in this moment when people are afraid of queerness to the point of being willing to take another person's life. Why do they feel danger? In the case below, also discussed at the outset of Part I, Misha, who intended to murder a gay person, Sergey, went with him to a remote area on the city outskirts for a picnic. Sergey said he had prepared a nice surprise:

> When they were in the meadow, Misha asked Sergey to explain what the surprise was about. Later on, Sergey explained that since Misha wanted to meet new friends and to have interesting conversations, he invited his associates to join them. This situation promised nothing good. Misha realised that he found himself in a very bad situation, namely that he was alone in the woods with a person with non-traditional sexual orientation, and Misha's relatives did not know where he was. Moreover, the closest town was far away, so if something bad happened, no help should be expected . . . Misha tried to look calm and show that he was not scared and anxious . . . Sergey said that the most interesting part of their get-together was still ahead and so he invited Misha to make himself comfortable, while Sergey excused himself to go pee. This last phrase convinced Misha that he must run away now . . . Misha understood that the danger was still urgent, because at any moment the people invited by Sergey might come. (1-121/2012, Severskaya, Krasnodar Territory)

The suspense described by the defendant in this story relates to some sort of danger he feels just by being face-to-face with a gay man. Or rather, he knows he is face-to-face with a gay man who is different from him, a heterosexual male. Thus, this danger is not simply the danger of merely being together, but, as I argue time and again, the danger of the asymmetrical positionality that is produced between the subjects of feelings as the encounter looks from the position of privilege. It is affects here that function as the mechanism of power relations because they produce this difference as inequality – that is, the asymmetry between two subjects. In addition, affects become violent when the subject who interprets their position as one of privilege begins to defend it, fearing they may be forced to cross to the other side. In the cases I review, privilege is always defended with violence.

What about women?

I have described the feelings shared among perpetrators and between perpetrators and their victims as if they involve only men.[3] Indeed, for reasons explained in Part II above, the information on women as victims or, in fact, as perpetrators is scarce. But while the feelings I analyse seem to be centred on masculinity, women participate in the circulation of these emotions in various roles, too, including as offenders: 'On entering the house, she saw two men and a woman lying naked in a bed, she disliked what she saw, because she did not respect "gays"' (1-4/2016, Birsk, Republic of Bashkortostan). Eventually, this woman beat up the men with a bat and stabbed them, participating in an assault with two of her male associates.

As perpetrators of violence, women express many of the emotions mentioned above. The feeling of respect that manifests in male drinking rituals, as highlighted above, also forms part of this palette: 'She said that by drinking with a homosexual they show disrespect to themselves and so hit [the victim] twice in his face' (1-17/2015, Ulan-Ude, Republic of Buryatia). While in this case of murder the woman clearly committed violence, her role in the legal process was only that of witness. This downplaying happens in many cases where women perpetrators of violence are involved. Remember, for example, the case that opened this book. Erasure of the role femininity plays occurs even at the level of women's contribution to a crime. Most importantly for my discussion, it is the role of women as instigators of violence that is manifested in the quote above. In this short phrase, the woman implies that a man who drinks with a homosexual man is not man enough – he disgraces himself through his proximity to a queer body. In a heteronormative system of gendered desire, this instigating role can be understood as controller or supervisor of heterosexuality and its borders. Male perpetrators feel obliged to act violently against queerness to prove their heterosexuality in front of women who challenge them and question their sexual affiliation. In such cases, women act as an element of the constellation that is there to evidence or challenge the heterosexuality of male perpetrators. Here is another illustration of this point, indicating the aggression felt by a male perpetrator arising precisely at the moment of challenge by a woman:

> She shouted at [the victim], said that he molested other men and that he was of non-traditional sexual orientation. [The defendant] immediately felt aggression to [the victim] and because of it hit him to his temple with a fist. [The victim] shook but stayed on his feet. So [the defendant] took a wooden chair, which was in the corridor close to the restroom, and hit twice to [the victim's] vertex. The chair broke in pieces. (1-331/2014, Neryungi, Republic of Sakha Yakutia)

Even when women are not present at a crime scene, male perpetrators tend to reference them for no reason. For example, they will frequently state they have a wife or girlfriend even without being asked. This is done to reassure the public and the court (and perhaps themselves) of their heterosexual masculinity, since involvement in something queer (even though it is the killing of a homosexual person) already implies uncertainty around their heterosexuality.

But this type of heterosexuality is not limited to fragile masculinity only. There are also female perpetrators who commit violence out of the feeling of possible loss of their heterosexual femininity when they are in situations that draw boundaries between heterosexual and lesbian desires. In this case, a party of three women in a private flat ended with two dead bodies:

> Further, they all went to bed, she lay on the bed to the left of the entrance, [victim-1] and [victim-2] lay on a sofa in the corner. Despite the fact that they were already sleeping, she still was very angry at [victim-1] and [victim-2]. When [victim-1] touched her genitals, this fuelled her anger, so she stood up and took a knife to kill [victim-1] and [victim-2]. As [victim-1] saw her taking the

> knife, she got up from her bed and approached [the defendant]. She stabbed her multiple times immediately, she did not remember how many. Then, she crawled to [victim-2] who she also stabbed many times, she did not recall how many. (2-93/2013, Krasnogorsk, Moscow Region)

According to the forensics report, the perpetrator stabbed the women at least 38 and 13 times respectively.

In the sample, there are also queer women who became victims of violence perpetrated by men. In an unfortunately classic story which I analysed in Chapter 2, a lesbian woman, Lyubov, met an old acquaintance, Anatoly, on the street. They walked and talked together for a while, reminiscing about the good old days, and she revealed her sexual orientation to him. In response, Anatoly decided to rape her. When she resisted, he stabbed her: 'the court established that a failed attempt to initiate intimate relationship and information about Lyubov's non-traditional sexual orientation . . . resulted in emerging unpleasant feelings to [the victim], argument and, subsequently, murder' (1-108/2011, Orekhovo-Zuevo, Moscow Region). In cases like this, male offenders see their societal function as guardians of heterosexuality, similarly to those women above who instigate violence. They feel that they can 'return' lesbian women to heterosexuality (as if it is a thing); once they discover they cannot, they 'freak out' and commit acts of violence – as in the case of a neighbour of two lesbian women who harassed and annoyed them for years before, eventually, causing serious injuries (1-22/2015, Artyom, Primorsky Territory).

In sum, women participate in cases of anti-queer violence as victims, perpetrators and instigators of violence, as witnesses and bystanders to whom perpetrators seek to prove their heterosexuality, and as potentially imaginary sexual partners brought up to corroborate the heterosexual orientation of defendants. What is important here is that, regardless of gender, affects seem to produce a sense of encounter between bodies and then turn the bodies into opposing communities of queers and heterosexuals or, eventually, victims and perpetrators. The affects that make this happen may be named in different ways by legal actors and by the perpetrators who give their accounts of past events. They may employ their formal names, such as 'hate' or 'unpleasantness', or use more everyday terms, such as 'disgust' or 'anger'. Whatever these affects are called, they do their work as *violent affections*. I argue that violent affections are a particular mechanism of power relations that produces difference between the subjects of an encounter, makes inequalities out of that difference and then results in violence when one of the subjects acts from a position of injured privilege.

In the above analysis of emotions expressed by perpetrators, I stressed the various forms of collectives produced by these feelings. The defendants share emotions with others, are affected by the queerness of others, and exhibit passionate protection of collective notions such as heterosexual masculinity when attacking their queer victims. This is another collective dimension that violent affections have. As a mechanism of power relations, violent affections are somehow triggered in susceptible bodies. In other words, they somehow circulate in a society and this circulation itself becomes the technique of power relations. In the Introduction to this book, I argued that the technique of power relations is currently changing from the organised panopticism of the disciplinary regime to a more unruly and messy circulation of memes. In what remains of the book, I turn to an analysis of how memes trigger violent affections, drawing on the situation in Russia. This will further help to demonstrate how power works in the neo-disciplinary configuration of power relations.

Notes

1   In 2013, defendants prosecuted under Criminal Articles 115–6 (comprising one category of minor criminal offences) mainly received fines (14,507) or community work (13,950), while 953 defendants were sentenced to imprisonment for a year or less and 857 sentences were suspended (Court Department 2013).
2   Notable exceptions exist (Knight 2020).
3   For an overview and analysis of issues related to the participation of women in crime, see Marianna Muravyeva's work (Muravyeva 2016; Muravyeva, Shon and Toivo 2020).

Part IV
Techniques of power

A vulnerable perpetrator

It was way after midnight in Novorossiysk when two women, Yuliya and Natasha, returned from a party to Yulia's luxurious condominium apartment. As they made their way across the hallway, Yuliya embraced Natasha, whispering something in her ear. When Yuliya opened the door to her apartment, an angry man attacked them from behind. He punched Natasha in the face and pushed Yuliya against the wall. The man, Kolya, pushed the women into the apartment and locked the door. There, he tortured them for an hour. He beat the women with his fists and feet, being especially harsh around their genitals. In the courtroom, it was revealed that he had hit Yuliya's genitals at least 20 times, causing wounds and injuries. At one point, Kolya threatened the women with a knife, dragging Yuliya by her hair and holding the blade to her face. Then he took off most of his clothes and went onto the balcony saying that he would jump, and the women would be charged with his murder. He demanded that Yuliya marry him. She agreed, just to stop the cruelty, but instead of calming down, Kolya stepped on Yuliya's hand, took her ring from her finger and threw some banknotes on the floor. Yuliya asked Kolya to call a taxi for Natasha as she was not supposed to be involved in this drama. Kolya agreed. When the cab arrived, the two women managed to escape from the apartment by locking the man inside and asked the driver to take them to the nearest police station.

When Kolya was called to testify in front of a judge, he stated that he and Yuliya had had an affair. She had often lent him the keys to her car so that he could drive her around, and often let him stay overnight. Once, they went alone to Dombay, a ski resort. Kolya even introduced her to his mother. He decided to propose to her on Valentine's Day. They went to buy an engagement ring and then invited friends to a restaurant. As he recalls, everything went perfectly, and everyone was happy. But their relationship soon deteriorated when Yuliya started to see her best friend Natasha more often and distanced herself from Kolya. He refused to believe that the two women were sleeping together, he claimed in the courtroom, although he had heard rumours about Yuliya's sexuality. She herself had even mentioned something about this to him, but he had only laughed. He told the judge that he had been presented with evidence of Yuliya and Natasha's relationship and decided to visit them to dispel his doubts. That was the night he ambushed the women in the dark corner of the condominium.

The judge barely noticed the sexual or romantic elements of this story and sentenced Kolya to at least 7 years' imprisonment.[1] This result is less interesting to me than the affective narrative of the testimonies and the ruling. I use the case as an entry point to discuss how violent affections circulate, reaching susceptible bodies, such as Kolya's in this criminal story. Both the victim and the perpetrator constantly refer to a very fragile object in their mostly concurring narratives: Kolya's masculinity. This is how Yuliya described the purchase of the ring that Kolya took from her finger that night:

> In a window of a jewellery shop, she saw a golden ring with yellow and black stones that she decided to buy . . . In January, she finally had enough money for the ring and made up her mind about purchasing it. Kolya rang her and she told him that she was on her way to the jewellery shop 'Golden Elite' to buy a ring. He met her by the entrance . . . Because she is a VIP-client of this jewellery shop and has a discount for their products, a shop assistant calculated the final price of the ring with this discount. The price was [redacted]. Since she was there together with Kolya and she did not want to embarrass him as a man, she gave him the money totalling [redacted] so that he could go and pay for the ring. The cashier gave a receipt and said that they could take the ring tomorrow. The next day, she went back to the jewellery shop 'Golden Elite' with her mother where she lodged the rest of the ring's price [redacted] and took the ring. This ring she bought with her own money. (1-18/2013, Novorossiysk, Krasnodar Territory)

In the courtroom, Kolya insisted that the ring had been his engagement present. Moreover, he suggested that Yuliya's 'allegations that she gave him money for the ring before entering into the jewellery shop were false. He believes that a woman can do such a thing to a man only if she wants to severely humiliate and offend him.' Although Kolya did not agree with Yulia's version of the facts, he shared with her the gender norms that ensure the unequal distribution of power between women and men. Both Kolya and Yuliya agreed that a woman paying for a ring with her own money in the presence of a man would somehow embarrass and even humiliate him.

Kolya's vulnerable masculinity is referred to throughout the text of the ruling, most prominently via his economic disadvantage in comparison to Yuliya. She was director of an insurance company; he was a court bailiff. The judge stated that Yuliya's monthly income was five or six times higher than Kolya's. Witnesses testified that when he arrived in Novorossiysk, he had no place to live and stayed with a friend of a friend; he had asked to stay for a week, but actually remained there for six months. When Kolya moved in, this friend of a friend 'noted that he had very few things and all of them were very old. Kolya had two shirts, one pair of trousers and a light jacket . . . When he started dating Yuliya, she bought him good clothes, she dressed him from head to toe.' This inequality bothered Kolya greatly: 'Before taking the ring, he took out money [redacted] from his wallet, threw it on a sofa and poked Yuliya's face into it saying that he was not poor.' Overall, Kolya said he 'felt humiliated and insulted, and this justified his actions'. The humiliation he felt due to his low economic status vis-à-vis a woman was reinforced by the feeling of anger he felt when he was rejected by her as a sexual partner:

> He was absolutely sober. He did not remember how the conversation started. But he asked about the relationship between Yuliya and Natasha. Natasha replied that it was none of his business. He lost control. He did not remember how and which one of them he hit first. He only remembered that he beat Yuliya in her genitals because of his anger toward her. How and who he beat up, what he was doing, he remembered poorly. Perhaps the victims gave an accurate description, but they exaggerated the number of hits. He talked about their non-traditional relationship in derogatory terms.

The constant gendered humiliation that Kolya reported feeling due to his economic status turned into a violent affection when it was reinforced by the 'insult' of being rejected by Yuliya as a sexual partner. According to all testimonies, Kolya seemed to be comfortable enough to receive presents from Yuliya and generally be under her direct provision. In fact, it was probably his plan to maintain this relationship with Yuliya until they were married, when he could officially take control of her wealth. But that had never been Yuliya's plan, although she had played along to protect some of his insecurities. On the contrary, Yuliya's independence and diverse sexual desires made the entire relationship (which lasted around four months) doomed to end sooner rather than later. Incapable of dealing with rejection, Kolya resorted to violence in an attempt to restore his fragile masculinity, which had been threatened by both his unfulfilled promise (to himself) of being a 'manly provider' and a challenge to his sexual manhood. What Kolya was defending by hitting Yuliya in her genitals was his own position, which he felt was on shaky ground. It was this unacknowledged vulnerability of male heterosexual masculinity in a diverse society that served as a condition for susceptibility to violent affections. In this case, the vulnerability clearly lay at the intersection of class, gender and sexuality.

7
'Gay propaganda' as a meme

The society of love

In the Introduction to this book, I suggested that the distinction between mechanisms and techniques of power is crucial for understanding and analysing current changes in neo-disciplinary power relations. I showed that power works not by simply classifying various sexualities, but by creating inequality between different categories through affective encounters. In other words, affect adds a certain quality or value to the relationship of difference that makes these relationships power relations. This is power as mechanism. The question nevertheless remains as to how various affections are distributed across societies to convert difference into inequality. Or in other words, how various knowledges are delivered to people to employ affects in their encounters. This is the question of power as technique. In the classic Foucauldian approach, knowledge circulates in a panopticon-like structure, with commonly recognised sources of information that disseminate expert knowledge and are upheld as legitimate. In contrast, in the neo-disciplinary situation as exemplified by contemporary Russia in my research, any information may become knowledge for different people in different circumstances. This chapter is devoted to the analysis of how this process occurs.

There are many more or less queer approaches to analysing the circulation of emotions that some of the authors whom I cite throughout this book have put forward. While my approach departs from them in key respects, it is worth taking a moment to appreciate how some of those approaches understand the movement of emotions. The main distinction between others' approaches and mine is that the former are adjusted to explain power in its panopticon-like configuration, not its neo-disciplinary form. I thus outline two approaches to the analysis of societal emotions, which can be referred to as the *liberal approach*, represented by Martha Nussbaum's work, and the *queer left approach*, represented by Sara Ahmed's political economy of emotions. While I find many helpful insights in the latter approach, I argue that in the neo-disciplinary frame, political economy alone cannot give an accurate account of the messy, fragmented and decentralised processes that seem to go into making emotions move. Instead, I use the lens of memetics to explain how violent affections circulate, and how they find and attach to susceptible bodies.

The liberal approach is based on a clear definition of various emotions as good or bad ones and assumes that there is a source of authority which can easily trigger certain emotions within a society. Indeed, we know of many examples where politicians have exploited existing societal sentiments to gain popular legitimacy and claim authority by manipulating people's emotions, from the rise of national socialism in Germany to the recent Trump presidency in the US. This approach presumes, however, that politicians are in full control of other people's emotions, which can be mastered with predictable results. Thus, depending on which kinds of emotion are triggered by public figures, a society as a whole may be driven towards an 'inclusionary' or 'exclusionary' path respectively. This position is expressed by, for example, Martha Nussbaum (2013) and can be summarised as follows:

> . . . whereas a fascist or segregated society will cultivate negative, hostile emotions towards a section or sections of its population, a decent society will cultivate emotions such as compassion, sympathy and love. To put this another way, a decent society will cultivate an *emotional* (as opposed to a merely rational) appreciation of the equal worth and status of all its citizens. Simultaneously, such a society will endeavour to keep at bay those emotions – like projective disgust, envy, fear, shame and humiliation – which would undermine the positive side of the emotion-shaping project. One consequence of Nussbaum's argument (though she seems not to say this explicitly) appears to be that societies are 'bad' or 'decent' in significant part *precisely to the extent that* they successfully cultivate the 'right' emotions and keep the 'wrong' ones at bay. (Neal 2019, 87–8)

I find this view not only naïve, but also barely accurate. The cases I have analysed illuminate the unstable understanding of both emotions and their qualities, which this approach refuses to embrace, as if the disgusting and the ugly can never be appreciated, and as if love can never lead to violence. This stable understanding, in turn, results in a simple solution to identify and restrict 'bad' feelings – through politico-legal measures – from societal circulation and to spread 'good' emotions instead, as if the people in power solely pursue the goal of building a blissful and happy citizenry. Such an idea legitimises the view that political institutions can be trusted in the way they identify certain qualities as worthy of spreading across society. It ignores the complex composition of societies in which emotions and affectionate states function in conflicting conditions of economic, political, cultural and other kinds of inequalities that make societies fragmented. It is also based on a simple conception of agency – as if there can be a subject in total control of the situation.

I argue that it is important to do away with assumptions that assign good and bad qualities to this or that emotion before an analysis of the multiple outcomes of their functioning takes place. Take love, for example. Laurie Essig suggested many different ways in which the current understanding of love is exploited by corporations, state bureaucracies and even the British Crown for financial gain, resulting in multi-billion businesses and holding citizens in the private sphere's thrall, ultimately keeping them away from political engagement (Essig 2019). In a different study, Sianne Ngai finds promising functions of what she calls 'ugly feelings', including disgust, that point at the symptoms of current issues and inequalities with great precision (Ngai 2005). Or consider the already classic idea of Lauren Berlant, who uncovered the cruelty of optimism – when something you want actually stands in your way (Berlant 2011) – which seems like an accurate characterisation of Nussbaum's interpretation of political emotions. I turn now to find alternative ways to analyse the circulation of affections without presumptively assuming their status to be good or bad.

A political economy of affections

Another way to conceptualise the workings of affect in a society is to follow Ahmed's lead in scrutinising a political economy of emotions (Ahmed 2004). Popular accounts may dismiss political manipulations of emotions as simple 'smokescreens' meant to obscure the 'real' advances that politicians make. Yet this is actually a way of saying that emotions do some kind of work that goes far beyond merely manipulating people (Karstedt 2011, 1). Within the political economy of emotions, it is argued that affects touch, they stick, and they produce effects that may not be entirely anticipated or planned (Ahmed 2004). In other words, making feelings, emotions and affects circulate means enacting relations of power that are productive beyond anyone's control. In her research into the US context, Paula Ioanide frames this in terms of affect:

> Dominant U.S. constituents came to desire and support shifts towards military carcerality because they generated the affective rewards of state protection, national security, and global dominance. These shifts enabled people to experience affectively aggressive thrills and enjoyments through their identification with the state's power, allowing them to vicariously feel the pleasures of punishing, policing, and excluding so-called illegal immigrants, suspected terrorists, and supposedly incorrigible criminals. (Ioanide 2015, 6)

Ioanide analyses this as an economy that promises to generate rewards for its participants: 'emotions attached to race and sexuality have their own unique logics of gain and loss. Thus emotions function much like economies; they have mechanisms of circulation, accumulation, expression, and exchange that give them social currency, cultural legibility, and political power' (Ioanide 2015, 2). In other words, when those different affects circulate, a process of trade and exchange is enacted, in which the feeling of security (no matter if only an illusory one) is exchanged for political support and, consequently, for other commodities such as legitimacy, competencies, funds and so forth.

Judith Butler recounts a similar story. She recalls a Tea Party meeting where a politician assured the public that 'those who have serious illness and cannot pay for health insurance, or "choose" not to pay, as he would put it, would simply have to die' (Butler 2015b, 12). In response, supporters joyfully cheered at someone else's – albeit possibly their own – prospects for disease and death. They excitedly shouted, as Butler contends, 'the kind of joyous shout that usually accompanies going to war or forms of nationalist fervor' (Butler 2015b, 12). Such instances of the political invocation of emotions form a pattern. Shona Hunter has found that in every recent election round in the UK, parties have competed to convince the public that the country is failing (S. Hunter 2015, 4). She lists social and economic decline as well as inequalities and general discontent as the most prominent indicators of failure that politicians use to scare the electorate and rally them to vote for them, implying, certainly, that they will make Britain great again.

In such accounts, good and bad affects circulate simultaneously, and it seems hard to distinguish between the qualities of circulating emotions.

As with Butler's example of 'joy', these affects are prompted by the promise of someone's death. There is always the ambiguity that makes itself evident as affects tend to pop up in various emotional categories while they are circulating. This is why I propose calling some feelings *violent affections* – rather than good or bad emotions – to signal their orientation towards grievous outcomes for someone, regardless of the apparently positive linguistic form in which the emotions come to our attention. On the other hand, 'bad' feelings may be more visible, especially due to their greater resonance online – the primary source of information today. For instance, empirical evidence suggests that current venues for the spread of information, such as online social networks, pass on violent affections with greater ease than messages of love within political discussions (Stoeckle and Albright 2019; Sanford et al. 2021). In brief, hate generates more clicks than love. Most importantly for my analysis, power manifests itself with greater clarity in these relations of extreme asymmetry, which usually are articulated under the heading of bad feelings. A political economy of emotions approach is good for tracking these feelings down.

Violent illusions

Within the political economy of emotions, affects 'stick' to bodies and this is how they circulate: a reference to such and such body enacts the entire system of cultural signs that position the body in a certain hierarchy (Ahmed 2004). Yet, as I showed above, it is the *mechanism* of power relations that makes us feel boundaries and difference between subjects that encounter each other, not the *technique* of circulation. In *Animacies*, Mel Chen (2012) demonstrates that such affectionate processes of drawing boundaries and producing subjectivity entail constructing hierarchies between the objects that appear to each other. Developing this argument further and regarding the affectionate relations as networks, Shona Hunter explains this process of delineation as the ordering or social structuration of affects:

> integral to creating hierarchies of power. They *bind* people within a social order, but at the same time because they also *move* people, they expose the fragility of these orders, highlighting their shifting dynamic nature. If we look at the emotions in this way then the feeling work can be viewed as ongoing, continuous, *co-ordinating, cohering, ordering* activity. Therefore, as well as feelings circulating

within governance networks, they are *constitutive* of those very networks. (S. Hunter 2015, 30–1)

Hunter goes on to say that this work of affects is concealed, which follows the more general Foucauldian understanding of how power works: it orders objects in hierarchies from behind a cloak of invisibility to ensure the work of ordering (Foucault 1978b, 86). This analysis clearly refers to a panopticon-like configuration of power relations that prioritises institutional structures: 'emotions are productive of power in the sense that they constitute part of the means by which the state comes to be, they are integral to its gendered and raced orderings and are in turn part of the means by which the state enacts gendered and raced power' (S. Hunter 2015, 22). This view puts a lot of emphasis on the state precisely because it is seen as a source of ultimate legitimate authority (Brown 2008, 83). Yet, my objective is to develop tools to understand the circulation of affects as a technique of neo-disciplinary power relations, which are much messier, more complex and more multifarious than Ahmed's Foucauldian-inspired political economy of emotions presumes. This technique of power is decentralised.

Let me offer an illustration that gets to this point, albeit in a circuitous manner. Among the myriad academic texts published by Russian pundits around 2013 – the year the federal 'gay propaganda' law was adopted – one of the most widespread feelings put forward was that of a speedily approaching disaster (Kondakov 2016; 2020b; Moss 2017; 2021):

> . . . today, gay activists demand that the world of a homosexual be attributed with all the provisions of the world of the heterosexual community (rights, institutions, guarantees and so on). In other words, they seek legal recognition of gay marriages, gay celebrations and gay propaganda in the public sphere. But this eventually leads to unacceptably wide interpretations and legal recognition of such fundamental institutions as 'marriage' and 'family' which in turn may cause a negative 'multiplication effect' in all social institutions and practices. (Shchelkin 2013, 140)

This articulation ticks all the boxes of the usual anti-queer alarmist sentiment that supports the status quo and existing societal structures. In order to produce this argument, the author has to present marriage as a stable, inviolable and valuable heterosexual privilege and assert that it is under attack. The argument is charged with a doomsday prediction: the change will ultimately result in the disintegration of the entire country because marriage is so central to society. Consequently, the expansion of marriage rights to same-sex partners is understood not simply as a legal issue of recognition, but as the tell-tale harbinger of a destructive catastrophe in which one group will inevitably lose all its privileges as the other group claims them, resulting in the traumatic dissolution of society as we know it.

I offer this example to show that these feelings can be both illusory and accurate at the same time, depending on one's perspective, and it is important to capture this ambiguity, messiness and fluidity. These affections are illusory because the Russian LGBT+ community is a long way off achieving legal recognition and any claim to privileges or rights. Same-sex marriage in particular is not recognised anywhere in Russian territory; on the contrary, the conditions are set for ensuring that this inequality continues, as a popular referendum amended the Russian Constitution to emphasise the heterosexual nature of marriage in 2020. Yet, these feelings are also accurate because to a great extent marriage is central to any heteronormative society. The feelings also indicate a somewhat accurate conclusion that if same-sex marriage were recognised, Russian society would necessarily have to change, perhaps dramatically. It would become less heteronormative, to the extent that same-sex marriage allows a society to be less heteronormative. Is a change like this catastrophic? The quote above shows that it depends on how you feel about it. It depends which side of the social structure you feel you belong on.

This example helps me to illustrate that the political economy of emotions approach captures only the feeling that manifests in the pundit's quote, not the multitude of possible reactions to the circulated affections. Indeed, the feeling manifested there posits a privileged heterosexual population as threatened despite its privileges, and a threatening homosexual population as the one to blame for taking those privileges away – regardless of the accuracy of the observation. For some, the described situation is a matter of survival: the loss of privileges signals total societal elimination. It therefore offers a chance to be a hero. Since the whole of society is on the edge of collapse and it is clear enough who is to blame for it, the job of saving society can be taken into one's own hands.

In the cases I reviewed, many perpetrators were entirely or partially driven by vigilantism: helping the police and the state to make society, as many defendants claimed, 'a brighter place' by getting rid of 'homosexuals'. But this is not the whole picture. In addition to those captured by my sample, there are undoubtedly others who simply delegate their power to defend society to someone else who promises to fix this problem. And yet another group may feel no threat, or they may even identify with the threatening population. In sum, the political invocation of violent affections produces many varied effects: feelings of belonging to abstract social structures; political gains for populist state officials; direct violence in the form of physical acts of brutality justified by the claim of saving society; indifference; and victimisation. Ahmed's political economy of emotions does not account for these multiple effects of power. Instead, it only explains what is already evident from conservative alarmist enunciations such as the one quoted above.

Violent affections as memes

Thus, the question still stands: how do violent affections circulate? Is it enough to just put a claim of a threat out there while simultaneously identifying a population to blame for the threat? If this is the technique of power, what is the place of law – such a promising institution in the previous configuration of power relations – in this picture? In the works I have relied on throughout, it is usually assumed that affects are spread via performative citations and, therefore, once they stick to something, they are reproduced in that form over and over, in continuous acts of repetition. Sara Ahmed, for example, shows that affectionate forms have no specific identifiable origin, but are still 'cited' in relatively similar shapes throughout time (Ahmed 2004, 162). The notion of repetitive performative acts does have this omnipotent tendency, when small deeds (e.g. wearing a skirt) are understood as citations enacting big and barely changeable rigid structures: womanhood in a particular form and together with it the whole system of gender inequality, historical oppression of women, binary logic, structures of kinship, etc. (Butler 1990). Eve Kosofsky Sedgwick suggested that, notwithstanding, with every act of repetition something goes slightly differently and, one might say, wearing a skirt every time enacts a fairly different form of womanhood, gender inequality, practices of oppression and so on (Sedgwick 1993). However, the affections reviewed in Chapter 6 are much messier and more inconsistent than citationality supposes.

Because we do not know the entire history of these repetitions, such explanations look convincing as we have techniques of both reproduction and change that account for the processes of emotions' circulation. In other words, if something comes to an analyst's attention in a recognisable form, we register a reproduction. When something appears in a different form, we register dynamism, whose history may or may not be uncovered through an 'archaeological' analysis. What we cannot explain, though, are the processes of fading away, intensifying or re-emergence of the circulating affections themselves; the multiplicity and inconsistency that they sometimes exhibit; the individual significance that they may assume for some people and not for others; the fragmented nature of resonances that the citationality entails; and their modes of storing ideas for better times to circulate. For example, the violent affections analysed in the previous chapter usually follow a pattern: perpetrators start with an interest in queerness, next comes fear of queerness, and then anger towards queer people in the simplest of incidents, followed by regret in some cases. This complexity demonstrates that affections arise and fade away in different forms producing not repetitive acts, but a chaotic variety of affectionate states that result in another feeling: the feeling of heterosexual vulnerability and the need for its violent defence.

As I argued in the Introduction, I see memetics as a helpful analytical strategy to track the circulation of violent affections. Eliot Borenstein (2004; 2019) has used it to analyse the spread of conspiracy theories. Indeed, the circulation of violent affections and the spread of conspiracy theories have a lot in common as techniques for the dissemination of information that (1) has an original meaning and message but (2) resonates differently with different people; (3) invokes emotional reactions (4) to the point of violence; and (5) circulates across societies in the form of unsubstantiated knowledges. Essentially, violent affections and conspiracy theories are threatening messages – implying disastrous societal consequences – spread publicly to touch people and produce conflicting parties with neatly distributed blame and vulnerability. Both adapt to dynamic circumstances to ensure resonance among various fragments of society. What is important for Borenstein, and I find matching my analytical objectives, is that memes do not require any particular authority to ensure their circulation, as they move around by themselves. Apparently, for Borenstein, memes circulate 'in the absence of any real agency at all':

> The memes of conspiracy are the familiar tropes, images, and phrases that, over the lifespan of a given theory, reach beyond the initiated, becoming part of the larger discourse . . . each phrase can theoretically be used in an entirely neutral context, but they are so thoroughly entangled in a conspiratorial semantic web that their very invocation serves as shorthand for a larger narrative. Whether

that narrative is taken seriously or not is, in this instance, unimportant: it is the constituent memes of conspiracy, rather than the theory itself, that most easily reach the largest number of people. (Borenstein 2019, 48)

In fact, this demonstrates distributed agency (Bennett 2010) rather than the absence of it: the situation where practices are made up of the contributions of an assemblage of various actors. Thus, I propose to understand the circulation of violent affections as this lifespan of memes and this lifespan of memes as a technique of power relations in the neo-disciplinary regime, or what I call *the Memeticon*. Various pieces of information that may or may not trigger violent affections are spread publicly. If they aren't 'sticky' enough they fall into disuse. On the other hand, if they are successful they spread further and transform to become more resonant (i.e. find a form that resonates). Once they enter this realm of resonance, though, their reach is barely under anyone's control. Some mutations of violent affections may be efficient in various situations, or under different conditions – they may work for one person and have no effect on another. In short, they may encounter little response or a fierce reaction. Their only purpose is to continue circulating by any means: changing form, adapting, transforming, igniting responses to deliver that 'larger narrative'. Those who are susceptible to them interpret these memes as pieces of knowledge, 'a truth' in the Foucauldian account. Those who are not susceptible dismiss them as mere memes and move on.

Law and the meme

In Chapter 1, I offered to define law as a field encompassing a vocabulary and certain set of practices applied by qualified legal professionals in their everyday job of creating the appearance of justice. This legal field is maintained by the authority of the institution of justice, which ultimately applies violence to make sure the law is followed. In the classic Foucauldian theory of power, this authority is understood as a way of structuring power relations around a few common sources of expert knowledge or, in other words, the ability to produce effective truths. I argue that neo-disciplinary power relations strongly challenge this position of law. Instead of taking on its conventional guise as an organising and ordering principle, law becomes one of many isolation chambers: a professional space, the legal field, in which legal vocabulary is employed for the internal production of authority. And in the outside world, law has to compete with other forms of circulating knowledges.

Legal concepts used by actors in the legal field are essentially memes – that is, pieces of information seeking to be reproduced, and they find this space for reproduction among the institutional edifices that will also guarantee and partially govern the extent of their efficiency. Thus, to pronounce someone's guilt in a courtroom is much like the successful reproduction of a meme. Here the meme is the particular idea of guilt narrated by the court drawing on many resources. But these (legal) memes have a greater ambition than merely spreading around the legal field. In fact, for memes, the boundaries of the legal field are non-existent; it is just an isolation chamber where their replicability is highly guaranteed. Meanwhile, their aspirations are bigger, even though outside the legal field legal memes are stripped of the institutional procedures that guarantee their effectiveness and replicability.

Thus, while legal memes outside of the legal field carry with them some of their original authority and meanings, they also readily adapt to new environments to continue circulating – with or without immediate success. In addition, memes from other fields may end up in the legal field, becoming legal concepts and demanding procedural responses. Many of the terms for queer sexualities in Russia that I identified in Chapter 4 are memes from prison and profane vocabularies that have ended up in the court rulings. Accordingly, common non-legal phrases or scientific concepts may prove applicable and ultimately catchy in the courtroom. Conversely, we may sometimes invoke legal notions to prove a point, stress an argument or, ultimately, frame a grievance to seek recognition outside the legal field too. The point is that memes resonate across fields but have different chances of reproducing in different surroundings. An invocation of memes – which always have a legacy of their own invocation – thus produces different outcomes in different fields. They produce certain kinds of knowledge in some of those fields and not in others.

I argue that when a certain field claims ownership of a meme (when it becomes legal in my example), that meme works in two ways. First, the legal field can prove efficient in enhancing migrating memes with its authority. Some of the most innovative precedents may be said to work this way. Hate crime – if understood as a result of the insistence of activists on addressing violence motivated by perpetrators' negative feelings towards particular kinds of victim – is a good case in point. Taken from disenfranchised groups' collective experience of political struggles against violence, this notion has become widespread. As a meme, hate crime is an extremely efficient one: its trajectory from activist circles and NGOs to the legal field in the US enabled its replication across both political and legal vocabularies to find resonance in various countries around the world. In terms of meme replication, hate crime is a success story. This does not mean that it is successful in terms of remedying or preventing violence against the populations it promises to defend. On the contrary, as my analysis in Chapter 1 showed, anti-queer hate crime in Russia is just a meme: a titbit of packaged information unimportant for the processing of criminal justice.

This leads me to the second point. When a certain field claims ownership of an idea, it may also start to limit the replicability of the meme. In other words, when a meme becomes a professional term, this may limit its resonance due to its reduced ability to mutate, as professional terms have more strictly defined meanings. Consequently, legal memes may be enhanced by legal authority and limited by that same legal authority simultaneously. In this case, memes receive a guarantee of circulation within the legal field, but also risk limiting their potential for reproduction outside the legal field. This is the effect that I refer to as an 'echo chamber' or 'isolation chamber' in my approach: the limited resonance and replicability of certain memes within the confines of a professional field.

Sara Ahmed suggests that emotions need to be in constant circulation to grow in value and bring benefits for those who invoke them for political gain (2004, 45–6). Drawing on this idea, other scholars have emphasised that when affects cease to circulate, their ability to touch people fades (S. Hunter 2015, 30; Ioanide 2015, 15). I contend that affections are often enacted through the circulation of memes and, if we understand the circulation of memes as a technique for this type of power relations, then affections always produce some effects, even though sometimes they can be small, too individualised or invisible. The thing is that while memes may circulate in just one particular sub-field or a very specific field, they always strive for a chance to spread further. We might think of memes as lying in wait, biding their time until they get a chance to resonate in other fields. What matters is that, as memes circulate, they try to reach out and affectively touch as many bodies as possible, even if they have to wait or mutate to achieve this end. Once they resonate, they have a better chance of reaching out to those who are susceptible to their messages and who may respond accordingly by enacting the mechanism of power. This is how memes fuel power and constitute it. Memes deliver a message, but their interpretation varies depending on which bodies they reach. In this process, enhancing memes with legal authority may play a crucial role in both improving their resonance and limiting their replicability. The analysis in this book is meant to illuminate this memetic circulation in one corner of the legal field in contemporary Russia.

What's in a meme?

In Chapter 2, I claimed that the rise in queer victims of violence in Russia starting in 2013 was connected to the introduction of the gay propaganda law that same year. Aside from the correspondence of year, I had no other proof to support this allegation. Certainly, it might all be mere coincidence or explained by many other factors. In the remainder of this chapter, I set aside the cases of anti-queer violence and get down to tracing the whereabouts of one meme to demonstrate how information circulates, how affects touch people and how violence erupts in response. Doing so will help me build the case for my claim. The meme under review is 'propaganda of non-traditional sexual relationships' and its derivatives (the meme complex). Let me begin with an analysis of the meme's apparent content. What is it actually trying to say? It consists of three elements: (1) sexual relationships; (2) non-traditional; and (3) propaganda.

The first element, 'sexual relationships', sounds like a perfectly neutral concept meant to signify an intimate association with a relatively stable character as opposed to, say, a short overnight encounter. Indeed, its implied stability suggests that the phrase refers to a sort of orientation rather than an act of sex – it is about relationships, not just a brief affair. In a way, sexual relationships stand somewhere in between the sexual act and sexual orientation and, in this sense, may already signal its implied inferiority in comparison to an 'inherent' sexual orientation. Importantly, though, the kinship between these notions points to the idea that it is still about the sex act: it is about having relationships centred on what people do with their genitalia in bed (or other places). Finally, 'sexual relationships' is a euphemism for something considered inappropriate to spell out publicly – it is an attempt to hide queerness behind the presumed neutrality of the phrase: it is synonymous with such categories as 'homosexuality' in certain contexts. Queerness, nonetheless, is signalled through the second element of the phrase – the adjective 'non-traditional'.

'Non-traditional' is certainly a very rich adjective. I can only highlight a few of its major facets. To begin with, nowadays it is possible to say that there are 'traditional sexual relationships' to refer to heterosexuality, as well as 'non-traditional' ones – which was the entire reason for creating the phrase in the first place. In other words, 'traditional sexual relationships' are only a deviation from 'non-traditional sexual relationships'. And yet, 'non-traditional' signifies the novelty of this sexuality in the sense of its otherness in terms of time. Supposedly, it is something that has not been done before (it is not learned from previous experience codified in traditions). The absence of tradition in these sexual relationships refers explicitly to a past when such relationships did not exist: it constructs (obviously, unfoundedly) a version of the past without queerness. Implicitly, it works with space, too. Since there was an illusory past without queerness, someone must have brought it here from the outside. Hence, 'non-traditional' also suggests foreignness and mixing. Altogether, this implies a loss of purity – the purity of that past state, which was free from this new object brought from the outside with unclear intentions.

The last element of the meme, 'propaganda', adds a clear political dimension. The word is intended to describe the act of bringing sexual relationships that have no place in Russia to its innocent soil. Its goal is to convince people to switch sides. Since propaganda is the spread of information with the purpose of recruiting new adherents, the fear that this meme plays on becomes clear: those who have so far had 'traditional sexual relationships' are being convinced to explore something new, to try 'non-traditional' sexual relationships. According to this story, there is a malicious plot unfolding with outside support, which is seeking to penetrate Russian borders. The idea of propaganda also suggests that the story is largely about information: propaganda is the dissemination of political messages, it is not a medical procedure. In this, the meme matches the moment.

Looked at as a whole, then, the phrase 'propaganda of non-traditional sexual relationships' communicates the presence of a hostile, invasive informational threat that is working to corrupt people's basic sexual instincts. All three elements of the meme employ vulnerability and penetrability as their fundamental concepts. 'Propaganda' suggests that hostile information can penetrate someone's mind and influence it. The adjective 'non-traditional' acts on the premise that an outside object enters a space where it has not been before: it suggests both the original purity of that space and its demise under the impact of external penetration. Lastly, 'sexual relationships', in the phallocentric model that this meme definitely obeys, presuppose penetrability of a body with someone's genitalia. Moreover, being open to penetration (by information, by foreign traditions, by other people's body parts) flags one's vulnerability. This vulnerability can definitely be read in a positive sense, but it can also provoke defensiveness, depending on one's position.

Where art thou?

Let me trace the trajectory and permutations of the meme 'propaganda of non-traditional sexual relationships' to show why it has proved so successful. In great part, its replicability and stickiness can be explained by the authority of law, which has backed its various incarnations at various stages. Yet the authority of law may also guarantee its ultimate limitations.[2] The first thing to consider is that the 'non-traditional sexual relationships' element was itself an unofficial legal notion that had been circulating within the legal field in the aftermath of the decriminalisation of male homosexuality. Within Soviet political and legal discourse, references to queerness as 'non-traditional' would not have made sense. On the contrary, Soviet ideology was rather hostile to tradition per se and Soviet law actively fought against traditions as 'vestiges of the past' that held society back from its inevitable path towards communism (Kondakov 2014a). Queerness, especially male homosexual desire, was interpreted as such a 'vestige of the past': a tradition of earlier pre-revolutionary and indigenous societies that would wither and die either by itself as people marched towards a brighter future, or with the help of the ruling Party that flagged this tradition for abolition through criminal censure (Alexander 2018b; Healey 2001). In this environment, the 'non-traditional sexual relationships' meme, if it existed at all, had slim chances of survival until Soviet ideologies loosened.

Indeed, by the end of the 1980s, Soviet ideological pressure had been eroded under Gorbachev's new policies of glasnost and pluralism. This allowed the circulation of alternative opinions to the Party line. It was a moment of the romantic revival of Russian 'traditions', reinterpreted as having been lost due to the 1917 Revolution (Borenstein 2019, 110). I believe that this is most likely the cradle of the term 'non-traditional sexual relationships' and its derivatives. One uncorroborated account puts the term in the form 'non-traditional sexual orientation' and dates it to this period, claiming that it was used to refer to homosexuality in the everyday language of the late 1980s and beginning of the 1990s (yakov_a_jerkov 2013). Importantly, though, whenever the meme originated, it picked up pace in the 1990s and 2000s. Describing what can be referred to as the Russian queer tradition, Dan Healey remarks in his 2001 book that '[t]he history of modern ideas of homosexuality is tied to a plethora of forms of what Russians currently call (without irony) "non-traditional sex"' (2001, 12). He goes on to analyse popular psychological literature where the meme 'non-traditional' was widely used to signify 'queer' or 'gay' (Healey 2008), including in sex education books for children published by major presses which included chapters like 'Non-Traditional Sexual Relationships' (Kondakov 2021a, 52).

What this brief account demonstrates is the availability of the meme 'non-traditional sexual relationships' and its modifications in discourse that – given memes' ability to replicate – made it capable of resonating across various fields, including the legal one. I argue that this is exactly what happened after the decriminalisation of male homosexuality in 1993, when the legal field required a term to deal with queerness without necessarily citing its formerly delinquent connotations. While Soviet jurisprudence had a codified term for homosexuality, *muzhelozhstvo* (buggery), which captured both forced and voluntary intercourse, in the post-Soviet Russian Criminal Code, the term applies only to same-sex rape. This does not, of course, mean that Russian lawyers do not use the term to refer to any manifestations of queerness, but it does mean that the conditions for differentiating between forced and voluntary homosexuality emerged. Hence, 'non-traditional sexual relationships' and its variants were given a viable opportunity to prove effective in the legal field.

In sum, the two elements of the meme, 'non-traditional' and 'sexual relationships' – or the derivative 'non-traditional orientation' – originated with the demise of the USSR to signify queer sexualities. They appear to form a phrase that was meant to serve as a euphemism for practices that were too provocative to be talked about in public. In the 1990s, the meme was commonly used in everyday language and in popular psychology. With the decriminalisation of male homosexuality and the introduction of the new Criminal Code, the law also required a new term to distinguish between criminalised forms of same-sex practices (rape) and consensual ones. As a result, by the beginning of the 2000s, the meme 'non-traditional sexual orientation' was being used in legal contexts to refer to homosexuality (Kondakov 2021a, 52). At the time, it was mutating to find the catchiest form that would ensure its resonance and replicability: 'non-traditional' orientation, relationships, love, etc. Yet the term was already in currency, working to mark queerness as alien, foreign, brought in from the outside to take advantage of heterosexual vulnerability. In a way, its eventual merger with the 'propaganda' element was an inevitable next step in this legal meme's continued replication, ensuring the delivery of the idea of malicious plans behind the spread of queerness.

A proper gate

At the beginning of the 2000s, Russian legislators returned to the matter of criminalising voluntary same-sex intercourse. Lawyers who assisted parliamentarians in that period appeared to be against the idea, and re-criminalisation bills were usually referred to as 'illogical' due to an absence of victims in consensual sexual encounters (see e.g. RIA Novosti 2002). Hence, the meme 'propaganda of non-traditional sexual relationships' emerged as a way to suggest victimhood and wicked intentions – in short, to fabricate an illusory heterosexual victim. Beginning in 2003, Duma parliamentarians initiated a number of unsuccessful attempts to criminalise the 'propaganda of homosexuality' (Healey 2018, 145). The initiatives were rejected again with a legal argument expressed in this official conclusion of the Duma Legal Department: 'liability for propaganda of homosexuality cannot be established due to the absence of liability for homosexuality itself'.[3] In other words, one cannot assume criminal responsibility for propagating something that is not criminal. A way around this ruling was found, however, and the Duma debuted it in the 2013 'propaganda' bill, which frames such behaviours not as criminal in themselves but as administrative offences – in Russian law, it is a category of wrongdoing prohibited by law without criminal liability.

During this initial period, legislators used the term 'propaganda of homosexuality' (or rather *gomoseksualizma*) in their proposals, but had already commented on it in the media as 'propaganda of non-traditional sexual relationships' in 2007 (Credo Press 2007). By then, it was a common term (especially in the form 'propaganda of non-traditional sexual orientation') in the legal field where it was used by law enforcement bodies to justify misrecognition of LGBT+ rights. And so, even without a specific law banning such 'propaganda', prosecutors, police and public officials used other pieces of legislation to restrict the free dissemination of information about queerness. Here is an example:

> In March 2006, the prosecutor's office of the Rostov Region issued a warning to two local TV channels (TRK Pul's and TV-Company EkspoVIM) for broadcasting text messages 'that contained propaganda of non-traditional sexual orientation'. In the prosecutor's warning, it was stated that 'propaganda of homosexuality is banned in Russia'.

Another example can be found in an official letter rejecting a registration application for a Tyumen organisation, 'Rainbow House', in 2006. The letter signed, by the Directorate of the Federal Registration Service in Tyumen Region, Khanty-Mansi and Yamal-Nenets Autonomous Districts, said, among other things: 'The activities of the organisation related to propaganda of non-traditional sexual orientation can result in the collapse of Russian society and the state.' The authors went on to assert that propaganda of non-traditional sexual orientation threatens the territorial integrity of the Russian Federation (Kochetkov and Kirichenko 2009, 70).

The above quote suggests that the message of the propaganda meme is understood and intended by the legal actors who enact it: queerness is a threat that may ultimately destroy Russia. In their attempts to defend country and society, these legal actors did not require any new statute: they were perfectly fine interpreting the laws they had. This is why even in the absence of a gay propaganda law in 2006, they could still easily ban such 'propaganda' and say the ban was legal. At that point, 'propaganda of non-traditional sexual orientation' played out in law enforcement bodies' censorship practices as a pure meme resonating in the legal field without statutory support. But that was to change.

The country's highest court of law proved crucial in incorporating the meme 'propaganda of non-traditional sexual relationships' into official legal vocabulary. First, in a 2006 Constitutional Court decision on same-sex marriage, the rejection of homosexuality based on Russian 'traditions' was established. Second, in a 2010 Constitutional Court ruling on the Ryazan 'propaganda' law, judges merged 'propaganda' and 'non-traditional marital relationships' (*brachnye otnosheniya*) in the same sentence. The word 'marital' stood for 'sexual', implying that sex can be performed only within marriage and also prominently endorsing the 'relationships' element of the phrase (Kondakov 2020a, 403–4). The authority of the court served as a gateway for the meme to go viral. When the federal legislature returned to the idea of banning 'propaganda' of queerness in 2013, it simply adopted the court's definition, modifying the meme's form to 'sexual relationships' and, ultimately, codifying the entire meme's structure in Article 6.21 of the Code of Administrative Offences (2001).

Going viral and its risks

The trajectory of the 'non-traditional sexual relationships' meme is a story of great success, but it can also be seen as the story of its own demise. In its lust for reproduction, the meme built an exceptional career, from (1) being a shameful reference to queerness in common speech in the 1990s to (2) acting as a questionable term in popular psychology at the beginning of 2000s and (3) circulating among everyday law enforcement in the mid-2000s to, finally, (4) worming its way into the language of the highest court in the country and its federal legislature by the end of the 2000s and the beginning of the 2010s. Yet, for all its adventures, it may have returned to where it started. As an official legal term, it can now be used more commonly in the application of law by legal professionals. If this is so, the meme reverted to its previous position after exhausting its capacity to reproduce, or even lost its reproductive possibilities as it is now a legal term to be used within the confines of the legal field by legal professionals. Certainly, though, it did its dark job on the way.

The popularity of the meme 'non-traditional sexual relationships' and its variations peaked during the federal legislature debates on the 'propaganda' bill. Elena Pronkina's study suggests that the word 'propaganda' in LGBT-related articles in major Russian newspapers was most common (25.7%) in 2012–14 (Pronkina 2016). In fact, the terms 'propaganda' and 'tradition' were rarely used together before 2013, then peaked in 2013 and fell thereafter (Weaver and Koch 2019). However, these studies look at media publications overall and include articles that merely discuss the 'propaganda' bill. It is impossible to discuss the bill without replicating the 'propaganda' meme itself. So, in order to measure meme's replicability, I studied its behaviour outside direct discussions of the gay propaganda law. This suggests the chances of the meme's survival in contexts that are not related to the application of the 2013 propaganda law. I once again used my sample of 314 anti-queer violence cases, but this time as a collection of legal vocabulary outside of the propaganda law's application. I supplemented it with another original sample of such cases, composed of media reports on anti-queer violent incidents. This sample contained all identified media publications, totalling 4,398 titles from Integrum (the largest media database in Russia), relating to attacks on LGBT+ people in 2011–16 (Kondakov 2021b; Sexuality Lab 2017). I performed content analysis of the meme complex in titles of media articles and in full texts of court decisions (Kondakov 2021a).

Figure 7.1 Frequency of the 'non-traditional' meme complex in the titles of media articles and in court rulings relating to anti-queer violence in Russia, 2011–16

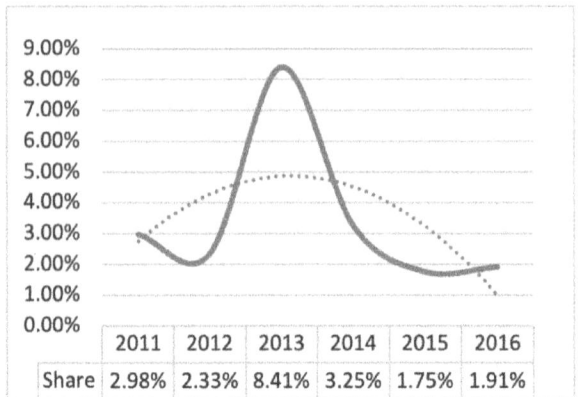

7.1a Percentage of media titles that include the term

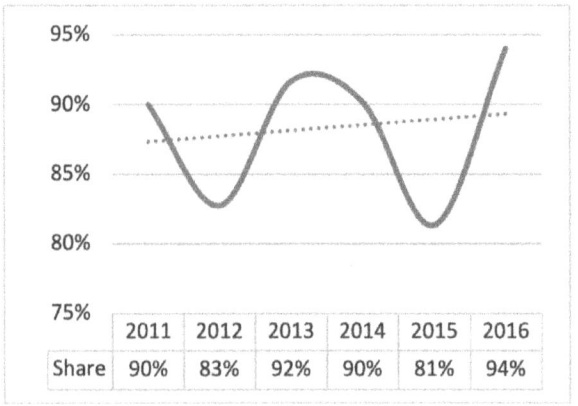

7.1b Percentage of court rulings that include the term

The frequency of the 'non-traditional' meme in media articles is represented in Figure 7.1a. The graph demonstrates that in these articles (which are not explicitly dedicated to the gay propaganda law), the meme complex referring to queer sexualities was used most often in 2013, the year the federal legislature's gay propaganda law was adopted. The analysis suggests that the meme had not been popular before 2013 and became even less so afterwards. Figure 7.1b represents the frequency of the same meme in court rulings on anti-queer violence. This graph shows a contrasting picture: the popularity of the meme was high even before the gay propaganda law, and it increased thereafter (notwithstanding some fluctuations). I include trend lines on the graphs in order to demonstrate this point and smooth the effects of the rather small sample.

One possible interpretation resulting from this comparison is that within the legal field, the meme 'propaganda of non-traditional sexual relationships' and its variants was already in common use prior to 2013. When the law was passed, it was simply reinforced as an official legal term and thus started to be used with even greater frequency. As for the media, they reacted positively to the meme at the very beginning as it was familiar. However, after the legalisation of the meme in 2013, the media opted out and stopped using it with the same frequency. This, at least, concerns those contexts in which the law on 'gay propaganda' was not being explicitly discussed.

This analysis demonstrates two important points for my study. First of all, it shows that the meme complex that I understand as a crucial conduit of violent affections did indeed spread widely at the time of the adoption of the gay propaganda law. It further indicates that the meme complex had the best chances of attaching itself to susceptible people around the same time, in 2013. This could explain the rise of anti-queer violence in that period encompassing the years spent on investigation, prosecution and adjudication of cases. Peaking anti-queer violence is one of the results of this meme's resonance, while we should add to this all the other effects that violent affections produced at the time, such as online bullying or displacement of LGBT+ people from Russia to other countries for refuge (Brock and Edenborg 2020; Lokot 2019; Novitskaya 2021; Mole 2021). Second, the comparison shows that the meme may have reached its zenith and that its demise was due to its codification in law. Anti-queer violence had also lessened somewhat by 2016, as my analysis in Chapter 2 attests, although of course all this may be subject to fluctuations in future. The decline, however, may be interpreted as the workings of the meme 'propaganda of non-traditional sexual relationships' and the subsequent slowing of its capacity to reproduce at the necessary pace outside of the legal field due to its meaning being narrowed to the legal definition of propaganda. The fewer people it reached, the less violence there was, it seems. I propose to attribute the demise of the meme to its narrower applicability after the adoption of the gay propaganda bill. When it became an official legal term and found itself increasingly enforced as such, it also fell into the trap of the legal field to an extent. While the meme is still quite powerful, its capacity to reproduce outside the legal field has waned somewhat. Considering its disturbing impact on violent affections, this is good news.

Why homosexuality?

As a central technique of power in the neo-disciplinary configuration of power relations, the circulation of the meme 'propaganda of non-traditional sexual relationships' proved successful in reaching as many people as possible. And because it reached so many people, it reached those susceptible to being touched by the meme in particular ways – signalling their vulnerability and penetrability and stimulating their need to defend themselves. In the cases I studied, the results of this were a turn to power and its mechanisms to produce asymmetrical relations through violent affections. In other words, the memetic spread of information is a technique of power, a technology. But the actual mechanism of power is impressing on those who are susceptible to violent affections.

The spread of the meme has been supported not only by the authority of the legal field and the interests of political elites, but also by favourable conditions for its flourishing. The timing coincided with a political crisis that was spawned in Russia after Putin's announcement that he would run for presidency for a third time. In 2011 and 2012 Putin's legitimacy was declining and people took to the streets to question parliamentarian and presidential election results, as well as Putin's fitness to rule (Clément 2015). In attempts to recover from this crisis and restore some legitimacy, the government initiated a number of smear campaigns that were meant to convince the populace of the current regime's capacity to protect them from a great variety of threats. In other words, Putin resorted to scapegoating queers among others. However, this alone is not enough to explain the rise of anti-queer violence in Russia and the resonance of the meme complex under analysis.

The meme 'propaganda of non-traditional sexual relationships' fell on fertile ground. Worldwide there was polarisation over LGBT+ rights which only reinforced the association of queerness with the 'West' and, for some countries that identified with the 'Eastern' end, with foreignness (Altman and Symons 2016; Edenborg 2021; Essig and Kondakov 2019). Those who wanted to read the meme's message as a message of foreign threat and the promise of protection had to invest very little effort. Most importantly, the meme played on the gnawing fear of a defeated Russian heterosexual masculinity. The meme sent a message of empowerment and community to those who felt their masculinity was injured. This is why the meme proved so prominent for Putin: while his message mutated over the years, its core was always the assurance of empowering defeated heterosexual masculinity injured by the dissolution of the USSR (Novitskaya 2017; Wiedlack 2020; Sperling 2014). Putin thus came to power with the message of restoring Russia's potency after the disastrous 1990s, continued with a revanchist promise of raising Russia 'from its knees', and now challenges the entire 'West' to finally establish the country's global domination. These messages have always been targeted at those who already feel injured – for people like Kolya introduced at the beginning of this chapter whose heterosexual masculinity was fragile due to his low class status (Morris and Garibyan 2021). Kolya's economic insecurities made him especially susceptible to threats towards his gender and sexuality. This susceptibility strongly resonates with the message of the 'gay propaganda' meme, especially in the context of Putin's geopolitical story. This time, the story went as far as to suggest Kolya's world domination.

Notes

1   The actual sentence was redacted from the file, but 7 years is the lower limit under Criminal Article 162 para. 3 and no extenuating circumstances were established in the courtroom. Suggesting a number involves pure guesswork, though, because sentencing could be influenced by a variety of factors.
2   A different version of this analysis looks at the traces of conservative discourse in the deployment of the term 'non-traditional sexual relationships' in law (Kondakov 2021a).
3   All documentation pertaining to the bills are published on the official Duma website. Any document can be reached by accessing the Duma database at http://duma.gov.ru/services/.

8
Conclusion: the global Memeticon

The Hate International

Two men got acquainted on Grindr, a gay dating app, and agreed to meet up for sex in a flat belonging to one of them. The invitee arrived with a drink and offered it to the host, who eagerly consumed it. A few moments later, the host fainted and fell unconscious. The guest let his associate, a young woman, into the flat. They immediately got down to searching the premises for valuables. They found credit cards and tried to use them to purchase diamonds online. In the courtroom, it was established that the defendants had used poison to knock their victim out, but ultimately murdered him due to an overdose.

Aside from the extravagant idea of buying diamonds, this type of story routinely features in my sample of 314 cases of anti-queer attacks in Russia. But this particular story occurred in London (Hutton 2021). The gay man, originally from Kilkenny in the Republic of Ireland, had been living in one of the central boroughs of England's capital for about 10 years prior to his death. His murderers were Londoners from the northern part of the city. None of them had any relevant connection with Russia.

A 2021 article in *The Guardian* suggested that anti-queer violence has been on the rise in the UK since 2015 (Brooks and Murray 2021). One of the activists interviewed for the article directly connected violent incidents with messy public discussions of reform bills pertaining to gender and sexuality, including the ban on conversion therapy, the Gender Recognition Act and sex education policies. Regardless of the intentions of the documents' authors, discussions around them spread quickly and resonated within a great many segments of British society, some of which were touched by violent affections and committed acts of violence. Moreover, the discussion fell on fertile ground for violent affections. The ground had been ploughed with polarising opinions on Brexit, which received official authorisation after the 2015 general election in the UK. In fact, the idea of Brexit – the Brexit meme – was almost entirely based on the protection of the British nation from outside penetration by EU bureaucracy, immigrants and foreign businesses (Creighton and Jamal 2020). While it had nothing to do with sexuality on a superficial level, it had an intimate and at times violent relationship with gender and sexuality – albeit discreetly. It seems that a very specific version of subjectivity proves most susceptible to violent affections when touched by the prospect of penetration. Whether in the UK or Russia, it is symbolically privileged heterosexual masculinity that goes on high alert at the very idea of penetration and yet, paradoxically, opens itself up to be penetrated with violent affections.

Parallels such as this can also be drawn with the 2016 election of Donald Trump in the US and the rise of violence there, especially violence perpetrated by white men (Bhambra 2017; Hodwitz and Massingale 2021; Sayer 2017). Scholars have even termed the rise of violent attacks on historically disadvantaged communities that are clearly connected to political speeches of the former US president 'the Trump Effect' (Warren-Gordon and Rhineberger 2021). Trump's rhetoric publicly espoused ugly sentiments such as fear and hate, as well as feeding on myriad conspiracy theories, memes and the misuse of social media to disseminate unsubstantiated information more generally – all resulting in incidents of both online and offline violence, as studies suggest (Keener 2019; Kelley-Romano and Carew 2019). These themes clearly mirror the situation in Russia that I have analysed throughout the book, and can also be found in places as diverse as Brazil, with its openly homophobic president Jair Bolsonaro; Ghana, where anti-queer sentiment in 2021 resulted in a reform that seeks to increase prison sentences to 10 years for homosexual practices and LGBT+ rights advocacy; and Hungary, which recently passed its own 'gay propaganda' law – an example of how the legal meme continues to resonate widely, now in other national contexts (Kováts and Pető 2017; McKenna 2020; Wahab 2021, 854; Akinwotu 2021; Walker 2021).[1]

Many analyses of the described phenomena centre on the idea of rhetorical manipulation, suggesting that politicians or their speech writers know exactly what they are doing. They know how to touch people and elicit the necessary reactions in response to their words; they deploy clear working strategies and consciously pursue very specific objectives. They are in total control of the situation. While I agree that many politicians and political strategists may indeed think they know what they are doing, I contend that much of what is happening is not under anyone's control. This does not exonerate those who disseminate hatred and fear, especially with manipulative intentions. On the contrary, they should be held accountable because they clearly exploit the opportunities that the current situation provides and unethically engage in stimulating public feelings for individual gain without thinking about the larger societal implications of their actions. What I want to say is that the Trump Effect, the success of the Russian 'gay propaganda' meme, the rise of hate crime in the UK, the anti-queer crackdown in Ghana, Bolsonarism and so on are all manifestations of a major shift that is taking place before our eyes. This shift is the reconfiguration of power relations from what Foucauldian theory describes as disciplinary power to a set of neo-disciplinary power relations characterised by fragmentation, fluidity and messiness.

What these stories have in common is that they occur because of a very specific technique of spreading hateful messages. To some people the messages sound bizarre and inaccurate; to others they are a much anticipated truth that had long been concealed. Those in the former group may not even believe that these messages could ever be taken seriously, until they see the quite real effects of their work. I argue that this technique of spreading information is not simply a method of delivering various messages to various factions in society. It is a technique of power relations and as such it involves a particular organisation of our societies in which the privilege of producing knowledge no longer belongs to the institutions of modernity (expert knowledge of science or state law). Rather, knowledge is something anyone can produce, but there is very little authority in any particular source of knowledge.

Ask Google

My investigation into this technique of power was conducted on a sample of anti-queer violent incidents. I concluded that prior to the introduction of the gay propaganda ban in 2013, the meme of gay propaganda was already in wide circulation across Russian society. While it was certainly enhanced and exploited by legal and political actors, it also moved around under its own steam in the search for resonance. As a result, cases of violence started to rise after 2013 because the 'propaganda' meme delivered a very specific message about malicious plans to undermine heterosexual masculinity, especially to those who were most susceptible to this message because of their insecurities. As the meme became a legal term, it had lost some of its power by 2016 due to a now narrower interpretation, and the violence decreased somewhat. In other words, as a *technique* of power the meme triggered a *mechanism* of power relations by touching people with violent affections, especially those who are susceptible to this kind of affective touch.

My research was devoted specifically to the study of violence. This does not mean, however, that the technique of neo-disciplinary power only produces violence or that it only enacts violent affections through the mechanism of its power relations. Power is productive, as Foucault famously claimed (1991, 194). It does not produce good or bad things, violence or non-violence. Rather, it produces subjects and asymmetries between them that may turn violent or affectionate or otherwise. On a more general level, it produces knowledge or truths: it structures the ways we know what we perceive and what to do about it. Meanwhile, our lives include more than violence. Neo-disciplinary power relations – just like any power relations – are not just productive of violent affections. As I have repeated time and again, Foucauldian disciplinary power worked on the premise of authoritative sources of knowledge assumed by the metaphor of the Panopticon. As this authority fades away, we can all probably feel how knowledge circulates differently in our everyday lives: we 'google' treatments instead of going to a GP; we watch short YouTube videos instead of learning from a history book; we click on a hashtag to study all the tweets about the latest news instead of watching a long and boring TV news show or picking up a newspaper. In these examples, medical professionals, historians and even TV anchors represent a type of expertise that has been a characteristic trait of various periods of modernity, from classic medical expertise to social science and humanities and conventional media. Professional fields with concentrated authority produced knowledge and offered it to populations.

Today, many people would rather trust random medical advice published on Instagram, an account of events from the past brought to you by the most technically advanced vlogger, or a political commentary from a next-door neighbour because their Twitter account is more popular than yours. In other words, the pillars of expertise are shaking and transforming into something new. Even if things do not work this way for everyone or in every instance, this technique of generating, circulating and consuming knowledge is becoming both increasingly widespread on the one hand, and individualised on the other: widespread because it is accessible to more people than ever before, and individualised because we search Google and watch YouTube on our own; we do not do these things collectively most of the time and – perhaps more importantly – these searches are increasingly tailored to our past individualised searches and viewing history. Therefore, what we do online, and how we find, interpret and otherwise consume information-which-becomes-knowledge is a socially conditioned practice usually performed in solitude but mediated by myriad networks of content producers, digital technology, AI algorithms and their human writers. There is no single panoptical guardian who will stop us watching that odd video or scrolling down to another inexplicably attractive Facebook opinion comment; instead there is a vast, diffuse, distributed network enabling and structuring these behaviours.

My claim in this book has been that the character of knowledge production is changing, and alongside this the configuration of power relations is also changing. I have described this in terms of the Panopticon's transformation into the Memeticon, which I further argued better captures contemporary fragmented, fluid and decentralised ways of crafting knowledge out of pieces of information. This change should be further investigated. What I show is that within this new configuration of power relations, older authorities compete with newer ones and find their messages both amplified and confined in isolation chambers. Medical and legal experts fight for the right to establish truth on an equal basis with random online commentators. Which truth will resonate? The arbiter here is no longer some expert, but the multifarious conditions in which various people receive, consume and interpret information – that is, the memes that are running across various fields in society and that are being read by fragmented society's portions.

My critical examples and comments about how knowledge is produced in multiple ways should not be read as dismissive of the new forms that truths and their generation are taking. In fact, I see a lot of democratising tendencies in these new processes. We now have greater access to ideas because many people have more opportunities to share their thoughts, views and feelings at their leisure. In order to publish an idea, one does not have to go through rigid and at times unfair procedures to verify one's privilege to generate knowledge, such as earning credentials or completing professional training, which usually depend on the amount of funds one can invest in obtaining them. In this sense, publicising ideas turns from the privilege of a few experts to the right of many people. This both diversifies and enlarges the pool of types of knowledge available for general consumption. Even though some of these pieces of information can be damaging, the diversity and accessibility that they ensure by circulating around is valuable in itself, and we need to find ways to deal with this tension – I sketch just a few below. Hence, rather than thinking about these new ways of producing knowledge as bad or good, it is more fruitful to think of the challenges and opportunities that the neo-disciplinary situation prompts. One of the major challenges is the difficulty of orienting ourselves in this immense and exponentially increasing pool of ideas. Which opinion deserves to be heard in a democratic society? What methods will governments and corporations find to exploit these new practices? How do citizens benefit from this knowledge rather than suffer from it?

We have already witnessed that many national governments and multinational corporations are aware of these processes and try to construe and use them for their own gain. The Russian government in particular is believed to be quite efficient online, organising troll factories to circulate memes and opinions glorifying Putin and undermining Western governments. The Western military alliance NATO defines a *troll factory* as 'an entity conducting disinformation propaganda activities on the Internet' and connects Trump's electoral victory directly to Russian internet trolls acting on Putin's command (NATO 2020, 1). In other words, these new power relations seem to employ memes and tweets rather than guns and bombs. Yet, as my analysis in this book shows, memes can and do kill. Moreover, the Russian invasion of Ukraine is another testament to the interrelated ties between bombs and memes. As the book also demonstrates, memes can have their own agendas that can be exploited by actors like Putin's trolls, but outside their effective control. Surely, the question of memes' agency demands further research. Such research may also shed light on whether it is possible for human actors to control memetic information more fully. My task in this book, however, is different. Instead, I look at the implications the Memeticon has in the legal field – a uniquely important social institution for the previous configuration of disciplinary power relations.

The old law in new circumstances

In the Introduction to this book, I suggested that my contribution could be referred to as queer criminology. Yet the version of queer criminology offered here does not simply focus on 'queer' identities or LGBT+ victims. Rather, my goal has been to decentre 'Western' arguments and issues from queer theory as outlined in Chapter 3 and to advocate for shifting the focus away from identity discussions and giving queer theory a global perspective. Hence, I proposed to do queer criminology with another objective in mind: to figure out new – queerer, perhaps – theoretical frameworks for rethinking law and conceptualisations of crime, violence, gender and sexuality. I thus proposed to look at the intersections between crime and sexuality through the idea of neo-disciplinary power. What does doing so bring to the table?

The idea of disciplinary power advocated by Michel Foucault reshaped criminology and studies of law more generally (Borch 2016; O'Malley and Valverde 2014; Valverde 2017; Leckey and Brooks 2010; Ashford and Maine 2020). It allowed analysts to engage critically with the law and, especially, with reformist thinking in law that gives the impression that criminal prohibition resolves many societal issues (Voruz 2011). Foucault's critical insights helped readers see that criminal prohibitions create new societal issues rather than resolve any, and reforms of law simply reinforce already authoritative actors such as the police at the expense of citizens' empowerment, including in the sphere of hate crime legislation (Spade 2015). Yet what happens if this disciplinary model of power is changing? Perhaps this change is not drastic, but it is distinct from power relations as we have known them so far. What new kind of framework could be used to look at law from the neo-disciplinary perspective?

The change in power relations that this book analyses seems to be deeply connected with the shift in information technologies (Miller et al. 2016). The internet made possible the empowerment of previously illegitimate sources of information by providing both a venue to speak and an audience to listen. Moreover, the invention of cheap individual devices that can easily connect online and provide a good user experience at a relatively low cost has amplified this connectivity. The coronavirus (Covid-19) pandemic, which was ongoing when this book was being written, only reinforced the tendency to be both ever more connected to the world and yet isolated from it. My central claim is that, in these circumstances, knowledge becomes any piece of information that means something deeply truthful and honest to some people and touches them with affections. Furthermore, new technologies and devices intensify these affective processes by delivering information to as many people as possible worldwide.

What would the old law's response to this shift be? One of the classical responses to a messy and disordered informational flood is censorship. Not unlike in Russia after the lawless 1990s, states and corporations worldwide are trying to create rules governing what can and cannot be published on the platforms they monitor or manage. Hate, disinformation and conspiracies are among the things that are being prohibited on some social networks but not others. New laws regulating personal data are being developed to craft the illusion of control remaining in the hands of internet users and states. These responses demonstrate that a struggle and negotiation is going on over who can determine the production and consumption of knowledges and how that can be done. At the same time, attempts to ban certain types of information and regulate how we deal with information more generally have created new, parallel spaces of resistance. The reshuffling is ongoing.

It is not only states or corporations that invest efforts in censorship. There are activist citizens who also try to censor information in an attempt to control it. This type of control proliferates in the universalisation of the demand for 'safe spaces': any space that is expected to be safe, that is free from homophobia, hatred, violence, triggers, sexual content, etc. In these spaces, information is closely policed to bar negative feelings from public discussions for all the best reasons. Yet, a side effect of such efforts is the same as states' and corporations' censorship attempts: fragmentation, cutting off opinions that do not confirm one's own worldview, and creating echo chambers. Meanwhile, violent affections still circulate and resonate with greater strength in spaces where it is now 'safe' to articulate homophobia. From those spaces violence erupts, as the analysis in this book has shown. While I argue that safe spaces should definitely exist, I also believe that the demand for safety cannot be universally applied to all spaces: there have to be spaces that are unsafe, to allow mixture, questioning and critique.

What might an alternative response to censoring or controlling messy and disordered memes be in the situation of shifting power relations? How can we deal with memes and the new ways of producing knowledge for purposes other than political manipulation or market exploitation? In other words, what does neo-disciplinary power look like outside the old legal approaches? While there might be many answers to these questions, I want to offer a general reflection resulting from what I have learned when reviewing my 314 cases of anti queer violence.

One of the main ideas forming the backdrop to my analysis was the idea of vulnerability, which may be a key for further theoretical, political and practical reflections. Vulnerability is a condition of feeling alive that is simultaneously the condition of being open to the workings of power (Ahmed 2004, 68–9; Butler 2015a, 76). Perpetrators of violence are afraid of their vulnerability actualised in the moment of affectionate encounters and imagined as a sign of imminent penetration that they try to stop. But what if we embrace this vulnerability rather than assume a defensive position? Can exposure and approximation to one's own vulnerability produce responses other than violent ones?

I propose this line of thinking as an alternative for queer criminology and studies of law and violence more generally. Instead of conceptualising legal responses in terms of prohibitions, what if we think about vulnerability and exposure in terms of dealing with them and coming out stronger? Law can be taken critically in this respect as unable to offer anything other than violent protection from violence. But I argue that it can be taken differently. It is the work of ethical systems to offer non-violent protection from violence. Therefore, in our epoch of intensifying neo-disciplinary power, law may become an ethical system of guidelines that is fluid, adaptive and receptive, facilitating careful and fruitful relationships into which people enter as vulnerable subjects by default.

The idea of vulnerability

The idea of vulnerability is the opposite of the idea of defence, or the idea of safety ensured through the old law of prohibition and through various forms of violence. It assumes openness and exposure to the outside world, which is unknown and can hurt. When such exposure is understood as dangerous, vulnerability may demand defence or enclosure in safer spaces in order to ensure survival. However, the belief that the state of vulnerability can be overcome is only an illusion. On the contrary, our very exposure and capacity for pain and pleasure prove that we are still in this world, that we are still alive, exposed to affects, that we are feeling subjects in relations with others. If – unlike the perpetrators of anti-queer violence – we can turn our vulnerability into an asset, perhaps we can find important routes to openness and exposure that will help us deal with neo-disciplinary power ethically and in a modality of collective care of the self. This would entail being predisposed to changes, messiness and mixtures. As well as not assuming the painlessness of our being in the world.

My individual journey towards writing these lines was indeed full of pain, but that pain has not made me a victim of endured violence. Coming from a working-class family in a rural setting, my intellectual career did not take off easily. In St Petersburg my regional accent was something to make fun of; in Spain, where I spent my formative years, I was sometimes not European enough, which somehow was supposed to make me weaker; and my interest in queer stuff was not appreciated by official Russian academia. Those same prejudices impacted on my relationship with queerness. Silencing and violent episodes around sexuality are things I know from both my everyday and activist experiences. Random strangers and the state attacked me, the latter especially when it made my partner a refugee running from state persecution (Shtorn 2020b) – an experience that has become inextricable from my own life story. Even though my privileges as a white cisgender male also impacted on my trajectories, at any point in time I could have just given up. Yet, these experiences made me relate to my vulnerability differently, to the point of going meticulously through 314 stories of much more brutal anti-queer violence than I have endured. It was not a safe and pleasant job – it was indeed full of suffering and tears – but I thought that I must expose myself to these stories in order to convey them further. My own experience did not make me ready for this work, but it did make me keep going and see it through. I argue that I kept going not because of some strength of mine, but because I acknowledged my vulnerability – through opening myself to the feeling of pain and still persisting.

A practice of exposure that embraces vulnerability concerns not only individuals or authors; it is about texts, too. For a text to embrace vulnerability means being open to various styles and genres of narrative. While this book is an academic text, it has opened itself up to penetration by elements of fictional genres – from detective stories to sensational pulp fiction – in its choice of words and style of presentation of some of the analysed materials. I contend that this departure from rigid academic styles does not make the book weaker or less factual, but rather opens it up for further interpretation, consumption and reworking outside of the university fortress. I might not be pleased by some of these interpretations and reworkings, but I shall always defend the book's right to stand its own ground. I know that its electronic copy will be made accessible to anyone for free to ensure this independent life of the book.

In fact, if I could, I would probably make this writing more fragmented and fluid than it is, by telling the stories of anti-queer violence through other forms of expression: painting, graffiti, dance, video, sound art, etc. I am not proficient in any of these types of art. As a part of the research project behind the book, St Petersburg-based feminist artist Polina Zaslavskaia created a series of watercolours (Zaslavskaia 2017).[2] She painted grey silhouettes of the weapons with which queer people were murdered in the cases under analysis. These shapes were hung in the air to speak to others. They might speak of violence and sexuality, but they can also speak about the everyday lives of different people across Russia. Here is a shovel to clear up a path in the snow. There is a pair of women's tights to wear on weekdays. That picture is of a simple clothes iron that almost everyone has in their home. Everyday objects speaking about everyday practices, including violence. I would imagine such art forms discussing violence as important in conveying myriad meanings and engaging audiences in co-production in more ways than an academic text can do. Such forms of expression offer to acknowledge one's vulnerability, allowing one to start working with violence to better understand it and, therefore, control it more effectively.

In my sample of anti-queer attacks in Russia, there are many more stories that are left untold. I do not know whether they will ever find their way outside the confines of my sample of criminal court rulings and in what form they might start circulating. A graphic novel? A crime show? What I do know is that these stories teach us in their queer ways not only about sexuality and violence in Russia, nor only about neo-disciplinary power relations as I understand them. They also teach us about the everyday lives of people in the most remote areas of Russia – about relationships that are not usually exposed to the outside gaze. These stories can tell us about the ways in which disability intersects with sexuality, age and masculinity. They offer a glimpse into relationships within a large family with three sons of different ages who have to live in a small bedroom and share their emerging desires. Or they can show us conditions of extreme poverty converted into the brutal murder of two people and arson simply for a pair of shorts. They expose misuses of institutionalised power by a gang of police officers who terrorise gay men for ransom. Or the stories of everyday choices made by sex workers who might radically reconsider their engagement in same-sex intercourse in the very process. And what about the intersections of ethnicity, race, migration status and class that produce a position which can too easily be taken advantage of and sexually abused? Here stories of cross-dressing homeless people and exiled lesbians seeking to return home circulate. One way or another, these stories will flow and offer their versions of truths to different people. Besides, many more such samples of stories can be created in other countries where anti-queer violence is recorded by the criminal justice system. These records are rich sources of information that become knowledge through the process of sharing.

Ideally these stories will be encountered by people prepared for the exposure. This exposure and preparedness will ensure that we react without defensiveness prompted by violent affections. Hence, one way to think beyond law is to figure out how to be vulnerable but keep going regardless of pain and suffering. Since for the most part we deal with memes as individuals and on our own, we need tools to assess and interpret this information. In these new circumstances, when any information may become knowledge, those who are equipped with critical thinking tools may be better off than others. It is indeed harder to orient ourselves in the ever-increasing flow of information. In Foucauldian terms, which also began this book, knowing how to distinguish trustworthy information from other kinds requires the technique of care of the self – a way to escape power relations. In this sense, if governments are eager to lay down new regulations to protect citizens from the current informational hazards of the online world, then they should think about investing more in teaching critical skills at all levels of education. This, however, puts these very same governments in danger of de-legitimisation. As I argue, the state is under pressure. It too is losing legitimacy along with the other institutions of authority that anchored modernity. Thus, perhaps we must also rethink the vulnerability of the state – a Russian, British, American, Brazilian, Ghanaian, etc. state, as well as the state as such. Rather than continue to act within the protective logic of classic prohibitive law, perhaps we need to ask how the state might find new ways to thrive through an acknowledegment of its own vulnerability. In these circumstances, critical thinking becomes more important than ever to make sense of the fragmented knowledge that is being produced without the backing of authoritative expertise found in the past.

One final thought. Earlier I showed that memes deliver their messages, but the interpretation of those messages depends on various circumstances, including context, situation and the environment in which they come to our attention. Thus, rather than try to embark on the impossible mission of selecting 'bad' memes and censoring them, when seemingly 'good' memes may still deliver violent affections, I suggest that it is possible to think of ways of changing these very circumstances. To do so would demand that we stop being afraid of words and rather start the work of reclaiming them. The idea of reclaiming in queer theory appears as a fruitful avenue to rethink how various memes are perceived. It seems that changing the use of a word may also change the interpretation of its quality, just like the case of 'queer' turning from a derogatory to a community notion. Hate, disgust or violence are all vulnerable to our reinterpretations, reclaiming and ownership. The work that the reclaiming of these feelings and practices can do may change the way we experience those very feelings and practices. Memes can be vulnerable, too.

Notes

1. It is important to remember as well that originally 'gay propaganda' was UK prime minister Margaret Thatcher's idea when she sought to prohibit discussions of LGBT+ topics in schools in the 1980s (Burridge 2004).
2. The illustrations were also used in a report published as a much earlier result of this analysis (Kondakov 2017c).

References

Legal documents

Code of Administrative Offences (2001) *Kodeks Rossijskoj Federacii ob administrativnyh pravonarushenijah* [Code of Administrative Offences of the Russian Federation].
Constitutional Court (2006) *Opredelene* [Decision], No 496-O.
Constitutional Court (2010) *Opredelene* [Decision], No 151-O.
Constitutional Court (2014) *Postanovlenie* [Decree], No 24-P.
Council of Europe (2006) *Advisory Committee on the Framework Convention for the Protection of National Minorities, Second Opinion on the Russian Federation.* ACFC/OP/II (2006)004, dated 11 May 2006.
Criminal Code (1996) *Ugolovnyj kodeks Rossijskoj Federacii* [Criminal Code of the Russian Federation].
Criminal Procedure Code (2001) *Ugolovno-processual'nyj kodeks Rossijskoj Federacii* [Criminal Procedure Code of the Russian Federation].
European Commission against Racism and Intolerance (2002) *General Policy Recommendation No 7*, dated 13 December 2002.
Federal Law (2013) *O vnesenii izmenenij v stat'ju 5 Federal'nogo zakona 'O zashhite detej ot informacii, prichinjajushhej vred ih zdorov'ju i razvitiju' i otdel'nye zakonodatel'nye akty Rossijskoj Federacii v celjah zashhity detej ot informacii, propagandirujushhej otricanie tradicionnyh semejnyh cennostej'* [On modification of Article 5 of the Federal Law 'On protection of children from information harmful to their wellbeing and development' and other normative acts of the Russian Federation for the purposes of protection of children from information that promotes negation of traditional family values], No 135-FZ, dated 29 June 2013.
Law of Ryazan Region (2006) *O zashhite nravstvennosti i zdorov'ja detej v Rjazanskoj oblasti* [On protection of the morality of children in Ryazan Region], No 41-OZ, dated 22 March 2006.
Law of St Petersburg (2012) *O vnesenii izmenenij v Zakon Sankt-Peterburga 'Ob administrativnyh pravonarushenijah v Sankt-Peterburge'* [On modifications of the Law of St Petersburg 'On administrative offences in St Petersburg'], No 108-18, dated 7 March 2012.
OSCE (2004a) *Combating Anti-Semitism*. Decision No 607, dated 22 April 2004.
OSCE (2004b) *Tolerance and the Fight Against Racism, Xenophobia and Discrimination*. Decision No 621, dated 29 July 2004.
Penal Code (1997) *Ugolovno-ispolnitel'niy kodeks Rossijskoj Federacii* [Penal Code of the Russian Federation].
RSFSR Criminal Code (1926) *Ugolovnyj kodeks Rossijskoj Socialisticheskoj Federativnoj Sovetskoj Respubliki* [Criminal Code of the Russian Socialist Federative Soviet Republic].
RSFSR Criminal Code (1960) *Ugolovnyj kodeks Rossijskoj Socialisticheskoj Federativnoj Sovetskoj Respubliki* [Criminal Code of the Russian Socialist Federative Soviet Republic].

Other sources

Adler, Libby. 2018. *Gay Priori: a queer critical legal studies approach to law reform*. Durham, NC: Duke University Press.
Ahmed, Sara. 2004. *The Cultural Politics of Emotion*. New York: Routledge.

Ajani, Gianmaria. 1995. 'By Chance and Prestige: legal transplants in Russia and Eastern Europe'. *American Journal of Comparative Law* 43(1): 93–117.

Akinwotu, Emmanuel. 2021. 'Ghana: anti-gay bill proposing 10-year prison sentences sparks outrage'. *The Guardian*. https://www.theguardian.com/global-development/2021/jul/23/ghana-anti-gay-bill-proposing-10-year-prison-sentences-sparks-outrage (accessed 8.2.2022).

Alaimo, Stacy, and Susan Hekman (eds). 2008. *Material Feminisms*. Bloomington, IN: Indiana University Press.

Alexander, Rustam. 2018a. 'Sex Education and the Depiction of Homosexuality under Khrushchev'. In *The Palgrave Handbook of Women and Gender in Twentieth-Century Russia and the Soviet Union*, edited by Melanie Ilic, 349–64. London: Palgrave Macmillan.

Alexander, Rustam. 2018b. 'Soviet Legal and Criminological Debates on the Decriminalization of Homosexuality (1965–75)'. *Slavic Review* 77(1): 30–52.

Altman, Dennis, and Jonathan Symons. 2016. *Queer Wars*. Cambridge: Polity.

Amico, Stephen. 2014. *Roll Over, Tchaikovsky! Russian popular music and post-Soviet homosexuality*. Urbana, IL: University of Illinois Press.

Amietta, Santiago Abel. 2021. 'In Ambiguous Times and Spaces: the everyday assemblage of lay participation to Argentine courthouses'. *Social & Legal Studies* 30(4): 605–26.

Andreevskikh, Olga. 2020. 'Non-Heteronormative Gender Performativity and the Discursive Value of Celebrity Brand Gesture: a case study'. In *Ethical Glamour and Fashion: styling persona brands*, edited by Samita Nandy, Kiera Obbard, and Nicole Bojko, 38–48. Toronto: Waterhill Publishing.

Andrianova, Varvara. 2018. 'The Everyday Experiences of Russian Citizens in Justice of the Peace Courts'. In *A Sociology of Justice in Russia*, edited by Agnieszka Kubal and Marina Kurkchiyan, 68–91. Cambridge: Cambridge University Press.

Anzaldúa, Gloria. 1999. *Borderlands/La Frontera: the new mestiza*. San Francisco, CA: Aunt Lute Books.

Aripova, Feruza. 2020. 'Queering the Soviet Pribaltika: criminal cases of consensual sodomy in Soviet Latvia (1960s–1980s)'. In *Decolonizing Queer Experience: LGBT+ narratives from Eastern Europe and Eurasia*, edited by Emily Channell-Justice, 95–113. London: Lexington Books.

Ashford, Chris, and Alexander Maine (eds). 2020. *Research Handbook on Gender, Sexuality and the Law*. Cheltenham: Edward Elgar.

Ayoub, Phillip M. 2016. *When States Come Out: Europe's sexual minorities and the politics of visibility*. Cambridge: Cambridge University Press.

Baer, Brian. 2002. 'Russian Gays/Western Gaze: mapping (homo)sexual desire in post-Soviet Russia'. *GLQ: A Journal of Lesbian and Gay Studies* 8(4): 499–521.

Baer, Brian. 2009. *Other Russias: homosexuality and the crisis of Post-Soviet identity*. Basingstoke: Palgrave.

Baker, James, Kelly Clancy, and Benjamin Clancy. 2019. 'Putin as Gay Icon? Memes as a tactic in Russian LGBT+ activism'. In *LGBTQ+ Activism in Central and Eastern Europe: resistance, representation and identity*, edited by Radzhana Buyantueva and Maryna Shevtsova, 209–38. Newcastle: Palgrave.

Bandes, Susan A. (ed). 1999. *The Passions of Law*. New York: New York University Press.

Bandes, Susan A., and Jeremy A. Blumenthal. 2012. 'Emotion and the Law'. *Annual Review of Law and Social Science* 8(1): 161–81.

Barad, Karen. 2007. *Meeting the Universe Halfway: quantum physics and the entanglement of matter and meaning*. Durham, NC: Duke University Press.

Barchunova, Tatiana, and Oksana Parfenova. 2010. 'Shift-F2: the internet, mass media, and female-to-female intimate relations in Krasnoyarsk and Novosibirsk'. *Laboratorium: Russian Review of Social Research* 2(3): 150–72.

Bennett, Jane. 2005. 'The Agency of Assemblages and the North American Blackout'. *Public Culture* 17(3): 445–66.

Bennett, Jane. 2010. *Vibrant Matter: a political ecology of things*. Durham, NC: Duke University Press.

Berlant, Lauren. 2011. *Cruel Optimism*. Durham, NC: Duke University Press.

Bhambra, Gurminder K. 2017. 'Brexit, Trump, and "Methodological Whiteness": on the misrecognition of race and class'. *British Journal of Sociology* 68(S1): S214–32.

Billé, Franck. 2010. 'Different Shades of Blue: gay men and nationalist discourse in Mongolia'. *Studies in Ethnicity and Nationalism* 10(2): 187–203.

Bingham, Natasha. 2017. '"Telling Our Stories": print media interpretations of Moscow lesbians' life stories in 2004 and 2005'. *Journal of Lesbian Studies* 21(1): 120–31.

Blackmore, Susan. 2000. *The Meme Machine: popular science*. Oxford: Oxford University Press.

Blix, Stina Bergman, Kathy Mack, Terry Maroney, and Sharyn Roach Anleu. 2019. 'Introducing an Interdisciplinary Frontier to Judging, Emotion and Emotion Work'. *Oñati Socio-Legal Series* 9(5): 548–56.

Bogdanova, Elena A. 2019. 'Objectives of Russian Law Schools Today: what is the "ideal jurist"?' *International Journal of the Legal Profession* 26(2–3): 295–320.

Bonacker, Thorsten, and Kerstin Zimmer. 2019. 'The Localization of Sexual Rights in Ukraine'. In *LGBTQ+ Activism in Central and Eastern Europe: resistance, representation and identity*, edited by Radzhana Buyantueva and Maryna Shevtsova, 153–84. Newcastle: Palgrave.

Borch, Christian. 2016. *Foucault, Crime and Power: problematisations of crime in the twentieth century*. London: Routledge.

Borenstein, Eliot. 2004. 'Survival of the Catchiest: memes and postmodern Russia'. *Slavic and East European Journal* 48(3): 462–83.

Borenstein, Eliot. 2008. *Overkill: sex and violence in contemporary Russian popular culture*. Ithaca, NY: Cornell University Press.

Borenstein, Eliot. 2019. *Plots against Russia: conspiracy and fantasy after socialism*. Ithaca, NY: Cornell University Press.

Borisova, Tatiana. 2008. 'Russian National Legal Tradition: Svod versus Ulozhenie in nineteenth-century Russia'. *Review of Central and East European Law* 33(3): 295–341.

Borozdina, Ekaterina, Anna Rotkirch, Anna Temkina, and Elena Zdravomyslova. 2016. 'Using Maternity Capital: citizen distrust of Russian family policy'. *European Journal of Women's Studies* 23(1): 60–75.

Bourdieu, Pierre. 1984. *Distinction: a social critique of the judgement of taste*. Cambridge, MA: Harvard University Press.

Bourdieu, Pierre. 1987. 'The Force of Law: toward a sociology of the juridical field'. *Hastings Law Journal* 38(5): 814–54.

Bourdieu, Pierre. 2013. *Outline of a Theory of Practice*. 28th ed. Cambridge: Cambridge University Press.

Brinkema, Eugenie. 2014. *The Forms of the Affects*. Durham, NC: Duke University Press.

Brock, Maria, and Emil Edenborg. 2020. '"You Cannot Oppress Those Who Do Not Exist": gay persecution in Chechnya and the politics of in/visibility'. *GLQ: a journal of lesbian and gay studies* 26(4): 673–700.

Brooks, Libby, and Jessica Murray. 2021. 'Spate of Attacks across UK Sparks Fear among LGBTQ+ Community'. *The Guardian*, 29 August 2021. https://www.theguardian.com/uk-news/2021/aug/29/spate-of-attacks-across-uk-sparks-fear-among-lgbtq-community (accessed 8.2.2022).

Brown, Wendy. 1993. 'Wounded Attachments'. *Political Theory* 21(3): 390–410.

Brown, Wendy. 1995. *States of Injury: power and freedom in late modernity*. Princeton, NJ: Princeton University Press.

Brown, Wendy. 2008. *Regulating Aversion: tolerance in the age of identity and empire*. Princeton, NJ: Princeton University Press.

Browne, Kath, and Catherine Nash (eds). 2010. *Queer Methods and Methodologies: intersecting queer theories and social science research*. Farnham: Ashgate.

Buist, Carrie, and Emily Lenning. 2016. *Queer Criminology*. New York: Routledge

Burridge, Joseph. 2004. '"I Am Not Homophobic But...": disclaiming in discourse resisting repeal of section 28'. *Sexualities* 7(3): 327–44.

Butler, Judith. 1990. *Gender Trouble: feminism and the subversion of identity*. New York: Routledge.

Butler, Judith. 1993. *Bodies That Matter: on the discursive limits of sex*. New York: Routledge.

Butler, Judith. 1997. *Excitable Speech: a politics of the performative*. New York: Routledge.

Butler, Judith. 2015a. *Senses of the Subject*. New York: Fordham University Press.

Butler, Judith. 2015b. *Notes Toward a Performative Theory of Assembly*. Cambridge, MA: Harvard University Press.

Buyantueva, Radzhana. 2018. 'LGBT Rights Activism and Homophobia in Russia'. *Journal of Homosexuality* 65(4): 456–83.

Buyantueva, Radzhana, and Maryna Shevtsova (eds). 2019. *LGBTQ+ Activism in Central and Eastern Europe: resistance, representation and identity*. Newcastle: Palgrave.

Cassiday, Julie A. 2014. 'Post-Soviet Pop Goes Gay: Russia's trajectory to Eurovision victory'. *The Russian Review* 73(1): 1–23.

Cassiday, Julie A., Helena Goscilo, and Jonathan Brooks Platt. 2019. 'Introduction'. *The Russian Review* 78(2): 183–200.

Chandler, Andrea. 2021. 'Russia's Laws on "Non-Traditional" Relationships as Response to Global Norm Diffusion'. *International Journal of Human Rights* 25(4): 616–38.

Channell-Justice, Emily (ed.) 2020. *Decolonizing Queer Experience: LGBT+ narratives from Eastern Europe and Eurasia*. London: Rowman & Littlefield.

Chen, Mel Y. 2012. *Animacies: biopolitics, racial mattering, and queer affect*. Durham, NC: Duke University Press.

Chernova, Dasha. 2016. 'The Right to Dance as the Right to the Body'. *Journal of Social Policy Studies* 14(3): 423–36.

Clech, Arthur. 2017. 'Homosexual Subjectivities in the Multinational USSR'. *Le Mouvement Social* 260(3): 91–110.

Clech, Arthur. 2019. 'Between the Labour Camp and the Clinic: *tema* or the shared forms of late soviet homosexual subjectivities'. In *Soviet and Post-Soviet Sexualities*, edited by Richard Mole, 32–55. London: Routledge.

Clément, Karine. 2015. 'Unlikely Mobilisations: how ordinary Russian people become involved in collective action'. *European Journal of Cultural and Political Sociology* 2(3–4): 211–40.

Connell, Raewyn. 1995. Masculinities. Berkeley, CA: University of California Press.

Coole, Diana, and Samantha Frost (eds). 2010. *New Materialisms: ontology, agency, and politics*. Durham, NC: Duke University Press.

Cooper, Davina. 2013. *Everyday Utopias: the conceptual life of promising spaces*. Durham, NC: Duke University Press.

Court Department. 2012. *Dannye Sudebnoy Statistiki* [Court Statistical Data]. http://cdep.ru/index.php?id=79&item=1776 (accessed 8.2.2022).

Court Department. 2013. *Dannye Sudebnoy Statistiki* [Court Statistical Data]. http://cdep.ru/index.php?id=79&item=2362 (accessed 8.2.2022).

Court Department. 2015. *Dannye Sudebnoy Statistiki* [Court Statistical Data]. http://cdep.ru/index.php?id=79&item=3418 (accessed 8.2.2022).

Court Department. 2021. *Otchet Ob Itogah Dejatel'nosti Sudebnogo Departamenta Pri Verhovnom Sude Rossijskoj Federacii Za 2020 God* [Report of Results of Activities of the Court Department of the Supreme Court of the Russian Federation in 2020]. http://www.cdep.ru/userimages/Otchet_SD_za_2020_g.pdf (accessed 8.2.2022).

Credo Press. 2007. "Spravedlivaya Rossiya" Predlagaet Ugolovno Nakazyvat' Za Reklamu "Netraditsionnykh Seksual'Nykh Otnosheniy" [The Just Russia Suggests to Criminalise Advertisement of 'Non-Traditional Sexual Relationships']. https://credo.press/82176/ (accessed 8.2.2022).

Creighton, Mathew J., and Amaney A. Jamal. 2020. 'An Overstated Welcome: Brexit and intentionally masked anti-immigrant sentiment in the UK'. *Journal of Ethnic and Migration Studies* 0(0): 1–21.

D'Emilio, John. 2012. *Sexual Politics, Sexual Communities*. 2nd ed. Chicago, IL: University of Chicago Press.

Darakchi, Shaban. 2021. 'Bulgarian LGBTQI Movement: generations, identifications, and tendencies'. *Sexualities*, March.

Davison, Kate. 2019. 'The Sexual (Geo)Politics of Loyalty: homosexuality and emotion in Cold War security policy'. In *From Sodomy Laws to Same-Sex Marriage: international perspectives since 1789*, edited by Sean Brady and Mark Seymour, 123–40. London: Bloomsbury.

Davison, Kate. 2021. 'Cold War Pavlov: homosexual aversion therapy in the 1960s'. *History of the Human Sciences* 34(1): 89–119.

Dawkins, Richard. 2016. *The Selfish Gene*. 40th Anniversary ed. Oxford: Oxford University Press.

de Lauretis, Teresa. 1991. 'Queer Theory: lesbian and gay sexualities. Introduction'. *Differences* 3(2): iii–xviii.

Deakin, Simon. 2002. 'Evolution for Our Time: a theory of legal memetics'. *Current Legal Problems* 55(1): 1–42.

Deakin, Simon. 2011. 'Legal Evolution: integrating economic and system approaches symposium on evolutionary approaches to (comparative) law: integrating theoretical perspectives'. *Review of Law and Economics* 7: 659–84.

Dezalay, Yves, and Mikael Rask Madsen. 2012. 'The Force of Law and Lawyers: Pierre Bourdieu and the reflexive sociology of law'. *Annual Review of Law and Social Science* 8(1): 433–52.

Dorogov, Dmitry. 2017. 'Po tu storonu antagonizma: gibrid kak model' postkolonial'noj kvir-sub"ektnosti'. *Zhurnal sociologii i social'noj antropologii* 20(5): 39–58.

Dubrovskiy, Dmitry. 2020. 'Akademicheskoe soobshhestvo i "gumanitarnaja" sudebnaja jekspertiza po jekstremizmu v sovremennoj Rossii'. *Journal of Social Policy Studies* 18(4): 721–36.

Duggan, Lisa. 2003. *The Twilight of Equality? Neoliberalism, cultural politics, and the attack on democracy.* Boston, MA: Beacon Press.

Dzmitryieva, Aryna. 2021. 'Becoming a Judge in Russia: an analysis of judicial biographies'. *Europe-Asia Studies* 73(1): 131–56.

Dzmitryeva, Aryna, Vadim Volkov, Kirill Titaev, and Mikhail Pozdnyakov. 2015. *Rossijskie sud'i: sociologicheskoe issledovanie professii.* St Petersburg: EUSP Press.

Edenborg, Emil. 2021. '"Traditional Values" and the Narrative of Gay Rights as Modernity: sexual politics beyond polarization'. *Sexualities*, April.

Eng, David L. 2010. *The Feeling of Kinship: queer liberalism and the racialization of intimacy.* Durham, NC: Duke University Press.

Engelstein, Laura. 1992. *The Keys to Happiness: sex and the search for modernity in fin-de-siècle Russia.* Ithaca, NY: Cornell University Press.

Engelstein, Laura. 1995. 'Soviet Policy toward Male Homosexuality'. *Journal of Homosexuality* 29(2–3): 155–78.

Essig, Laurie. 1999. *Queer in Russia: a story of sex, self, and the other.* Durham, NC: Duke University Press.

Essig, Laurie. 2014. '"Bury Their Hearts": some thoughts on the specter of homosexuality haunting Russia'. *QED: a journal in GLBTQ worldmaking* 1(3): 39–58.

Essig, Laurie. 2019. *Love, Inc.: dating apps, the big white wedding, and chasing the happily neverafter.* Berkeley, CA: University of California Press.

Essig, Laurie, and Alexander Kondakov. 2019. 'A Cold War for the Twenty-First Century: homosexualism vs. heterosexualism'. In *Soviet and Post-Soviet Sexualities*, edited by Richard C.M. Mole, 79–102. London: Routledge.

Favarel-Garrigues, Gilles. 2021. '"Vigilante Shows" and Law Enforcement in Russia'. *Europe-Asia Studies* 73(1): 221–42.

Favarel-Garrigues, Gilles, and Ioulia Shukan. 2019. 'Perspectives on Post-Soviet Vigilantism. Introduction'. *Laboratorium: Russian review of social research* 11(3): 4–15.

Fedorovich, I., Y. Yoursky, and V. Djuma. 2020. *Permit Do Not Forbid. How laws on the prohibition of 'gay propaganda' operate in the Russian Federation.* Tallinn: ECOM.

Fejes, Nárcisz, and Andrea P. Balogh (eds). 2012. *Queer Visibility in Post-Socialist Cultures.* Bristol: Intellect.

Fiks, Yevgeniy. 2020. *Dictionary of the Queer International.* Ontario: Guelph.

Floyd, Kevin. 2009. *The Reification of Desire: toward a queer Marxism.* Minneapolis, MN: University of Minnesota Press.

Foucault, Michel. 1978a. *The Care of the Self. Volume 3 of The History of Sexuality.* 1st American ed. New York: Pantheon Books.

Foucault, Michel. 1978b. *An Introduction. Volume I of The History of Sexuality.* New York: Pantheon Books.

Foucault, Michel. 1988. *The Use of Pleasure. Volume 2 of The History of Sexuality.* 1st Vintage Books ed. New York: Vintage Books.

Foucault, Michel. 1991. *Discipline and Punish. The Birth of Prison.* 2nd ed. New York: Vintage Books.

Foucault, Michel. 2021. *Confessions of the Flesh. Volume 4 of The History of Sexuality.* New York: Pantheon Books.

Fried, Michael S. 1999. 'The Evolution of Legal Concepts: the memetic perspective'. *Jurimetrics* 39(3): 291–316.

Garstenauer, Therese. 2018. 'Gendernye i Kvir-Issledovanija v Rossii'. *Sociology of Power* 30(1): 160–74.

Gdeetotdom. 2011. *Rejting samyh 'seksual'nyh' rajonov Moskvy* [Rating of the most 'sexual' districts of Moscow]. https://www.gdeetotdom.ru/articles/1850173-2011-11-09-rejting-samyih-seksualnyih-rajonov-moskvyi/ (accessed 8.2.2022).

Gessen, Masha. 1994. *The Rights of Lesbians and Gay Men in the Russian Federation: an International Gay and Lesbian Human Rights Commission report*. San Francisco, CA: International Gay and Lesbian Human Rights Commission.

Godwin Phelps, Teresa. 2016. 'The Evolving Rhetoric of the Gay Rights and Same-Sex Marriage Debate'. In *Rhetorical Processes and Legal Judgments: how language and arguments shape struggles for rights and power*, edited by Austin Sarat, 54–82. Cambridge: Cambridge University Press.

Golder, Ben, and Peter Fitzpatrick. 2009. *Foucault's Law*. London: Routledge.

Golunov, Ivan. 2020. '"Drinking Heroin": the witnesses against *Meduza* correspondent Ivan Golunov were part of a setup. Here's how Russia's police abuse a system that empowers them to jail virtually anyone.' *Meduza*. https://meduza.io/en/feature/2020/11/10/drinking-heroin (accessed 8.2.2022).

Goodwin, Jeff, James M. Jasper, and Francesca Polletta (eds). 2001. *Passionate Politics: emotions and social movements*. Chicago, IL: University of Chicago Press.

Gorbachev, Nikolay. 2019. '"Pidor mechty." Nikolay Gorbachev o rekleiminge rugatel'stv i gomofobii' ["The Dream Fag". Nikolay Gorbachev on reclaiming of slurs and homophobia]. *SpidCenter*. https://spid.center/ru/articles/2595/ (accessed 8.2.2022).

Gradskova, Yulia. 2020. 'Personal is Not Political? The sexual self in Russian talk shows of the 1990s'. *Sexuality & Culture* 24(2): 389–407.

Gradskova, Yulia, Alexander Kondakov, and Maryna Shevtsova. 2020. 'Post-Socialist Revolutions of Intimacy: an introduction'. *Sexuality & Culture* 24(2): 359–70.

Gregg, Melissa, and Gregory J. Seigworth. 2010. 'An Inventory of Shimmers'. In *The Affect Theory Reader*, edited by Melissa Gregg and Gregory J. Seigworth, 1–25. Durham, NC: Duke University Press.

Grigoryeva, Irina, L.A. Vidyasova, Alexandra Dmitriyeva, and Ol'ga Sergeyeva. 2015. *Pozhilyye v Sovremennoy Rossii: Mezhdu Zanyatost'yu, Obrazovaniyem i Zdorov'yem*. St Petersburg: Aleteya.

Gulevich, Olga A., Evgeny N. Osin, Nadezhda A. Isaenko, and Lilia M. Brainis. 2018. 'Scrutinizing Homophobia: a model of perception of homosexuals in Russia'. *Journal of Homosexuality* 65(13): 1838–66.

Halberstam, Jack. 2005. *In a Queer Time and Place: transgender bodies, subcultural lives*. New York: New York University Press.

Halberstam, Jack. 2018. *Trans*: a quick and quirky account of gender variability*. Oakland, CA: University of California Press.

Hall, Casey D., Umedjon Ibragimov, Minh N. Luu, and Frank Y. Wong. 2020. 'Actives, Passives and Power: heteronormative gender norms and their implications for intimate partner violence among men who have sex with men in Tajikistan'. *Culture, Health & Sexuality* 22(6): 630–45.

Halperin, David M. 2012. *How To Be Gay*. Cambridge, MA: Harvard University Press.

Halperin, David M., and Valerie Traub. 2009. *Gay Shame*. Chicago, IL: University of Chicago Press.

Hartblay, Cassandra. 2014. 'Welcome to Sergeichburg: disability, crip performance, and the comedy of recognition in Russia'. *Journal of Social Policy Studies* 12(1): 111–25.

Haynes, Amanda, Jennifer Schweppe, and Seamus Taylor (eds). 2017. *Critical Perspectives on Hate Crime: contributions from the island of Ireland*. Basingstoke: Palgrave.

Healey, Dan. 2001. *Homosexual Desire in Revolutionary Russia: the regulation of sexual and gender dissent*. Chicago, IL: University of Chicago Press.

Healey, Dan. 2002. 'Ischeznovenie Russkoy "Tyotki," Ili Kak Rodilas Sovetskaya Gomofobiya' [Disappearance of the Russian "Tyotka", or How Soviet Homophobia Was Born]. In *O Muzhe(n)Stvennosti* [On Masculinity], edited by Sergei Oushakine, 414–31. Moscow: Novoye literaturnoye obozreniye.

Healey, Dan. 2006. 'Can We "Queer" Early Modern Russia?'. In *Queer Masculinities, 1550–1800: Siting Same-Sex Desire in the Early Modern World*, edited by K. O'Donnell and M. O'Rourke, 106–24. Basingstoke: Palgrave.

Healey, Dan. 2008. '"Untraditional Sex" and the "Simple Russian": nostalgia for Soviet innocence in the polemics of Dilia Enikeeva'. In *What Is Soviet Now? Identities, legacies, memories*, edited by Thomas Lahusen and Peter H. Solomon, 173–91. Munster: Lit Verlag.

Healey, Dan. 2009. *Bolshevik Sexual Forensics: diagnosing disorder in the clinic and courtroom, 1917-1939*. DeKalb, IL: Northern Illinois University Press.

Healey, Dan. 2014. 'Love and Death: transforming sexualities in Russia, 1914–22'. In *Cultural History of Russia in the Great War and Revolution 1914–22*, edited by Murray Frame, Boris Kolonitskii, Steven Marks, and Melissa Stockdale, 2:151–78. Bloomington, IN: Slavica Publishers.

Healey, Dan. 2018. *Russian Homophobia from Stalin to Sochi*. London: Bloomsbury.

Heller, Dana. 2007. 'T.A.T.u. You! Russia, the Global Politics of Eurovision, and Lesbian Pop'. *Popular Music* 26(2): 195–210.

Hendley, Kathryn. 2012. 'Who Are the Legal Nihilists in Russia?' *Post-Soviet Affairs* 28(2): 149–86.

Hendley, Kathryn. 2017. *Everyday Law in Russia*. Ithaca, NY: Cornell University Press.

Hendley, Kathryn. 2018a. 'A Profile of Russian Law Students: a comparison of full-time versus correspondence students'. *Journal of Legal Education* 67(4): 1005–34.

Hendley, Kathryn. 2018b. 'Mapping the Career Preferences of Russian Law Graduates'. *International Journal of the Legal Profession* 25(3): 261–77.

Hodwitz, Omi, and Kelley Massingale. 2021. 'Rhetoric and Hate Crimes: examining the public response to the Trump narrative'. *Behavioral Sciences of Terrorism and Political Aggression* 0(0): 1–18.

Horne, Sharon, Elin Ovrebo, Heidi Levitt, and Sonja Franeta. 2009. 'Leaving the Herd: the lingering threat of difference for same-sex desires in postcommunist Russia'. *Sexuality Research and Social Policy* 6 (June): 88–102.

Hunt, Alan, and Gary Wickham. 1994. *Foucault and Law: towards a sociology of law as governance*. London: Pluto Press.

Hunter, Rosemary. 2015. 'More than Just a Different Face? Judicial diversity and decision-making'. *Current Legal Problems* 68(1): 119–41.

Hunter, Shona. 2015. *Power, Politics and the Emotions: impossible governance?* London: Routledge.

Hutton, Brian. 2021. 'Murdered All-Ireland Irish Dance Champion "an Explosion of Colour"'. *The Irish Times*. https://www.irishtimes.com/life-and-style/people/murdered-all-ireland-irish-dance-champion-an-explosion-of-colour-1.4527441 (accessed 8.2.2022).

Iarskaia-Smirnova, Elena, Pavel Romanov, and Valentina Yarskaya. 2015. 'Parenting Children with Disabilities in Russia: institutions, discourses and identities'. *Europe-Asia Studies* 67(10): 1606–34.

Ingbrant, Renata. 2020. 'Michalina Wisłocka's *The Art of Loving* and the Legacy of Polish Sexology'. *Sexuality & Culture* 24(2): 371–88.

Ioanide, Paula. 2015. *The Emotional Politics of Racism: how feelings trump facts in an era of colorblindness*. Paolo Alto, CA: Stanford University Press.

Ivanova, Ekaterina. 2015. 'Gendernyj disbalans v rossijskom sudejskom korpuse: feminizacija professii'. *Journal of Social Policy Studies* 13(4): 579–94.

Janssen, Diederik F. 2021. 'Homosexual/Heterosexual: first print uses of the terms by Daniel von Kászony (1868–1871)'. *Journal of Homosexuality* 0(0): 1–6.

Jones, Tiffany. 2020. 'Double-Use of LGBT Youth in Propaganda'. *Journal of LGBT Youth* 17(4): 408–31.

Jong, Ben De. 1982. '"An Intolerable Kind of Moral Degeneration": homosexuality in the Soviet Union'. *Review of Socialist Law* 8(1): 341–57.

Kadri, Aavik. 2019. 'Negotiating Uncertainty: sexual citizenship and state recognition of same-sex partnerships in Estonia'. In *LGBTQ+ Activism in Central and Eastern Europe: resistance, representation and identity*, edited by Radzhana Buyantueva and Maryna Shevtsova, 127–52. Newcastle: Palgrave.

Kahn, Jeffrey. 2018. 'The Richelieu Effect: the Khodorkovsky case and political interference with justice'. In *A Sociology of Justice in Russia*, edited by Marina Kurkchiyan and Agnieszka Kubal, 231–58. Cambridge: Cambridge University Press.

Karstedt, Susanne. 2002. 'Emotions and Criminal Justice'. *Theoretical Criminology* 6(3): 299–317.

Karstedt, Susanne. 2011. 'Handle with Care: emotions, crime and justice'. In *Emotions, Crime and Justice*, edited by Susanne Karstedt, Ian Loader, and Heather Strang, 1–19. Oxford: Hart.

Katsuba, Sergei. 2021. 'Hate Crimes against LGBT in Russia: legal status and research problems'. *Pravo i politika*, No 3: 61–78.

Katz, Daniel Martin, Michael James Bommarito, Julie Seaman, Adam Candeub, and Eugene Agichtein. 2011. 'Legal N-Grams? A simple approach to track the "evolution" of legal

language'. SSRN Scholarly Paper ID 1971953. Rochester, NY: Social Science Research Network.
Keener, Kayla. 2019. 'Alternative Facts and Fake News: digital mediation and the affective spread of hate in the era of Trump'. *Journal of Hate Studies* 14(1): 137–51.
Kelley-Romano, Stephanie, and Kathryn Carew. 2019. 'make america hate again: donald trump and the birther conspiracy'. *Journal of Hate Studies* 14(1): 33–52.
Kerf, Justine De. 2017. 'Anti-Gay Propaganda Laws: time for the European Court of Human Rights to overcome her fear of commitment'. DiGeSt. *Journal of Diversity and Gender Studies* 4(1): 35–48.
Khodzhaeva, Ekaterina, and Yulia Shesternina Rabovski. 2016. 'Strategies and Tactics of Criminal Defenders in Russia in the Context of Accusatorial Bias'. *Russian Politics & Law* 54(2–3): 191–226.
Kirichenko, Kseniya, and Valery Sozayev. 2013. *Doklad ob implementacii Rossijskoj Federaciej Rekomendacii CM/Rec(2010)5 Komiteta Ministrov Soveta Evropy gosudarstvam-uchastnikam o merah po bor'be s diskriminaciej po priznaku seksual'noj orientacii ili gendernoj identichnosti* [Report on the implementation of CM/Rec(2010)5 by the Russian Federation]. St Petersburg: Rossijskaja.
Kislitsyna, Polina. 2020. 'Religious Experiences in Life Stories of Homosexuals and Bisexuals in Russia'. In *Decolonizing Queer Experience: LGBT+ narratives from Eastern Europe and Eurasia*, edited by Emily Channell-Justice, 173–88. London: Lexington.
Knight, Kyle. 2020. 'Russian Court Rules Transgender Woman's Firing Unlawful'. Human Rights Watch. https://www.hrw.org/news/2020/06/25/russian-court-rules-transgender-womans-firing-unlawful (accessed 8.2.2022).
Kochetkov, Igor, and Kseniya Kirichenko. 2009. *Polozhenie lesbiyanok, geev, biseksualov, trasgenderov v Rossiyskoy Federatsii* [The Situation of Lesbians, Gay Men, Bisexuals and Transgender People in Russia]. Moscow: Moscow-Helsinki Group.
Kon, Igor. 2006. *Liki i maski odnopoloy lyubvi: Lunnyi svet na zare* [Facets and Masks of Same-Sex Love: moonlight on the dawn]. 2nd ed. Moscow: AST.
Kon, Igor. 2009. *Muzhchina v menjajushhemsja mire* [Men in the Changing World]. Moscow: Vremya.
Kon, Igor. 2010. *Klubnichka na berezke: Seksual'naja kul'tura v Rossii* [Strawberry on a Birch Tree: sexual culture in Russia]. Moscow: Vremya.
Kon, Igor. 2011. 'Tri v odnom: Seksual'naja, gendernaja i semejnaja revoljucii' [Three in One: sexual, gender and family revolutions]. *Zhurnal Sociologii i Social'noj Antropologii* [Journal of Sociology and Social Anthropology] 14(1): 51–65.
Kondakov, Alexander. 2012. 'Legal Wounds: the meaning of human rights for lesbians and gay men in Russia'. *Laboratorium: Russian review of social research* 4(3): 84–104.
Kondakov, Alexander. 2013a. 'Do Russians Give a Damn about Homosexuality?'. *OpenDemocracy*. https://www.opendemocracy.net/en/odr/do-russians-give-damn-about-homosexuality/ (accessed 8.2.2022).
Kondakov, Alexander. 2013b. 'Resisting the Silence: the use of tolerance and equality arguments by gay and lesbian activist groups in Russia'. *Canadian Journal of Law and Society / Revue Canadienne Droit et Société* 28(3): 403–24.
Kondakov, Alexander. 2014a. 'Formirovanie kvir-arhiva issledovanij seksual'nostej' [The Formation of a Queer Archive of Sexuality Studies]. In *Na pereputye: Metodologia, teoria i praktika LGBT i lvir-issledovaniy* [On the Crossroads: methodology, theory and practice of LGBT and queer studies], edited by Alexander Kondakov, XI–XXII. St Petersburg: Centre for Independent Social Research.
Kondakov, Alexander. 2014b. 'The Silenced Citizens of Russia: exclusion of non-heterosexual subjects from rights-based citizenship'. *Social & Legal Studies* 23(2): 151–74.
Kondakov, Alexander. 2016. 'Teaching Queer Theory in Russia'. QED: a journal in *GLBTQ worldmaking* 3(2): 107–18.
Kondakov, Alexander. 2017a. 'Javljajutsja li LGBT social'noj gruppoj?: Sociologicheskie kriterii ponjatija dlja sudebnyh interpretacij' [Are LGBT a Social Group? Sociological criteria for adjudication]. *Sravnitel'noe konstitutsionnoe obozrenie* [Comparative Constitutional Review] 6(121): 131–44.
Kondakov, Alexander. 2017b. 'Konfiguracii prava: Kak dejstvuet zakon o "propaganda" v shkolah' [The Configurations of Law: how the 'propaganda' law functions in schools]. *Zhurnal sociologii i social'noj antropologii* [Journal of Sociology and Social Anthropology] 20(5): 187–206.

Kondakov, Alexander. 2017c. *Prestupleniya na pochve nenavisti protiv LGBT v Rossii* [Hate Crimes against LGBT in Russia]. St Petersburg: Centre for Independent Social Research.

Kondakov, Alexander. 2017d. 'The Feminist Citizen-Subject: it's not about choice, it's about changing it all'. *Feminist Legal Studies* 25(1): 47–69.

Kondakov, Alexander. 2017e. 'Rabstvo i gospodstvo kak vzaimnye otnoshenija: analiz dogovornyh otnoshenij v BDSM' [Slavery and Domination as Mutual Relationships: an analysis of consent in BDSM]. *Novoe literaturnoe obozrenie* [The New Literary Observer] 147(5): 170–83.

Kondakov, Alexander. 2018a. 'Crip Kinship: a political strategy of people who were deemed contagious by the shirtless Putin'. *Feminist Formations* 30(1): 71–90.

Kondakov, Alexander. 2018b. 'Spatial Justice: how the police craft the city by enforcing law on prostitution'. In *Understanding Sex for Sale: meanings and moralities of sexual commerce*, edited by May-Len Skilbrei and Marlene Spanger, 199–214. London: Routledge.

Kondakov, Alexander. 2019a. 'Chechnya, Detention Camps In'. In *Global Encyclopedia of Lesbian, Gay, Bisexual, Transgender, and Queer (LGBTQ) History*, 315–18. Boston, MA: Charles Scribner's Sons.

Kondakov, Alexander. 2019b. 'Rethinking the Sexual Citizenship from Queer and Post-Soviet Perspectives: queer urban spaces and the right to the socialist city'. *Sexualities* 22(3): 401–17.

Kondakov, Alexander. 2019c. 'The Censorship "Propaganda" Legislation in Russia'. In *State-Sponsored Homophobia*, edited by L. Ramon Mendos, 213–15. Geneva: ILGA-Europe.

Kondakov, Alexander. 2020a. 'Regulating Desire in Russia'. In Research *Handbook on Gender, Sexuality and the Law*, edited by Chris Ashford and Alexander Maine, 396–408. Cheltenham: Edward Elgar.

Kondakov, Alexander. 2020b. 'The Queer Epistemologies: challenges to the modes of knowing about sexuality in Russia'. In *The SAGE Handbook of Global Sexualities*, edited by Zowie Davy, Ana Cristina Santos, Chiara Bertone, Ryan Thoreson, and Saskia E. Wieringa, 82–98. Thousand Oaks, CA: SAGE.

Kondakov, Alexander. 2021a. 'Non-Traditional Sexual Relationships: law, forgetting and the conservative political discourse in Russia'. In *Conservatism and Memory Politics in Russia and Eastern Europe*, edited by Katalin Miklóssy and Markku Kangaspuro, 45–61. London: Routledge.

Kondakov, Alexander. 2021b. 'The Influence of the "Gay-Propaganda" Law on Violence against LGBTIQ People in Russia: evidence from criminal court rulings'. *European Journal of Criminology* 18(6): 940–59.

Kondakov, Alexander. 2021c. 'Challenging the Logic of Progressive Timeline, Queering LGBT Successes and Failures in Ireland and Russia'. *Sexualities*, October.

Kondakov, Alexander, and Evgeny Shtorn. 2021. 'Sex, Alcohol, and Soul: violent reactions to coming out after the "gay propaganda" law in Russia'. *The Russian Review* 80(1): 37–55.

Kondakov, Alexander, and Yulia Subbotina. 2017. *Otchet. Kolichestvennye dannye monitoringa diskriminacii po SOGI* [Report. The Quantitative Data of the Monitoring of Discrimination Based on SOGI]. Russian LGBT Network. https://lgbtnet.org/library/reports/otchet_kolichestvennye_dannye_monitoringa_diskriminatsii_po_sogi/ (accessed 8.2.2022).

Kováts, Eszter, and Andrea Pető. 2017. 'Anti-Gender Discourse in Hungary: a discourse without a movement?' In *Anti-Gender Campaigns in Europe: mobilizing against equality*, edited by Roman Kuhar and David Paternotte, 117–32. London: Rowman & Littlefield.

Kowalska, Alicja. 2011. 'Polish Queer Lesbianism: sexual identity without a lesbian community'. *Journal of Lesbian Studies* 15(3): 324–36.

Kozlovsky, Vladimir. 1986. *Argo Russkoy Gomoseksual'noy Subkul'tury: Source Materials* [Argot of the Russian Gay Subculture]. Benson, VT: Chalidze Publications.

Kubal, Agnieszka. 2018. 'In Search of Justice: migrants' experiences of appeal in the Moscow City Court'. In *A Sociology of Justice in Russia*, edited by Agnieszka Kubal and Marina Kurkchiyan, 92–117. Cambridge: Cambridge University Press.

Kubal, Agnieszka. 2019. *Immigration and Refugee Law in Russia: socio-legal perspectives* (Law in Context). Cambridge: Cambridge University Press.

Kulpa, Roberto, and Joanna Mizielinska (eds). 2011. *De-Centring Western Sexualities: Central and Eastern European perspectives*. London: Routledge.

Kuntsman, Adi. 2009. '"With a Shade of Disgust": affective politics of sexuality and class in memoirs of the Stalinist gulag'. *Slavic Review* 68(2): 308–28.

Kurkchiyan, Marina. 2009. 'Russian Legal Culture: an analysis of adaptive response to an institutional transplant'. *Law & Social Inquiry* 34(2): 337–64.

Latour, Bruno. 2005. *Reassembling the Social: an introduction to actor-network-theory*. Oxford: Oxford University Press.

Latour, Bruno. 2013. *The Making of Law: an ethnography of the Conseil d'Etat*. Cambridge: Polity.

Latypov, Alisher, Tim Rhodes, and Lucy Reynolds. 2013. 'Prohibition, Stigma and Violence against Men who Have Sex with Men: effects on HIV in Central Asia'. *Central Asian Survey* 32(1): 52–65.

Lawrence, Frederick M. 1999. *Punishing Hate: bias crimes under American law*. Cambridge, MA: Harvard University Press.

Leckey, Robert, and Kim Brooks (eds). 2010. *Queer Theory: law, culture, empire*. London: Routledge.

Ledeneva, Alena. 2008. 'Telephone Justice in Russia'. *Post-Soviet Affairs* 24(4): 324–50.

Levin, Eve. 1989. *Sex and Society in the World of the Orthodox Slavs, 900–1700*. Ithaca: Cornell University Press.

Levy, Denise L., and Corey W. Johnson. 2012. 'What Does the Q Mean? Including queer voices in qualitative research'. *Qualitative Social Work* 11(2): 130–40.

Liu, Petrus. 2015. *Queer Marxism in Two Chinas*. Durham, NC: Duke University Press.

Lokot, Tetyana. 2019. 'Affective Resistance Against Online Misogyny and Homophobia on the RuNet'. In *Gender Hate Online: understanding the new anti-feminism*, edited by Debbie Ging and Eugenia Siapera, 213–32. Cham: Springer International Publishing.

Low Reyna, Zachary. 2020. 'Toward a More Robust New Materialist Politics: how the practice of criminal animal trials can inform contemporary politics'. *Stasis* 9(1): 105–27.

McCarthy, Lauren A. 2015. *Trafficking Justice: how Russian police enforce new laws, from crime to courtroom*. Ithaca, NY: Cornell University Press.

McCarthy, Lauren A. 2018. 'Decision-Making in the Russian Criminal Justice System: investigators, procurators, judges and human trafficking cases'. In *A Sociology of Justice in Russia*, edited by Agnieszka Kubal and Marina Kurkchiyan, 205–30. Cambridge: Cambridge University Press.

McKenna, Elizabeth. 2020. 'Taxes and Tithes: the organizational foundations of bolsonarismo'. *International Sociology* 35(6): 610–31.

McRuer, Robert. 2006. *Crip Theory: cultural signs of queerness and disability*. New York: New York University Press.

Madsen, Mikael Rask, and Yves Dezalay. 2013. 'Pierre Bourdieu's Sociology of Law: from the genesis of the state to the globalisation of law'. In *Law and Social Theory*, edited by Reza Banakar and Max Travers. 2nd ed. 111–28. Oxford: Hart.

Martin, Fran, Peter Jackson, Mark McLelland, and Audrey Yue (eds). 2010. *AsiaPacifiQueer: rethinking genders and sexualities*. Urbana, IL: University of Illinois Press.

Martsenyuk, Tamara. 2012. 'The State of the LGBT Community and Homophobia in Ukraine'. *Problems of Post-Communism* 59(2): 51–62.

Mason, Gail. 2009. 'Hate Crime Laws in Australia: are they achieving their goals?' *Criminal Law Journal* 33(6): 326–40.

Mason, Gail. 2014a. 'Legislating against Hate'. In *The Routledge International Handbook on Hate Crime*, edited by Nathan Hall, Abbee Corb, Paul Giannasi, and John Grieve, 59–68. London: Routledge.

Mason, Gail. 2014b. 'The Hate Threshold: emotion, causation and difference in the construction of prejudice-motivated crime'. *Social & Legal Studies* 23(3): 293–314.

Massad, Joseph Andoni. 2002. 'Re-Orienting Desire: the gay international and the Arab world'. *Public Culture* 14(2): 361–85.

Massumi, Brian. 2002. *Parables for the Virtual: movement, affect, sensation*. Durham, NC: Duke University Press.

Massumi, Brian. 2015. *Politics of Affect*. Cambridge, MA: Polity.

Mayhew, Nick. 2020. 'Queering Sodomy: a challenge to "traditional" sexual relations in Russia'. In *Queer-Feminist Solidarity and the East/West Divide*, edited by Katharina Wiedlack, Saltanat Shoshanova, and Masha Godovannaya, 77–96. Oxford: Peter Lang.

Mažylis, Liudas, Sima Rakutienė, and Ingrida Unikaitė-Jakuntavičienė. 2015. 'Two Competing Normative Trajectories in the Context of the First Baltic Gay Pride Parade in Lithuania'. *Baltic Journal of Law & Politics* 7(2): 37–76.

Menkel-Meadow, Carrie. 2021. 'Feminist Legal Academics: changing the epistemology of American law through conflicts, controversies and comparisons'. In *Gender and Careers in the Legal Academy*, edited by Ulrike Schultz, Gisela Shaw, Margaret Thornton, and Rosemary Auchmuty, 475–510. Oxford: Hart.

Mestvirishvili, Maia, Tinatin Zurabishvili, Tamar Iakobidze, and Natia Mestvirishvili. 2017. 'Exploring Homophobia in Tbilisi, Georgia'. *Journal of Homosexuality* 64(9): 1253–82.

Meyer, Doug. 2015. *Violence Against Queer People: race, class, gender, and the persistence of anti-LGBT discrimination*. New Brunswick, NJ: Rutgers University Press.

Mielke, Tomas. 2017. *The Russian Homosexual Lexicon: consensual and prison camp sexuality among men*. CreateSpace Independent Publishing Platform.

Mikhaylova, Oxana R., and Galina V. Gradoselskaya. 2021. 'Radical Self-Representation in a Hostile Setting: discursive strategies of the Russian lesbian feminist movement'. *Social Media + Society* 7(1): https://doi.org/10.1177/2056305121989253 (accessed 8.2.2022).

Miller, Daniel, Elisabetta Costa, Nell Haynes, Tom McDonald, Razvan Nicolescu, Jolynna Sinanan, Juliano Spyer, Shriram Venkatraman, and Xinyuan Wang. 2016. *How the World Changed Social media*. London: UCL Press.

Mitrofanova, Anastasia. 2020. 'Questioning the European Path: orthodox political radicalism in contemporary Moldova'. *Religion, State and Society* 48(2–3): 107–24.

Mole, Richard. 2011. 'Nationality and Sexuality: homophobic discourse and the "national threat" in contemporary Latvia'. *Nations and Nationalism* 17(3): 540–60.

Mole, Richard. 2021. 'Rethinking Diaspora: queer poles, Brazilians and Russians in Berlin'. In *Queer Migration and Asylum in Europe*, edited by Richard Mole, 57–77. London: UCL Press.

Moon, Steven, and Adriana Helbıg. 2018. 'Listening Technology and The Gay Male Body in Azerbaijan'. *Etnomüzikoloji Dergisi* 1: 49–67.

Morozov, Viatcheslav. 2005. 'Russia's Changing Attitude toward the OSCE: contradictions and continuity'. *Sicherheit Und Frieden (S+F) / Security and Peace* 23(2): 69–73.

Morris, Jeremy, and Masha Garibyan. 2021. 'Russian Cultural Conservatism Critiqued: translating the tropes of "gayropa" and "juvenile justice" in everyday life'. *Europe-Asia Studies* 73(8): 1487–507.

Moss, Kevin. 2017. 'Russia as the Savior of European Civilization: gender and the geopolitics of traditional values'. In *Anti-Gender Campaigns in Europe: mobilizing against equality*, edited by Roman Kuhar and David Paternotte, 195–214. London: Rowman & Littlefield.

Moss, Kevin. 2021. 'Russia's Queer Science, or How Anti-LGBT Scholarship is Made'. *The Russian Review* 80(1): 17–36.

Mozzhegorov, Sergey. 2014. 'Narrativy o gomoseksual'nom raskrytii v zapadnom i rossijskom sociokul'turnom kontekste' [Coming Out Narratives in Western and Russian Sociocultural Contexts]. *Sotsiologicheskiy Zhurnal* [Sociological Review] 1: 124–40.

Muñoz, José Esteban. 2009. *Cruising Utopia: the then and there of queer futurity*. New York: New York University Press.

Muravyeva, Marianna. 2012. 'Personalizing Homosexuality and Masculinity in Early Modern Russia'. In *Gender in Late Medieval and Early Modern Europe*, edited by Marianna Muravyeva and Raisa Maria Toivo, 205–25. London: Routledge.

Muravyeva, Marianna. 2013a. 'Introduction. Russian Law Today: at the crossroads of past and present'. *Review of Central and East European Law* 38(3–4): 209–16.

Muravyeva, Marianna. 2013b. 'Sex, Crime and the Law: Russian and European early modern legal thought on sex crimes'. *Comparative Legal History* 1(1): 75–103.

Muravyeva, Marianna. 2014. 'Legal Definitions of Sex Crimes in the Laws and Commentaries of Russian Lawyers (1860s–1910s)'. In *Women's History in Russia: (re)establishing the field*, edited by Marianna Muravyeva and Natalia Novikova, 28–49. Cambridge: Cambridge Scholars.

Muravyeva, Marianna. 2016. 'Gender and Crime in Russian History'. *Russian History* 43(3–4): 215–20.

Muravyeva, Marianna, Phillip S. Shon, and Raisa Maria Toivo. 2020. *Parricide and Violence against Parents: a cross-cultural view across past and present*. London: Routledge.

Naiman, Eric. 1997. *Sex in Public: the incarnation of early Soviet ideology*. Princeton, NJ: Princeton University Press.

Nartova, Nadya. 2008. 'Drugoe (li) telo: Proizvodstvo lesbijskogo tela v lesbijskom diskurse' [(Is) the body different: The production of lesbian body in the lesbian discourse]. In *V teni tela* [In the Shadow of the Body], edited by Nadya Nartova and Elena Omelchenko, 93–110. Ulyanovsk: Ulyuanovsk State University Press.

NATO. 2020. Media – (Dis)Information – Security: troll factories. https://www.nato.int/nato_static_fl2014/assets/pdf/2020/5/pdf/2005-deepportal2-troll-factories.pdf (accessed 8.2.2022).
Neal, Mary. 2019. 'Discovering Dignity: unpacking the emotional content of "killing narratives"'. In *The Emotional Dynamics of Law and Legal Discourse*, edited by Heather Conway and John Stannard, 83–103. London: Bloomsbury.
Ngai, Sianne. 2005. *Ugly Feelings*. Cambridge, MA: Harvard University Press.
Novitskaya, Alexandra. 2017. 'Patriotism, Sentiment, and Male Hysteria: Putin's masculinity politics and the persecution of non-heterosexual Russians'. *NORMA* 12(3–4): 302–18.
Novitskaya, Alexandra. 2021. 'Sexual Citizens in Exile: state-sponsored homophobia and post-Soviet LGBTQI+ migration'. *The Russian Review* 80(1): 56–76.
Nussbaum, Martha C. 2004. *Hiding from Humanity: disgust, shame, and the law*. Princeton, NJ: Princeton University Press.
Nussbaum, Martha C. 2010. *From Disgust to Humanity: sexual orientation and constitutional law*. New York: Oxford University Press.
Nussbaum, Martha C. 2013. *Political Emotions: why love matters for justice*. Cambridge, MA: Harvard University Press.
Nussbaum, Martha C. 2016. *Anger and Forgiveness: resentment, generosity, justice*. New York: Oxford University Press.
O'Malley, Pat, and Mariana Valverde. 2014. 'Foucault, Criminal Law, and the Governmentalization of the State'. In *Foundational Texts in Modern Criminal Law*, edited by Markus Dirk Dubber, 317–33. Oxford: Oxford University Press.
Omelchenko, Elena. 1999. 'Ot "pola" k "genderu": Opyt analiza seks-diskursov molodezhnykh rossiyskikh zhurnalov' [From "Sex" to "Gender": analysis of sexual discourse in Russian journals for youth]. In *Zhenshchina ne sushchestvuyet: Sovremenniye issledovaniya polovogo razlichiya* [Woman Does Not Exist: contemporary theories of sex diversity], edited by Irina Aristarkhova, 77–115. Syktyvkar: Syktyvkar University Press.
OSCE, ODIHR. 2005. *Combating Hate Crime in the OSCE Region: an overview of statistics, legislation, and national initiatives*. Warsaw: OSCE.
OSCE, ODIHR. 2006. *Challenges and Responses to Hate-Motivated Incidents in the OSCE Region*. Warsaw: ODIHR.
Pallot, Judith. 2012. 'Changing Symbolic and Geographical Boundaries between Penal Zones and Rural Communities in the Russian Federation'. *Journal of Rural Studies, Rural Realities in the Post-Socialist Space* 28(2): 118–29.
Paneyakh, Ella, Kirill Titaev, and Maria Shklyaruk. 2018. *Traektorija ugolovnogo dela* [Trajectory of a Criminal Case]. St Petersburg: EUSP Press.
Patton, Cindy. 1993. 'Tremble, Hetero Swine!' In *Fear of a Queer Planet: Queer Politics and Social Theory*, edited by Michael Warner, 143–77. Minneapolis, MN: University of Minnesota Press.
Perry, Barbara. 2001. *In the Name of Hate: understanding hate crimes*. London: Routledge.
Petri, Olga. 2019. 'Discipline and Discretionary Power in Policing Homosexuality in Late Imperial St Petersburg'. *Journal of Homosexuality* 66(7): 937–69.
Plummer, Ken. 1996. '"I Can't Even Think Straight": "queer" theory and the missing sexual revolution in sociology'. In *Queer Theory/Sociology*, edited by Steven Seidman, 64–82. Oxford: Blackwell.
Posner, Richard. 1999. 'Emotion versus Emotionalism in Law'. In *The Passions of Law*, edited by Susan A. Bandes, 309–29. New York: New York University Press.
Pronkina, Elena. 2016. 'Osobennosti LGBT-diskursa v rossijskih media, iniciirovannogo diskussijami o regulirovanii seksual'nosti' [Peculiarities of LGBT Discourse in the Russian Media Initiated by the Discussion to Regulate Sexuality]. *The Journal of Social Policy Studies* 14(1): 71–86.
Raj, Senthorun Sunil. 2020. *Feeling Queer Jurisprudence: injury, intimacy, identity*. London: Routledge.
Rao, Rahul. 2020. *Out of Time: the queer politics of postcoloniality*. Oxford: Oxford University Press.
Rarog, A.I. 2015. *Ugolovnoe parvo Rossii. Chasti obshchaya i osobennaya* [The Russian Criminal Law. Common and special chapters]. Moscow: Prospect.
RIA Novosti. 2002. 'Gruppa "Narodnyy deputat" predlagayet vernut' v Ugolovnyy kodeks Rossii stat'yu, predusmatrivayushchuyu nakazaniye za gomoseksualizm' [The Group "People's

Deputy" suggests to recriminalise homosexuality]. https://ria.ru/20020423/124042.html (accessed 8.2.2022).

Rose, Nikolas, Pat O'Malley, and Mariana Valverde. 2006. 'Governmentality'. *Annual Review of Law and Social Science* 2(1): 83–104.

Rostokinsky, A.V. 2007. 'Evolutsiya motivatsii: Ot lichnoy nepriyzni do vrazhdy i nenavisti k chasti obshchestva' [The Evolution of Motives: from personal unpleasant feelings to animosity and hatred to a societal faction]. *Zhurnal nauchnykh publikatsiy aspirantov* i doktorantov [Journal of Academic Publications for Graduate Students] 12(18): 87–89.

Rotkirch, Anna. 2000. *The Man Question: loves and lives in late 20th century Russia*. Helsinki: University of Helsinki.

Sanford, Mary, James Painter, Taha Yasseri, and Jamie Lorimer. 2021. 'Controversy around Climate Change Reports: a case study of Twitter responses to the 2019 IPCC report on land'. *Climatic Change* 167(3): 59.

Sarajeva, Katja. 2011. *Lesbian Lives: sexuality, space and subculture in Moscow*. Stockholm: Stockholm University.

Sayer, Derek. 2017. 'White Riot – Brexit, Trump, and post-factual politics'. *Journal of Historical Sociology* 30(1): 92–106.

Schaefer, Donovan O. 2015. *Religious Affects: animality, evolution, and power*. Durham, NC: Duke University Press.

Schaefer, Donovan O. 2019. *The Evolution of Affect Theory: the humanities, the sciences, and the study of power*. Cambridge: Cambridge University Press.

Schaper, Marcel GH. 2014. 'A Computational Legal Analysis of Acte Clair Rules of EU Law in the Field of Direct Taxes'. SSRN Scholarly Paper ID 2805710. Rochester, NY: Social Science Research Network.

Schluter, Daniel. 2002. *Gay Life in the Former USSR: fraternity without community*. New York: Routledge.

Schultz, Ulrike, Gisela Shaw, Margaret Thornton, and Rosemary Auchmuty (eds). 2021. Gender and *Careers in the Legal Academy*. Oxford: Hart.

Schweppe, Jennifer, and Mark Austin Walters (eds). 2016. *The Globalization of Hate: internationalizing hate crime?* Oxford: Oxford University Press.

Sedgwick, Eve Kosofsky. 1990. *Epistemology of the Closet*. Berkeley, CA: University of California Press.

Sedgwick, Eve Kosofsky. 1993. 'Queer Performativity: Henry James's The Art of the Novel'. *GLQ: a journal of lesbian and gay studies* 1(1): 1–16.

Sedgwick, Eve Kosofsky. 2003. *Touching Feeling: affect, pedagogy, performativity*. Durham, NC: Duke University Press.

Sedgwick, Eve Kosofsky. 2011. *The Weather in Proust*. Durham, NC: Duke University Press.

Seidman, Steven. 2013. *Beyond the Closet: the transformation of gay and lesbian life*. New York: Routledge.

Sekerbayeva, Zhanar. 2020. 'Stifled Monstrosities: gender-transgressive motifs in Kazakh folklore'. In *Decolonizing Queer Experience: LGBT+ narratives from Eastern Europe and Eurasia*, edited by Emily Channell-Justice, 135–54. London: Lexington Books.

Serykh, Dasha. 2017. 'Homonationalism before Homonationalism: representations of Russia, Eastern Europe, and the Soviet Union in the US homophile press, 1953–1964'. *Journal of Homosexuality* 64(7): 908–27.

Sexuality Lab. 2017. *Nasilie protiv LGBT v Rossi po dannym media. Otchet* [Violence against LGBT People in Russia According to Media Publications. A Report]. St Petersburg: Sexuality Lab.

Shchelkin, A.G. 2013. 'Netraditsionnaya seksual'nost' (opyt sotsiologicheskogo analiza)' [Non-Traditional Sexuality (An Experience of Sociological Analysis)]. *Sotsiologicheskie issledovaniya* [Sociological Research] 6: 132–42.

Shirinian, Tamar. 2018. 'Queer Life-Worlds in Postsocialist Armenia: alternative space and the possibilities of in/visibility'. *QED: a journal in GLBTQ worldmaking* 5(1): 1–23.

Shoshanova, Saltanat. 2021. 'Queer Identity in the Contemporary Art of Kazakhstan'. *Central Asian Survey* 40(1): 113–31.

Shtorn, Evgeny. 2017. 'Jesse o "sublichnosti": Dvukratnaja popytka pogovorit' o nasilii' [Essay on Sub-Personality: a double attempt to talk about violence]. *Zhurnal sociologii i social'noj antropologii* [Journal of Sociology and Social Anthropology] XX(5): 207–21.

Shtorn, Evgeny. 2018. 'Murders of Non-Heterosexuals as a Hate Crime (Based on Court Decisions)'. *Sociology of Power* 30(1): 60–78.

Shtorn, Evgeny. 2020a. 'From Evgeny to Yevgeniy about a Particular Type of Blue'. In *Dictionary of the Queer International*, edited by Yevgeniy Fiks, 1–6. Ontario: Guelph.
Shtorn, Evgeny. 2020b. *Khroniki bezhenstva* [Refugee Chronicles]. St Petersburg: Poriadok Slov.
Silbey, Susan. 1998. 'Ideology, Power, and Justice'. In *Justice and Power in Sociolegal Studies*, edited by Bryant G. Garth and Austin Sarat, 272–308. Evanston, IL: Northwestern University Press.
Slobodenyuk, Ekaterina. 2017. 'Posledstvija krizisa 2015 goda: obednenie ili prekarizacija?'. *Journal of Social Policy Studies* 15(2): 183–200.
Slootmaeckers, Koen, Heleen Touquet, and Peter Vermeersch (eds). 2016. *The EU Enlargement and Gay Politics: the impact of Eastern enlargement on rights, activism and prejudice (Gender and Politics)*. Cham: Palgrave Macmillan.
Soboleva, Irina V., and Yaroslav A. Bakhmetjev. 2015. 'Political Awareness and Self-Blame in the Explanatory Narratives of LGBT People Amid the Anti-LGBT Campaign in Russia'. *Sexuality & Culture* 19(2): 275–96.
Solomatina, Irina, and Tatsiana Shchurko (eds). 2014. *Kvir-seksual'nost': Politiki i praktiki* [Queer Sexuality: politics and practices]. Minsk: Galijafy.
Solomon, Peter H. 2018. 'Accusatorial Bias in Russian Criminal Justice'. In *A Sociology of Justice in Russia*, edited by Agnieszka Kubal and Marina Kurkchiyan, 170–204. Cambridge: Cambridge University Press.
Sozayev, Valery. 2011. *Mify i fakty o geyakh, lesbiyankakh i biseksualakh* [Myths and Facts about Gays, Lesbians and Bisexuals]. 4th ed. St Petersburg: Raduga.
Sozayev, Valery. 2012. '"Kvir" dolzhen umeret' ["Queer" Must Die]. *Outloudmag*. https://outloudmag.eu/events/item/kvir-dolzhen-umeret (accessed 8.2.2022).
Spade, Dean. 2015. *Normal Life: administrative violence, critical trans politics, and the limits of law*. Durham, NC: Duke University Press.
Sperling, Valerie. 2014. *Sex, Politics, and Putin: political legitimacy in Russia*. New York: Oxford University Press.
Stähle, Hanna. 2015. 'Between Homophobia and Gay Lobby: the Russian Orthodox Church and its relationship to homosexuality in online discussions'. *Digital Icons* 14: 49–71.
Stake, Jeffrey Evans. 2001. 'Pushing Evolutionary Analysis of Law or Evolving Law: design without a Designer'. *Florida Law Review* 53(5): 875–92.
Stella, Francesca. 2013. 'Queer Space, Pride, and Shame in Moscow'. *Slavic Review* 72(3): 458–80.
Stella, Francesca. 2015. *Lesbian Lives in Soviet and Post-Soviet Russia: post/socialism and gendered sexualities*. Basingstoke: Palgrave.
Stephenson, Svetlana. 2015. *Gangs of Russia: from the streets to the corridors of power*. Ithaca, NY: Cornell University Press.
Stoeckle, Thomas, and Jonathan Albright. 2019. 'Public Relations, Political Communication and Agenda Setting: the rise of the micro-propaganda machine'. In *The Global Public Relations Handbook*, edited by Krishnamurthy Sriramesh and Dejan Verčič. 3rd ed. 293–308. New York: Routledge.
Štulhofer, Aleksandar, and Theo Sandfort. 2005. *Sexuality and Gender in Postcommunist Eastern Europe and Russia*. New York: Haworth Press.
Suchland, Jennifer. 2018. 'The LGBT Specter in Russia: refusing queerness, claiming "whiteness"'. *Gender, Place & Culture* 25(7): 1073–88.
Sultanalieva, Syinat. 2020. 'Escaping the Dichotomies of "Good" and "Bad": chronotopes of queerness in Kyrgyzstan'. In *Decolonizing Queer Experience: LGBT+ narratives from Eastern Europe and Eurasia*, edited by Emily Channell-Justice, 135–54. London: Lexington Books.
Sundstrom, Lisa McIntosh, Valerie Sperling, and Melike Sayoglu. 2019. *Courting Gender Justice: Russia, Turkey, and the European Court of Human Rights*. New York: Oxford University Press.
Suyarkulova, Mohira. 2019. 'Translating "Queer" into (Kyrgyzstani) Russian'. In *Sexuality and Translation in World Politics*, edited by Caroline Cottet and Manuela Lavinas Picq, 42–56. Bristol: E-International Relations.
Swader, Christopher S., and Vaida Obelene. 2015. 'Post-Soviet Intimacies: an introduction'. *Sexuality & Culture* 19(2): 245–55.
Sweet, Denis M. 1995. 'The Church, the Stasi, and Socialist Integration'. *Journal of Homosexuality* 29(4): 351–68.
Szulc, Lukasz. 2018. *Transnational Homosexuals in Communist Poland: cross-border flows in gay and lesbian magazines*. Basingstoke: Palgrave.

Takács, Judit. 2015. 'Disciplining Gender and (Homo)Sexuality in State-Socialist Hungary in the 1970s'. *European Review of History: Revue Européenne d'histoire* 22(1): 161–75.

Takács, Judit, Roman Kuhar, and Tamás P. Tóth. 2017. '"Unnatural Fornication" Cases under State-Socialism: a Hungarian–Slovenian comparative social-historical approach'. *Journal of Homosexuality* 64(14): 1943–60.

Takács, Judit, and Tamás P. Tóth. 2021. 'Liberating Pathologization? The historical background of the 1961 decriminalization of homosexuality in Hungary'. *Hungarian Historical Review* 10(2): 267–300.

Taşcıoğlu, Ezgi. 2021. 'States of Exception: legal governance of trans women in urban Turkey'. *Social & Legal Studies* 30(3): 384–404.

Timofeeva, Oxana. 2018. *The History of Animals: a philosophy*. London: Bloomsbury.

Tlostanova, Madina. 2018. *What Does it Mean to be Post-Soviet?: decolonial art from the ruins of the Soviet Empire*. Durham, NC: Duke University Press.

Tolkachev, Dmitrii, and Tamar Tolordava. 2020. 'Shared Past, Different Future? Russian and Georgian authorities' discourse concerning homosexuality'. *Sexuality & Culture* 24(2): 447–64.

Tuana, Nancy, and Sandra Morgen (eds). 2001. *Engendering Rationalities*. New York: SUNY Press.

Tuller, David. 1996. *Cracks in the Iron Closet: travels in gay and lesbian Russia*. Chicago, IL: University of Chicago Press.

Turovsky, Daniil. 2018. 'The Trans Man whose Pioneering Surgery was a State Secret for Decades'. *BuzzFeed News*. https://www.buzzfeednews.com/article/turovsky/soviet-doctor-trans-history (accessed 8.2.2022).

Umali, Violeda, and Emerson Bañez. 2013. 'Evolving Democracy: a memetic analysis of the latest proposal for constitutional change in the Philippines'. In *Political Marketing: strategic 'campaign culture'*, edited by Kostas Gouliamos, Antonis Theocharous, and Bruce I. Newman, 74–96. London: Routledge.

Utkin, Roman. 2021a. 'Introduction. Illegal Queerness: Russian culture and society in the age of the "gay propaganda" law'. *The Russian Review* 80(1): 7–16.

Utkin, Roman. 2021b. 'Queer Vulnerability and Russian Poetry after the "Gay Propaganda" Law'. *The Russian Review* 80(1): 77–99.

Valodzin, Uladzimir. 2020. 'Criminal Prosecution of Homosexuals in the Soviet Union (1946–1991): numbers and discourses'. Working Paper. Florence: European University Institute.

Valverde, Mariana. 2010. 'Specters of Foucault in Law and Society Scholarship'. *Annual Review of Law and Social Science* 6(1): 45–59.

Valverde, Mariana. 2017. *Michel Foucault*. London: Routledge.

Vērdiņš, Kārlis, and Jānis Ozoliņš. 2019. 'The Latvian LGBT Movement and Narratives of Normalization'. In *LGBTQ+ Activism in Central and Eastern Europe: resistance, representation and identity*, edited by Radzhana Buyantueva and Maryna Shevtsova, 239–64. Newcastle: Palgrave.

Vincent, Mark. 2020. *Criminal Subculture in the Gulag: prisoner society in the Stalinist labour camps*. London: Bloomsbury.

Volkov, Vadim. 2002. *Violent Entrepreneurs: the use of force in the making of Russian capitalism*. Ithaca, NY: Cornell University Press.

Volkov, Vadim, and Aryna Dzmitryieva. 2015. 'Recruitment Patterns, Gender, and Professional Subcultures of the Judiciary in Russia'. *International Journal of the Legal Profession* 22(2): 166–92.

von Boemcken, Marc, Hafiz Boboyorov, and Nina Bagdasarova. 2018. 'Living Dangerously: securityscapes of Lyuli and LGBT people in urban spaces of Kyrgyzstan'. *Central Asian Survey* 37(1): 68–84.

Voronkov, Viktor, Boris Gladarev, and Liliya Sagitova (eds). 2011. *Militsiya i etnicheskie migranty: Praktiki vzaimodeystviya* [The Police and Ethnic Migrants: practices of interactions]. St Petersburg: Aleteya.

Vorontsov, Dmitri. 2017. 'Seksual'nost' kak etnichnost': Kul'turnyj resurs genderizovannoj seksual'nosti' [Sexuality as Ethnicity: the cultural resource of gendered sexuality]. *Zhurnal sociologii i social'noj antropologii* [Journal of Sociology and Social Anthropology] XX(5): 59–74.

Voruz, Veronique. 2011. 'Politics in Foucault's Later Work: a philosophy of truth; or reformism in question'. *Theoretical Criminology* 15(1): 47–65.

Wahab, Amar. 2021. 'Affective Mobilizations: pinkwashing and racialized homophobia in "Out There"'. *Journal of Homosexuality* 68(5): 849–71.

Walker, Shaun. 2021. 'Hungary's Viktor Orbán Will Hold Referendum on Anti-LGBT Law'. *The Guardian*. https://www.theguardian.com/world/2021/jul/21/hungarys-viktor-orban-will-hold-referendum-on-anti-lbgt-law (accessed 8.2.2022).

Warren-Gordon, Kiesha, and Gayle Rhineberger. 2021. 'The "Trump Effect" on Hate Crime Reporting: media coverage before and after the 2016 presidential election'. *Journal of Ethnicity in Criminal Justice* 19(1): 25–45.

Weaver, Cai. 2019. '"I'm Gay, but I'm Not Like Those Perverts": perceptions of self, the LGBT community, and LGBT activists among gay and bisexual Russian men'. In *LGBTQ+ Activism in Central and Eastern Europe: resistance, representation and identity*, edited by Radzhana Buyantueva and Maryna Shevtsova, 101–26. Newcastle: Palgrave.

Weaver, Cai, and Timo Koch. 2019. 'The Aftermath of the Gay Propaganda Law: mapping trends in the Russian media'. *European Conference on Gender and Politics*. Madrid.

Weeks, Jeffrey. 2002. *Sexuality and its Discontents: meanings, myths, and modern sexualities*. London: Routledge.

Weeks, Jeffrey. 2017. *Sex, Politics and Society: the regulation of sexuality since 1800*. London: Routledge.

Wickes, Rebecca L., Sharon Pickering, Gail Mason, Jane M. Maher, and Jude McCulloch. 2016. 'From Hate to Prejudice: does the new terminology of prejudice motivated crime change perceptions and reporting actions?' *British Journal of Criminology* 56(2): 239–55.

Wiedlack, Katharina. 2017. 'Gays vs. Russia: media representations, vulnerable bodies and the construction of a (post)modern West'. *European Journal of English Studies* 21(3): 241–57.

Wiedlack, Katharina. 2020. 'Enemy Number One or Gay Clown? The Russian president, masculinity and populism in US media'. *NORMA* 15(1): 59–75.

Wilkinson, Cai. 2014. 'Putting "Traditional Values" into Practice: the rise and contestation of anti-homopropaganda laws in Russia'. *Journal of Human Rights* 13(3): 363–79.

Wilkinson, Cai, and Anna Kirey. 2010. 'What's in a Name? The personal and political meanings of "LGBT" for non-heterosexual and transgender youth in Kyrgyzstan'. *Central Asian Survey* 29(4): 485–99.

Wirtz, Andrea L., Anna Kirey, Alena Peryskina, Fabrice Houdart, and Chris Beyrer. 2013. 'Uncovering the Epidemic of HIV among Men who Have Sex with Men in Central Asia'. *Drug and Alcohol Dependence* 132 (November): S17–24.

Woods, Jordan Blair. 2014. '"Queering Criminology": overview of the state of the field'. In *Handbook of LGBT Communities, Crime, and Justice*, edited by Dana Peterson and Vanessa R. Panfil, 15–41. New York: Springer New York.

yakov_a_jerkov. 2013. 'Netraditsionnye seksual'nye otnosheniya' [Non-traditional sexual relationships]. https://yakov-a-jerkov.livejournal.com/756240.html (accessed 8.2.2022).

Yavorskiy, M.A. 2014. 'Interpretatsiya gendernogo (polovogo) ekstremizma' [Interpretation of Sexual Extremism]. *Chelovek: Prestuplenie i nakazanie* [The Human: crime and punishment] 85(12): 129–33.

Zaslavskaia, Polina. 2017. 'Veshchdok' [Physical Evidence]. *Polina Zaslavskaia* (blog). https://polinazaslavskaya.wordpress.com/%d0%bf%d1%80%d0%be%d0%b5%d0%ba%d1%82%d1%8b/veschdok/ (accessed 8.2.2022).

Zdravomyslova, Elena, and Anna Temkina. 2003. 'Gendernoye (gendered) grazhdanstvo i sovetsky etakratichesky poryadok' [Gendered Citizenship and the Soviet Etacratic Order]. In *Transformatsiya gendernykh otnosheny: Zapadniye teorii i rossiyskiye praktiki* [Transformation of Gender Relationship: Western theories and Russian practices], edited by Lyudmila Popkova and Irina Tartakovskaya, 27–61. Samara: Samara University Press.

Zhaivoronok, Daniil. 2016. '"Solidarity with all the Trainer-Killers!": de-individualization and de-subjectivation of politics within the animal liberation movement'. *Journal of Social Policy Studies* 14(3): 393–408.

Zylan, Yvonne. 2011. *States of Passion: law, identity, and social construction of desire*. Oxford: Oxford University Press.

Index

actions of sexual character 109, 114, 122, 164
active vs passive dichotomy 91, 99, 106, 108, 114-5, 119, 154
activism LGBT+ 38, 86, 96, 180
    the first wave of 34
actors legal 13, 18, 30-2, 42-5, 55, 147, 184, 192, 204
    judges as legal actors 34, 41, 113
    vocabulary of legal actors 35, 90, 109
Adygea Republic of 24, 26
affect, affection 3, 21, 137, 139, 146, 164, 168, 175, 183, 206
    as a mechanism of power 4, 103, 130, 139, 142, 145, 166, 201
    murder 50t, 52, 113, 153, 164-5
    theory 17, 137-9, 177, 179, 186
    violent 21-2, 70, 143-4, 146, 153, 169, 173, 179, 195, 199
    see also emotion
affective bond 102, 143, 155, 160, 182
agency 17, 19, 139, 183, 203
    distributed 18, 95, 177, 184
aggravating circumstances 28, 36, 40, 49, 57, 148
Ahmed Sara 17, 142-4, 155, 176-7, 180, 186
alcohol 1-2, 56, 75, 106, 113-5, 117, 126, 154, 157, 159-61, 163-4
amnesty due to 70th Anniversary of Victory 54, 58, 72, 151, 165,
amoral behaviour 92, 109-10, 112-3
Amur Region 24, 26, 118
anus 2, 91, 119, 158
Arkhangelsk Region 100
Article 6.21 of the Code of Administrative Offences 97, 191-2
assemblage 18, 93, 184
asymmetry 11-2, 101, 130, 142, 145, 157, 159, 166, 201
    see also inequality, hierarchy
Astrakhan Region 111
authority legitimate 4, 10, 29, 94, 176, 180, 185-6, 196, 200-2, 209
    of law, legal 13-5, 20, 31-2, 49, 88, 184, 189
Bashkortostan 117, 119, 166
battery 41, 50t, 54, 148
beer *see* alcohol

Belgorod Region 71
bias *see* prejudice
bio-power *see* disciplinary power
bisexual persons 4, 79, 104, 107, 123
    see also LGBT+, lesbian, gay man, transgender
body 132, 134-5, 137-42, 145, 160, 167, 98
    as appearance 102, 111-2, 163
    dead 1, 24, 41, 51-2, 119, 126, 135, 156, 167
    as embodiment 10, 30-1, 45, 80, 82, 136, 144, 148, 168, 179
    susceptible 12, 17, 169, 172, 176, 179, 186, 188
Borenstein Eliot 15, 183-4
boundary 83, 98, 117, 133, 142-3, 155, 158-62, 167, 179
Bourdieu Pierre 13-4, 20, 30-1, 34-5
buggery 48, 88-9, 97, 109, 126, 154, 190
    see also muzhelozhstvo
Buryatia 71-2, 154, 166
Butler Judith 8, 30, 81, 137, 178
care 70, 102, 152, 206, 209
case criminal 3, 8, 20, 27-9, 33-4, 39, 41-3, 45, 48-9, 51-8, 68, 70, 91, 102, 111, 113-4, 119, 122-3, 129, 133, 148, 150, 168, 193
    homicide 61-2, 67, 79, 166
catchphrase (*also* catchy, catchiness) 16-8, 185, 190
category discursive 5, 9, 15, 77-80, 82, 84-6, 88-9, 92, 97-8, 102, 104-5, 107, 123, 136, 142, 146, 149, 187
censorship (*also* self-) 7, 8, 97, 192, 204-5
centralised source of power (*see* hegemony)
Chechnya 124
Chelyabinsk Region 63, 110, 117, 120, 155, 158, 162
children protection of 97, 190
circulation of power 6, 10, 12, 14-8, 90, 96, 137, 169, 175-6, 178-80, 183-6, 193, 196, 201-2, 205
citizenship 33, 143, 177, 205
class working, social 64-5t, 66-8, 174, 197
clerk court 42, 54-5, 79, 103, 122
club gay 118, 159

collective 68, 104, 143, 147-8, 155-8, 160, 169, 206
colonisation of knowledge (*also* decolonisation, provincialisation) 22, 82-3, 86, 99
Russian (*also* imperialism) 46, 99
community LGBT+ 4, 79, 82, 84, 92-3, 103-5, 107-8, 143, 147, 152, 168, 180
complexity 10, 81, 86, 95, 98, 180, 183
concept 15-9, 21, 37, 39, 53, 62, 91, 96, 102, 116, 131, 183, 185-8, 199, 202-3, 210
   see also meme
configuration of power 3, 10, 22, 95-6, 101, 123, 175, 180, 202
see also reconfiguration of power relations
conscious, -ness 11, 55, 131, 136-7, 139-40, 142, 160
conspiracy theory 15, 183
constitution -al Court 39-40, 46-7, 49, 97, 192
of the Russian Federation 94, 181
control power of 12, 14, 18, 89, 95-6, 131, 136, 167, 176-8, 184, 199, 203, 205
court decision (*see* ruling)
criminal justice system
Criminal Code 35-7, 40, 49, 88-9, 99, 149, 151, 190
court 2, 4, 9, 31, 36, 39, 41-5, 49, 51, 54-5, 57-8, 66, 78, 101, 106, 112, 115, 120, 135, 152, 165, 185
law 4-5, 7, 29, 36, 49, 89-90
Penal Code 36, 46, 88-9
procedure (Code) 36, 40-4, 54, 68, 70, 103, 121, 149, 151, 185
criminalisation of male homosexuality (*see* decriminalisation)
Critical Theory 5, 21, 83, 94, 134, 204, 209
cruising strip 92-4
Dagestan 118
data 15, 19, 29, 46, 51
-base 'Justice' (*also* 'Rosjustice') 48, 71, 193
-base of Media Articles 193
dating website/application 24, 27, 53, 57, 109, 121, 150-1, 154, 156, 198
decriminalisation of male homosexuality 89, 94, 189-91
decolonisation (*see* colonisation)
decentralised source of power (*see* hegemony)
disciplinary power 7-9, 11-2, 14, 30-2, 80, 82, 87-8, 90, 93, 98, 101, 175, 200-1, 204
discourse 6, 8, 17, 20, 30, 89-91, 96, 140-1, 189-90
discrimination (anti-) 37-8, 46, 57, 145, 151
discursive field 4, 13-4, 16, 31, 138
disgust 132-6, 143-4, 154-5, 168, 176-7
doctrine legal 16, 130-1, 147-8, 152
documents as evidence 28, 42-6, 51, 56
   see also ruling
dystopia queer 87, 93, 95, 98
   see also utopia
East vs West, -ern Europe 82, 87, 197
   see also West vs East
echo chamber *see* isolation chamber
Ekaterinburg *see* Sverdlovsk Region
emancipation 13, 82
emotion 3, 21, 70, 129-36, 139-40, 146, 153, 155, 159-60, 164, 166, 176, 183

circulation of (*also* political economy of) 175-9, 182, 186
collective 156, 158
juridical 147-52, 164-5
see also affect
encounter 21, 105, 112, 123-4, 130, 136, 139-45, 153, 155, 158-60, 163-4, 166, 168-9, 179, 205
enhanced sentence 27, 40, 49, 130, 147, 151
erasure *see* silencing
Essig Laurie 82-4, 86, 94, 177
ethnic bias 36-40, 46, 57, 71-2, 111
against Asian people 57-8, 71-2, 117-8
antisemitism 37, 107
against people from the Caucasus region 71-2, 111, 117-8
expert knowledge/expertise 12, 80, 140, 175, 184, 200-2, 209
legal and medical 9-10, 88-92, 202
expression sexual, gender, queer 15, 76, 95-6, 98-9, 104, 106, 121, 152
extenuating circumstances 44, 109-10, 112-3, 153
extortion 50t, 54, 59, 62, 66, 68-9
family
heterosexual vs same sex 14, 97, 114-8, 180-1, 192
feeling *see* affect, emotion
femininity 3, 76-7, 82, 114-5, 166-7
fluidity of sexuality 10, 15, 80-2, 84-5, 93, 95, 98-9, 116-7, 181, 200
forensic examination 2, 89, 91, 119
Foucault Michel 6-7, 10-14, 29-32, 80, 88-9, 93, 102, 139, 143, 175, 180, 184, 201, 204, 209
Fragmentation, -ted, -ments 10, 20, 89-90, 93, 96, 141, 143, 176-7, 183, 200, 202, 205, 209
gay-bashing 54, 150-1
gay man/people 2, 4-5, 10, 24, 27-8, 54, 57, 68-9, 76-7, 79, 84, 91-2, 104-6, 108, 110-1, 116, 123, 135, 150-1, 161, 164-6, 198
   see also LGBT+, lesbian, bisexual, transgender
gay propaganda (*also* propaganda of non-traditional sexual relationships, homosexual propaganda)
law (federal) 4, 7, 48, 53, 70, 98, 180, 187, 193, 200
law (regional) 97, 100
meme (also concept) 96, 187-9, 191-2, 195-7, 199, 210
gender 49, 75-80, 82, 95-7, 101, 103, 107, 109, 111-2, 114-5, 119, 123, 140, 152, 158, 167, 172-4, 182, 197-8
see also expression
goluboi 79, 92, 104, 108
gomoseksualizm 48, 89, 106-7, 109, 124, 191
   see also homosexuality
grievance 143, 185
Grindr *see* dating website
habitus 30, 55
hate
as a feeling 28, 70, 129-30, 146-7, 149-52, 179, 199, 204

crime 3, 27-9, 35-40, 49, 55-7, 70-1, 107, 129-30, 147-8, 150-2, 185-6, 204
motive 28-9, 36, 40, 49, 57, 62, 113, 129, 149, 151
speech 8, 40, 46, 50t, 71, 107
Healey Dan 89, 96, 189-91
hegemony -ic 6, 9-10, 13-5, 29, 32, 124, 176, 180, 202
heteronormative -ity, non- 3, 19, 35, 80, 144, 167, 181
hierarchy 3, 12, 17-8, 21, 57-8, 62-3, 92, 123, 130, 140, 142-3, 146, 179-80
homeless 45, 64-5t, 67, 75, 78, 102
homicide 50t, 52-4, 60t, 61-3, 77
  see also murder
homosexual panic defence 112, 114, 124
homosexuality 3, 17, 19, 33-4, 48, 53-5, 69, 77-9, 83-4, 88-94, 98, 104-10, 114-5, 124, 127, 133-5, 155, 160-4, 167, 181, 187, 189-90, 192, 196
  see also LGBT+, gay man, bisexual, transgender
human rights 37, 94
Hunter Shona 178-80
idea *see* concept
identity gender, sexual 5-6, 9, 15, 21, 49, 76, 79-80, 82-8, 90, 93, 95, 97-8, 104, 108, 123, 151-2
impact *see* touch
impress *see* touch
income 66-7, 172
  see also inequality
indifference 69-71, 103, 124, 145, 150, 182
inequality 12, 34, 58, 63, 124, 130, 157, 161, 166, 169, 175, 177, 182
  see also asymmetry, hierarchy
information as knowledge 6-8, 10-1, 13, 15-9, 29, 32, 96-8, 140, 175, 179, 183-5, 187-8, 196, 199-200, 202-5, 209
  see also data
intercourse sexual 3-4, 88-90, 94, 96, 106, 109, 115, 118-21, 154-6, 162, 164, 190-1
investigation police 24-7, 41-5, 51, 54-6, 120, 130, 195
Irkutsk Region 100, 161
isolation chamber 32, 184-6, 202, 205
  see also meme, replicability
Ivanovo Region 159
judge 9, 13, 27-36, 40-4, 49, 54-9, 61-3, 66, 68-70, 76, 78-9, 104, 109-10, 112-4, 122, 127, 129-30, 147-52, 164, 192
justice (injustice, romantic, social, telephone) 29, 31-2, 34-6, 43-6, 49, 52, 55, 58, 62-3, 70, 113, 152, 184
Kaluga Region 119, 165
Kamchatka Territory 59, 115
Kemerovo Region 162
Kirov Region 123
knowledge *see* expert knowledge
Kostroma Region 100
Kozlovsky Vladimir 84, 92, 99
Krasnodar Territory 24-5, 28, 100, 112, 156, 165-6, 172
Krasnoyarsk Territory 107, 122, 159
Kurgan Region 113, 153, 159

Kursk Region 114, 153
larceny 50t, 52-3
law definition of 4, 6-9, 11-4, 16-7, 29-32, 34-5, 48-9, 131-2, 146, 184-5, 203-4
  criminal (*see* criminal justice system)
  enforcement 30, 38, 41, 51, 54, 62, 64-5t, 70, 119, 191-3
  everyday 33-4, 55, 63, 184, 193
  see also positivism, modality of law
  legal field 4, 13-4, 16, 20, 29-32, 34-5, 41-3, 45, 48-9, 55, 57-8, 69, 103, 123, 184-7, 189-93, 195-6, 203
  see also juridical
legitimacy -te 10, 13, 31-5, 49, 89-91, 93, 141, 175, 178, 180, 196, 204
lesbian 4, 48, 56, 79, 84, 91-3, 97, 104, 109-10, 114-5, 122-3, 167-8
  see also LGBT+, lesbian, gay man, bisexual, transgender
LGBT+ 3-5, 7-9, 27, 36, 38-9, 49, 70-1, 79-80, 84-5, 88, 94-7, 104-5, 106, 110, 143-4, 147-52, 181, 193, 195-6, 203
  see also lesbian, gay man, bisexual, transgender
lifespan 22, 184
Liu Petrus 86, 88
Magadan Region 100
manslaughter 2, 50t, 56, 60t, 61, 63, 79, 161
  see also homicide, violence
Mari El Republic 108, 120, 162
marriage (*see* family)
masculinity (*also* male, manhood, masculine) 31, 77-8, 82, 91, 106, 111-2, 114-5, 134, 144, 156-60, 162, 166, 169, 172-4, 199, 200
  fragile 3, 167, 173-4, 197
meaning 6, 9-10, 13-4, 17, 20, 32, 80, 88, 90, 93, 123-4, 141, 183-6, 196, 200-2, 208
  see also concept
mechanism of power 6, 10-2, 21-2, 99, 101-3, 124, 130, 138, 142-3, 145-6, 155, 166, 169, 175, 179, 186, 196, 201
  see also disciplinary power, techniques of power
media (*also* social) 53-4, 94, 97, 191, 193-5, 199, 201
meme 6, 11, 14-9, 96, 169, 183-97, 199, 201-3, 205, 208-9
  complex 17, 19, 22, 187, 193, 194t, 196
  legal 16, 185-6, 190, 199, 201
Memeticon the 6, 11, 14, 20, 29, 184, 202
memetics 15-7, 19, 176, 183
messiness 6-7, 10, 15, 81, 101, 181, 200, 206
modality of law sovereign vs disciplinary 7-8, 14, 30-1
  see also law, positivism
modernity (*also* premodern, postmodern) 10-1, 13, 20, 84-5, 88-90, 99, 139, 200-1, 209
morality (*see* amoral behaviour)
Moscow 43, 75-6, 102-4, 107-8, 112, 117-9, 122, 161
Moscow Region 55-6, 69, 108, 114-5, 148, 153-4, 164, 168
motive (*see* hate motive)
Muravyeva Marianna 88-9, 169

murder 1-2, 21-2, 24, 27-8, 33, 41, 45, 49, 51-2, 55, 61-3, 67-8, 75-7, 79, 102, 110, 112, 126-7, 129, 164-6, 168, 198
  Criminal Article 105, paras. 1 and 2 28, 36-7, 40, 50t, 56, 60t, 130
  see also homicide, manslaughter, violence
muzhelozhstvo 48, 88-9, 97, 109, 119, 190
  law on 89, 91, 96
  see also buggery
nashi 92, 100, 104
nature vs the social (*also* New Materialism) 131-2, 136, 138-9, 142, 145
Neo-disciplinary power 3, 6-8, 10, 13-5, 17, 30, 81, 130, 139-41, 175-6, 180, 184, 196, 200-1, 204-6
New Materialism (*see* nature)
Nizhny Novgorod Region 159
non-traditional sexual relationships (*also* sexual orientation, traditional sexual relationship) 9, 17, 19, 28, 48, 77, 97-8, 104, 107-9, 113, 117, 122, 151, 187-97
norms legal (*also* procedural) 7, 11, 30-1, 35, 43, 45, 55, 103, 147, 151-2
  see also law, ruling
Novgorod Region 105
Novosibirsk Region 57, 100, 109, 129, 148, 156, 159
Nussbaum Martha 132-8, 141, 176-7
object (*see* subject)
Occupy Paedophilia 53, 68, 71
Omsk Region 154
opushchenny (*see* prison subculture)
Orenburg Region 157
Oryol Region 1
Panopticon the 6, 10-5, 29, 32, 140-1, 175, 180, 201-2
  see also Memeticon the
pardon (*see* amnesty)
passive (*see* active vs passive dichotomy)
Penal Code (*see* criminal justice system)
penetration 91, 109, 122, 133, 144, 162, 188, 199, 205, 207
Penza Region 104
performative power (*also* performativity) 4, 7-8, 13-4, 30, 82, 91, 95, 142, 144, 182
Perm Region 115-6
perpetrator 3, 27-8, 41, 49, 59, 61-2, 65t, 66-70, 111-3, 119, 122-3, 133-4, 144, 147-50, 155, 160, 163, 166-8, 171-2, 181, 205
  see also victim
petukh (*see* prison subculture)
pidor (*see* prison subculture)
police 13, 24, 27-31, 41-3, 51, 54, 68-9, 118, 124, 181, 191
  see also investigation
politics everyday (*also* grassroots) 29, 32-5, 70, 90, 94, 103, 143-4, 147-52, 177, 188
positivism legal 7, 14, 16, 30
Posner Richard 131, 134, 140-1
poverty (*also* poor) 63, 66-9, 173
  see also class
power relations 3-17, 29-30, 32, 43-4, 58, 68, 80-2, 86-7, 90, 95-6, 98, 101, 123-4, 130, 137-46, 166, 169, 175, 179-80, 182, 184, 186, 196, 200-5, 208-9

power-knowledge (*see* expert knowledge)
practices 12-3, 29-32, 44-5, 62, 70, 82, 85-9, 102, 108-9, 182, 184, 202, 207, 209
prejudice in adjudication (*also* bias) 34-9, 58, 63, 69, 114, 147, 149-50, 152
Primorsky Territory 115, 163, 168
prison subculture, vocabulary (*also* opushchenny, petukh, pidor, pedik) 90, 92-3, 98, 105-6, 108, 185
procedural norms (*see* norms)
productive -ity power, of power 10, 12, 90, 143, 145, 157-9, 163-4, 178, 201
propaganda (*see* gay propaganda)
prosecution (*also* prosecutors) 27, 31, 41-5, 51-2, 54-9, 77, 91, 119-20, 191, 195
  see also investigation
provincialisation (*see* colonisation)
Putin Vladimir 32-4, 96, 196-7, 203
queer as category of practice (*also* queerness) 6, 15, 17, 32-3, 38-9, 48-9, 51-4, 59, 61-3, 66-7, 70-1, 83-5, 88-92, 96-8, 101, 103-4, 107-24, 134-5, 144, 148, 150, 152-5, 158-61, 163-5, 167-8, 183, 185, 187-93, 197
  criminology 4-5, 129, 203-4, 206
  theory (*also* approach) 6, 79-82, 84-7, 93-5, 99, 130, 137, 140, 142, 145, 175-6, 209
  umbrella category 5, 9, 85, 97-9, 104, 107
rape 56, 99, 105, 161, 168, 190
re-criminalisation of male homosexuality (*see* decriminalisation)
reconfiguration of power relations 82, 84, 87, 90, 93-6, 98-9, 200
regional gay propaganda ban (*see* gay propaganda)
replicability (*see* resonance)
resonance of memes 22, 137, 179, 183-7, 189-90, 193, 195-6, 200
  see also meme, isolation chamber
respect 102-3, 114, 157-8, 166
Rostov Region 105, 111, 154, 156, 159-60, 163, 191
ruling (*also* court decision, sentencing) 4, 8-9, 22, 27-30, 32-7, 40-2, 44-5, 48-9, 54, 57-9, 61-3, 67-70, 72, 77-8, 99, 103-4, 106, 121-3, 130, 146-9, 165, 193
Ryazan Region 96, 100, 192
Sakha Yakutia Republic of 72, 167
Samara Region 100
Saratov Region 106, 114, 119
self 80, 93, 95, 101, 153, 206, 209
sentencing (*see* ruling)
sexual minority 48, 92, 107, 118, 148
sexual orientation (*see* non-traditional)
shame 107, 110, 122, 132, 154-5, 193
silencing (*also* erasure) 76, 78, 89-90, 93, 96, 102, 121-4, 150, 152, 166-7
Smolensk Region
social group 36, 39-40, 47, 49, 55, 57, 70, 107, 110, 148, 151-2
social media (*see* media)
social the vs nature (*see* nature)
sodomy (*see* buggery)
sovereign law vs disciplinary law (*see* modality of law)

Soviet 19, 35, 37, 89-93, 99, 104, 109, 119, 124, 189, 197
  Post- 79, 83, 86, 94-6, 99, 119, 149, 151, 190
St Petersburg 97, 100, 118, 121
stab wounds 56, 59, 106, 129, 157, 161-3, 166, 168
statistics hate crime 37, 48, 51-4, 60-1, 67, 122
Stavropol Region 24-6, 120, 161
Stella Francesca 84, 86, 92
subject -ivity 10, 12, 17-8, 83-4, 86, 90, 94, 102-4, 108, 116, 121, 123-4, 133, 135-40, 144-6, 153, 157, 166, 169, 177, 179, 199, 201, 206
subversion *see* reconfiguration of power relations
susceptible body 12, 17, 137, 169, 172, 174, 176, 184, 186, 195-7, 199-201
Sverdlovsk Region 120, 122
targeting 27, 70, 95, 123, 147, 150-1
Tatarstan 72
techniques of power 6, 11-5, 17-8, 29, 82, 101, 169, 175, 179-80, 182-4, 186, 196, 200-2
  see also mechanism of power
tema 92, 100, 108
text legal *see* ruling, procedural norms
Tomsk Region 111, 118, 151, 163
touch 12-3, 16-8, 131, 135-45, 158-9, 177, 183, 186-7, 196, 198-9, 201, 204
traditional *see* non-traditional
traditional values 39, 97
trans* /transgender person 4, 48, 68, 75-6, 78-9, 82-3, 91, 97, 102, 104, 112, 123
  see also LGBT+, lesbian, gay man, bisexual
truth *see* meaning
Tula Region 114
Tuva Republic 72, 105
Tver Region 108, 157
Tyumen Region 113, 149, 192
Udmurtia 108
unconscious *see* conscious
United Kingdom the 178, 198-9, 210
United States of America the 15, 21, 79, 81-2, 84-8, 94, 133, 151, 176, 178, 186, 199
unpleasant feelings 28, 127, 129-30, 146-7, 149-53, 158, 168
USSR *see* Soviet
utopia queer 19, 82, 87, 93-5, 98-9
  see also dystopia
victim 2-4, 9, 27, 41, 48-9, 50t, 51-4, 58-9, 62-3, 64t, 66-8, 69-70, 77-8, 91, 102-3, 106, 109, 113-4, 119, 123, 129, 144, 147-8, 150, 152, 156, 166, 168-9, 191
  see also perpetrator
vigilante, -ism 33, 53-4, 181
violence anti-queer 1, 3-4, 9, 29, 36, 40, 48-9, 50t, 52-3, 62, 69-70, 76, 95, 102-3, 112, 123-4, 129-30, 144-6, 149-51, 163-4, 166-7, 169, 177, 183, 186-7, 195-6, 199, 201, 205-6, 208
violent affections *see* affect
Vladimir Region 100, 116, 161
vodka *see* alcohol
Volgograd Region 126

vulnerability 53-4, 70, 93, 132-3, 143, 147, 150, 152, 164, 172, 174, 183, 188-9, 190, 196, 205-10
West vs East /Western 5, 37, 79-80, 83-5, 87, 94, 197
  see also East vs West
Zabaykalsky Territory 114, 150, 155

www.ingramcontent.com/pod-product-compliance
Lightning Source LLC
LaVergne TN
LVHW050008140426
836100LV00010B/59